Atlantic
Ocean
BAHAMA
ISLANDS
GREAT BAHAMA BANK
ELEUTHERA
Nassau
NEW PROVIDENCE
ANDROS
CAT I.
SAN SALVADOR
RUM CAY
GREAT EXUMA
LONG I.
CROOKED I.
ACKLINS I.
GREAT INAGUA
ARCH. DE CAMAGÜEY
Morón
Ciego de Ávila
CAMAGÜEY
Camagüey
Nuevitas
Victoria de las Tunas
Holguín
Banes
ORIENTE
Manzanillo
Bayamo
Sierra Maestra
Guantánamo
Baracoa
Santiago de Cuba
Guantánamo Bay
U.S. NAVAL STATION
WINDWARD PASSAGE
DE LA REINA
HAITI
JAMAICA
Sea
V. Gray

Eye on Cuba

Edwin Tetlow

EYE
ON
CUBA

Harcourt, Brace & World, Inc.   *New York*

To the Cuban People

Contents

Eye on Cuba

1 ❖ Change
in the Night

A MAN'S circumstances—his attitudes, his career, his very
life—are often transformed by the merest chance. How often
has each of us said how extraordinary it was that he should
have knocked at that other door, taken that train or airplane
instead of another, gone to that dreary-sounding party after
all. Momentous consequences indeed can follow such trivial
moves and decisions.

Flukes operate with especially critical importance, and sometimes mischief, in the effervescent and haphazard life of the
foreign correspondent, a man like myself, who most of the time
has to realize on awakening in the morning that he really does
not know for certain where on earth he may be at the end of

the day; goodness knows how many potentially profitable or
disastrous decisions he will have made in pursuit of whatever
story might have come his way.

Nobody should be surprised that so many important and
seemingly miraculously contrived exclusive reports have burst
upon the world by accident, and that some of the most breath-
taking journalistic opportunities have arisen so freakishly that
a man can scarcely believe them to have been there for the
taking. That was how it fell with me in Cuba.

Like millions of other people who followed the meanderings
of Fidel Castro and his band of bearded rebels in eastern and
central Cuba between early 1956 and late 1958, I met with
apathy and some irritation what I read in the newspapers and
magazines and what I saw in the occasional pictures. To me
these men looked and behaved like delinquents who had taken to
the hills because the city offered no scope for their brand of
playacting and capering. One wished with growing irritation
that Fidel Castro would either *do* something or stop playing the
ineffectual bandit in a country that, outwardly at least, seemed
to have little time for him. A general strike that he called in
Havana by remote control from the Sierra Maestra in the
spring of 1958 had been a humiliating flop. For months after
that disaster there appeared to be scant chance indeed that he
was ever going to unseat Fulgencio Batista or gather even part
of the island into his fold. Then, as the debilitating summer
heat ebbed, he and his cause revived. Toward the end of 1958
the fragmentary reports reaching the United States, and the
even briefer ones going into Europe (where interest in the Castro uprising had earlier been just about as intense as preoccupation with, say, the fortunes of the New York Yankees), began
to suggest success. The raids upon the sugar mills, the blowing
up of main roads, and the hit-and-run attacks upon Cuban
Army barracks were beginning to affect the morale of Batista's
men after all. Soldiers seemed to be deserting and joining the

rebels. Castro's forces in the mountains and on the plains were growing in power as well as in human strength. In November, 1958, it began to look as if these forces might eventually do enough to inspire the disorganized and presently lukewarm pro-Castro underground into some kind of coordinated action.

But the world was reluctant to believe that anything much would yet be happening. Even in the last week of 1958 Cuba was still an interesting but not urgent topic of discussion and observation. One editor sitting in the foreign room of a newspaper in distant London on December 29 was smitten with an idea as he sat reading one of the scrappy reports reaching him from the Caribbean. It would be a good idea if I, as a British correspondent, went from New York to Havana—the very word was an alluring synonym in damp and foggy England for luxurious warmth, gambling, naughty gaiety, and worse—to describe how the carefree city would celebrate the coming of the New Year despite the growing threat from a gang of bearded tatterdemalions working their way slowly closer to the capital from the east. I well remember the admonition in the service message from London that carried my marching orders: "DON'T WRITE TOO MUCH." The man who sent that advisory clearly did not have an inkling of what was afoot; neither he nor I knew that within twenty-four hours he would be clamoring for every word I could bellow into the telephone line under the Atlantic between Havana and London.

There was not the slightest hint in the United States on that last day of 1958 that Fulgencio Batista had decided that his game was up. Probably a few people in the State Department in Washington knew something, but, if so, they were not sharing it with anybody. I picked up all the New York newspapers before taking a taxi to Idlewild and read them as I waited, interminably it seemed, while Cubana Airlines made ready for the afternoon flight of their Britannia to Havana. (I did not know for days that the delay was caused by a notification to the airline from its main office in Havana that the documents

and luggage of every intending passenger had to be scrupulously checked before the plane could leave, on orders from the
Presidential Palace.)

The newspapers were all saying approximately the same
thing: that still another effort by Castro and his men to cut
the island in two across the province of Las Villas, on a line
about 150 miles from Havana, was being decisively blocked.
The impression given by everything one read was that the
government forces continued to be in firm control of Cuba, and
that there was nothing out of the ordinary to be worried about;
the Castro revolt was being contained just as it had been for
the last two years.

The reason for this soothing delusion was, of course, that
only one side of the story was being told. If there were one or
two independent observers in the field with Fidel Castro at
that time, they were getting no chance of sending out what they
knew because the government was in charge of all communications between Cuba and the outside world. Castro's primitive
propaganda machine was putting out bulletins by short-wave
radio but, having heard it all before, nobody was paying attention. The so-called reporting that Americans were able to
read in their papers or hear on their radios about the struggle
going on for possession of the city of Santa Clara in Las
Villas Province was coming from Havana, and it was coming
from tainted sources. Even at this final stage the government
was still pumping out lie after lie. Batista was already getting
ready to fly, but naturally not a word about that was being
said. Nor were the American and other reporters penned in
Havana being told how disastrously the fight had gone out of
the government troops facing the rebels, and that now nothing
stood between Fidel Castro and early victory. I still thought
as I sat, one of only three first-class passengers aboard the
Britannia, that my mission when I got to Havana would be
merely to write a light-hearted account of how the New Year
was welcomed in the night clubs and the casinos.

All seemed normal enough at Havana Airport. I remember nothing out of the ordinary about the way the handful of passengers went through the usual formalities, which were as complex as I have always found them in Latin America. Porters scurried about to earn their pesos by taking us and our luggage to the waiting taxis. I shared a big Buick with a tall young American—somewhat of a playboy, I deduced—who was joining a party of his friends for a New Year binge. The dark-skinned driver was humming softly to the music from his car radio as he drove us gaily at a good clip into the city.

The illusion of normalcy still seemed valid when I reached the Hotel Nacional, where a modest room was available—at the immodest rate of $26.00 a night. Celebrants were everywhere. The dining room was full of urbane men and elegantly gowned women enjoying an almost limitless menu, and under the massive chandeliers of the casino gaming tables were being well patronized by Cuban and American welcomers of the imminent New Year. A bar just off the casino was doing really splendid business, amid such a hubbub that you almost had to yell to make yourself heard by your neighbor. Cubans love noise—or used to! This night their talent for shouting instead of merely talking was being supplemented by the pounding and blasting of a four-piece band and the uninhibited contralto contribution of a lusty Cuban songstress who was taxing the capacity of a microphone only a few yards from the mob around the bar.

The gambling in the casino was intense. When in a fleeting moment of excitement somebody made a particularly pretty haul at a roulette table or hit the jackpot at one of the many slot machines lining the walls of the casino, only then did heads turn and faint, envious smiles lighten tight-lipped mouths. I vividly recall one incident that fascinated me as a nongambler. From the dining room emerged a young man twirling a fifty-dollar bill. Hardly breaking step, he approached the roulette table at which I was standing, placed the bill on red, and continued his quick march round the room. He came back to the

table just as red showed, collected his due hundred, and walked
out. I never saw him again that night.

The casino was still very full when I went to bed soon after
2 A.M. There had been only a perfunctory halt in activity at
midnight, but the band had now mercifully evaporated and
the songstress had gone. The gamblers were still around the
tables and at the slot machines, and a dwindling party of New
Year revelers, becoming more disarrayed almost by the minute,
were keeping surviving barmen busy.

At just about this time Batista and some forty members of
his family and close friends were leaving the Presidential Palace and their homes around the city for the airfield. At least
they knew that Fidel Castro was not to be fended off this time.
They flew from Camp Columbia, the military citadel on the
fringe of Havana, for the Dominican Republic, a short hop
across the water to the east-south-east. Batista would have
preferred to take the traditional route to the north-east to
the United States. But, justifiably or not, he had acquired an
unsavory name as a monster and a tyrant, and his acceptance
as a refugee within the United States would have raised an
awful yell in almost the whole of Spanish America. The Dominican Republic was one of the few places in the Caribbean to
which Batista could safely go. At that time it was firmly held
by Generalissimo Rafael Trujillo, one of the last surviving
despots of the hemisphere and a most unlovely and ridiculous
representative of his dying kind. He was to be ambushed and
mown down by a group of disgruntled army officers as he was
driving away from or to a visit to his mistress in Santo Domingo two years later.

How does a conquest such as Fidel Castro's emerge? I was
awakened before 8 A.M. by Robert Perez, my resident correspondent, who gave me the electrifying news that Batista had
gone. "He's just gone with the night," Perez said. I looked out
of the bedroom window after we had spoken and saw that the
city was deadly quiet. The old order had passed in the night,

and the new had not yet taken over. It was not to do so, indeed, for almost a week, and in the interval Havana completely changed its civic aspect. Batista had tried to bequeath power to a junta of three uncommitted men. Presumably he hoped they might be able to stop Castro from taking over full control and—who knew?—might even manage to keep the door open for a return to the good-old days. The hope flickered only briefly. Castro must have seen straight through the ruse, for that day he broadcast a flamboyant victory speech from somewhere near Santa Clara and announced to Havana that he did not accept the residual junta as a bargaining agent. He said he would be coming to the city soon and in the interval was arranging for an advanced guard of his rebel force to hold the city for him.

Then he began a fantastic amble by jeep over the western half of the island that had fallen to him. He had no planned route, only a general drift in the direction of the capital, and he had no purpose except to ensure that as many Cubans as possible saw him and talked to him. He had become almost a god overnight, but the resulting power had not yet even begun to corrupt him. I believe that on this day, and for quite a time after he eventually came to Havana, the purer elements in the nature of Fidel Castro were in control. Warmth, impulsiveness, idealism, unselfishness—these were the qualities that were guiding him. He *was* almost Christlike, during this first simple pilgrimage, in his love and concern for the people. In this fleeting moment of purity, before others began to work on him and exploit his glaring weaknesses, he wanted to show himself to his Cubans—to talk to them, to assure them that the bad-old days had gone, to show his concern for them. He was drunk with triumph, but glowingly drunk.

Yet, even allowing for all that, his pronouncements and his very movements were already carrying the stamp of vagueness and uncertainty that was to cause so much anguish later to those who would try to work with and for him; and he clearly had no plans whatever to meet the responsibilities of victory. It was difficult then—because of the confusion and the lack of communications between one part of Cuba and another—to find out what was happening within the Castro camp, and it is now impossible to do so, but I think it reasonable to deduce that the collapse of Batista took even Castro by surprise, as it had taken almost everybody else. If he or his makeshift staff in the field had had any inkling that total victory was imminent they would have had plans ready for the seizure of Havana and the take-over of power.

On that deliciously cool New Year's Day of Castro's victory nobody was in charge in Havana. Cubans there reacted to the flight of Batista exactly as one would expect seasoned victims of Latin American upheavals and riots to react. They put up their shutters and boarded themselves in until they saw which way the wind was going to blow, toward disturbance and bloodshed or toward peace and jubilation. Until early afternoon it looked as if the happier direction would be the chosen one. Until then all the streets in the heart of the city, between the waterfront and Vedado, were eerily quiet. A man or woman would venture out occasionally but only because of some demanding task that justified the risk. I noticed that most of these venturesome people walked as closely as they could to walls and doors of buildings and made maximum use of whatever cover was offered. One exception was a handsome, full-bosomed young Negro woman who, with all the pride and confidence of youth, swung along a side street close to the University of Havana. I watched her progress in fascination and admiration from a window on the third floor of the Hotel Colina where I had been awaiting with growing fury a long-promised telephone call to London. The girl's bottom, exaggerated by a skirt very cunningly tightened halfway down, jutted what seemed to be a full eight inches horizontally from her spine. I could scarcely believe that the anatomy was real. But this was the first time I had stayed for long in Havana,

and nobody had advised me in advance about the shape of the
female Cuban bottom. In the many visits I was to pay to the
island after the onset of the revolution, I was to become as
used to it as any man can, but I was never to hear a satis-
factory explanation of how it was achieved. Is it a biological,
dietary, or just a sartorial phenomenon? I do not know. Whatever it is, it is uniquely Caribbean.

The superficial situation in Havana changed for the first
time that day around 2:30 P.M. In a movement that seemed to
begin in the suburbs, where there was understandably never
the same tension as gripped the inner city, people began ventur-
ing from their homes. They got into their cars and opened a
crazy motorized game of follow-the-leader up and down and
around the narrow thoroughfares of old Havana. They had
decided, quite wrongly as it soon turned out, that the replace-
ment of Batista by Castro was to be a safe and peaceful and
enjoyable transition. I was staggered by their childlike mani-
festation of relief and happiness. They draped their American-
made cars with Cuban flags. If the car was a convertible they
wound down its hood. Anything up to a dozen passengers
climbed into or upon each car. One slow procession after another grew longer and longer and gave birth to more as the
infection of delusion spread. Doors opened and Cubans swarmed
out into the streets, many in their gayest clothes. The din became hard to bear.

As is common throughout Latin America, these people re-
joicing at the ouster of a dictator used the word *"libertad"*
as their theme. They sent back my memory to a day in Buenos
Aires in 1955 when President Juan Perón at last went up the
Paraná River in a gunboat. Then the Argentinos tramped up
and down city streets chanting *"li-ber-tad"* and clapping their
hands together in a monotonous rhythm until I thought I'd
go out of my mind.

The only variation on the theme of liberty I have met in
Latin America was in Santo Domingo around 1961, and the

explanation of the variation was that the Dominicans were re-
joicing not at the assassination of their disgusting oppressor
but were further on the road of emancipation. They were campaigning for the dismissal of his residual heir, the comparatively harmless Joaquin Balaguer. So they went up and down
their historic streets chanting a rhythm that went "tum-tum-
tum—tum-tum," divided into three "tums" and then two. I de-
coded it thus: "Ba-la-guer, boo-boo." The interesting point
about this was that the rhythm was the same as that used by the
Algerians when that country was seeking its independence so
bloodily. Their war cry, I am told, was *"Al-gé-rie Fran-çaise."*
Now it is a long way from Algiers to Santo Domingo and, so
far as I have been able to establish, there has never been any
contact between the demonstrators in the two cities; yet they
were prompted to use the same rhythm to vent their boiling
feelings. I do not try to explain why. I merely record the fact
and shall leave it to the psychologists and sociologists to tell
us what it all might mean.

In Havana the Cubans could not clap their hands to the
chant of *"li-ber-tad,"* since they were hanging precariously
onto cars. It was left to drivers to provide the refrain by
sounding the syllables on their horns. The result was quite
appalling, especially to one not accustomed to the daily hubbub
of Havana, which used to be one of the noisiest cities of either
the Old or New Worlds. Happily from the point of view of
the sensitive listener, but unhappily for Cuba, the noise did not
last long that day. It was halted by terrorism.

I saw the first sinister omen while walking, without much confidence in the rousing good fellowship that seemed to have
blessed the day, along the Prado, where there was incidentally
plenty of cover in case of need. There had been a minor traffic
jam outside the Restaurant Miami and this had brought a lull
in activity along the Prado. I was dismayed to see an untidy
young Cuban walking warily into the broad avenue from Calle
Neptuno, a narrow street, holding a rifle aslant in front of him.

It was a very old battered rifle that, I imagine, the young ruffian had kept hidden for just such an occasion as this. I felt as sure as I could be that he was only the forerunner, the herald, of others of his kind. Soon it proved so.

The villains of the Cuban underworld began to seep into the open. Most had a weapon of some kind, with decrepit and dangerous old rifles and shotguns in the majority. I had an unpleasant feeling as I watched more and more of these unwholesome characters appear in the streets that they were coming out of the sewers, and the certainty that they intended to seize physical control of Havana in the absence of any kind of civic order raised nasty possibilities. They were without doubt the riffraff of Havana, and there may be lower kinds than that but not, I feel, very many. They very soon finished off the pathetic public rejoicings. The sight of only the first few of these dirty and menacing men with guns was enough for most Cubans. Cars were quickly driven out of the center of Havana. People went back into their homes and once again locked doors and windows and put up shutters. The brief moment of happy intoxication was over, and, as I now look back years later, I realize that it was the only moment of pure joy that the Castro revolution produced for most Cubans. The course thereafter for most of them was downhill all the way, as the new revolution faltered and was betrayed and then finally obliterated.

The young gangsters made quick and simple work of taking over the city. Some of them even managed a few home-sewn armbands carrying initials proclaiming membership of the Students' Union, the 26th of July Movement, and other bodies that had never been heard of before and were never to be heard of again. They formed themselves into little gangs, each assuming authority over a small section of city territory. Men took positions at street junctions, with their guns at the ready, and established their authority by directing whatever wheeled traffic still moved and giving orders to pedestrians at gunpoint. There was not by this time one uniformed police officer anywhere. Batista's hated force had vanished. Officers and men had fled, fearful of what would happen to them if they stayed. Not all were quick enough in getting away, for I heard later that several of them were shot or beaten to death in some of the rougher districts of the capital.

Now the bandits settled into the real business of the day—looting. Parking meters were the first target. They were smashed or even sawn apart and their contents pocketed by small bands of looters, who were usually guarded by one or more armed escorts, just in case anybody tried to interfere. Next it was the turn of the pinball machines in the downtown arcades and the slot machines in some of the casinos that could readily be entered, such as one close to the Sevilla Biltmore Hotel. I saw one gang breaking open a slot machine on the sidewalk by bashing at it with jagged metal from a looted parking meter. It was an interesting illustration of the well-known theory that money makes money.

Physical danger to anybody who risked going out of doors increased as the gangsters gained confidence and got their hands on rum and other liquor. Shooting began. Mostly it was wild and pointless, but occasionally it meant that an old debt was being paid. Ambulances began to make their screaming runs through the almost deserted streets and hospitals and mortuaries became busy. Some of the shooting was the most futile and frightening I have ever seen in war or so-called peace. One man's rifle would go off because it was defective, because he had forgotten his finger was on the trigger, or even because of some whimsical idea of showing off. Each shot seemed to start a chain reaction. Everybody else with a gun anywhere near would fire off a shot and bullets and pellets would start ricocheting off walls and sides of houses or cracking through windows. All for nothing.

One of the most senseless, but illuminating, episodes of all during this mad and dangerous period of near-anarchy happened in the late afternoon of January 2. I was standing in the shelter of an arcade on one side of the Parque Central, noting the devastation of shattered windows and ransacked shop fronts left by the looters, when I became aware of a hubbub on the corner close to the Sevilla Biltmore Hotel. Shots began cracking. The square emptied of the few hardy Cubans who had ventured outdoors. I peeped cautiously out of the cover of my arcade and saw a squad of young men firing rifles and machine pistols at a window on an upper floor of one of the buildings on the side of the square opposite me. The firing was wildly inaccurate, bullets squelching into stonework far below, above, and around the target window. The wild assault continued for almost an hour without, as I carefully noted, one single shot being fired back at the attackers. Parties of American tourists who had holed up inside the Sevilla Biltmore in obedience to advice given to them from the United States Embassy could hear it all but could see almost nothing. The facts emerged later.

The militiamen had been told that somebody had taken refuge inside the room behind the window. At first, the story was that only one fugitive was there, but very soon it was that at least a dozen armed followers of Rolando Masferrer, a particularly unpopular member of the Batista regime, were in the room. That caused the shooting. When it was all over one of the militiamen told me proudly that all twelve had been killed. I decided to check the story that evening. I then found that nobody whatever had been behind that window, and that the whole affair was totally without point. It always served me afterward as a kind of cautionary signpost. On all the fourteen visits I paid to Havana between 1959 and 1965, I made a point of always glancing up at that pockmarked building, with the same old riddled blind flapping at the paneless window, and remembering that mad episode. It helped me to avoid taking everything I heard at face value, particularly anything told me by a Cuban or anybody else with a case to put either for or against Fidel Castro and his revolution. It served also to remind me that

there is an element of, let us say, irresponsibility in the Cuban
character that must always be taken into account in assessing
that revolution.

Bandit rule lasted in Havana until about midnight that second day of revolution. The city remained broodingly quiet for
most of the time, the sinister and unnatural calm being broken
intermittently by the clanging bell of an ambulance, a flurry
of shots, or the screeching tires of a commandeered car being
driven with defiant showiness as a squad of self-appointed mas-
ters of Havana careered through the streets, watched with
varying degrees of fear and uneasiness by Cubans sheltered behind their boarded windows. Relief from this mob rule came
very soon after the first small advance unit of rebels, promised
by Fidel Castro in one of his many radio messages from somewhere in the countryside, reached the capital from the province
of Las Villas. I happened to catch a very early sight of them,
simply because I had been arrested by the bandits an hour or
two earlier.

I had been writing until fairly late in the evening in the one
secure refuge I knew in downtown Havana, the offices of the
Havana *Post*, in an area near the waterfront of the Malecon
drive at the junction of the old streets of Animas and Lealtad.
About 9 P.M. a small group, all Americans except myself, decided to walk home through the silent city to our hotel, the
Havana Hilton, a mile and a half away uptown in Vedado.
Walking was the only way of getting anywhere, and the hotel
would be cheerless enough when we arrived, for all bars, restaurants, and public places had closed down in obedience to
a radio call for a general strike from Fidel Castro. To this
day, I do not know any valid reason why he should have called
that strike. I believe the explanation is that he wanted to make
sure of the loyalty of the mass of workers in the capital. He
had called just such a general strike many months earlier while
still battling inconclusively in the Sierra Maestra, and it had
been a dismal failure. He was presumably not taking a chance

this time. He must have been very stimulated by the reports of the almost total success of the second strike. Of course the bandits had helped by making it hazardous for anybody to do anything, open any establishment, or place himself within range of any of the hundreds of untrustworthy firearms being paraded around the city. Nonetheless the strike was almost unanimous. Like many other visiting foreigners I had to exist for a day and a half on a few scraps of biscuits and chocolate.

We had walked about two-thirds of the way to the Hilton when we ran into bandits and difficulties. A voice called out of the darkness in grating Cuban Spanish, "Hands up." As we peered ahead we could make out three figures covering us with rifles, two of them down on a knee at the sides of the street and the other, who turned out to be in charge of the little detail, barring the way straight ahead.

I was hungry and bad tempered—and I suppose prompted by some instinctive contempt for amateur warriors—and was all for pushing on and defying them. The gangsters of Havana had been doing this kind of nonsensical playacting all day, often holding up people simply to feed self-importance, and I felt convinced they would do nothing if we marched ahead and talked matters over with them. My companions had cooler and perhaps wiser heads. They raised their hands. I followed their lead, half-heartedly. The desperadoes rounded us up and escorted us to the passageway of an apartment house where their group had set up rough-and-ready operational headquarters. Now started a complicated argument with an unshaven young man seated at a desk. It was very hot indeed in that passageway. I left the arguing and protesting to those of our party who spoke far better Spanish than I and sauntered to the doorway to get some air. If chances looked favorable, I planned to make a break for freedom and my cosy bed at the Hilton. But boys with guns were still out in the street and I had to give up any idea of dashing off.

After an hour the disagreeable news was given to us. Our

gangsters claimed that it would not be safe for them to let us go on our way because their writ covered only one small area around the apartment house and, they said, they did not want us to fall into the hands of an adjacent gang that controlled the next stretch of territory. Actually, I'm quite sure they were making the most of a chance, possibly the first in their lives, of lording it over Americans. They said we should have to stay the night at a place of their choice. They took us to it in a car they had acquired during their busy day, making the maximum possible noise and commotion. It turned out to be a dingy flop-house of a hotel in a street running diagonally off the Malecon, on the seafront. I found later that it had been used as a refuge for agents of Castro and other fugitives from Batista's police, and this explained the appearance there, as I was reluctantly resigning myself to going upstairs to a mean little bedroom that had been allotted to me by my captors, of the very first bearded rebels I was to see.

As I was walking to the desk of the hotel to claim my key I noticed a small utility truck standing outside the door of the building, with half a dozen tough, well-armed and laughing soldiers unloading their kit from it. Two of them had black hair hanging down so long at the back that I should have taken them for girls, were it not for their flowing beards. They were all very young, none more than eighteen, and they all looked to be in magnificent physical condition. They looked all the better to me because their coming meant that the rule of the desperadoes would soon be over, and they had brought food with them. They hauled it all into the hotel and spread it along the counter. There were great hams, sausages, fresh bread, butter, beer . . . Not many minutes had passed before some twenty of us—Cuban soldiers, American and British detainees, and the inevitable lucky ones who just happened to be there— were digging in. There was much laughter, backslapping and talk of friendship between the nations. It was a memorable episode.

It was akin to one I experienced in 1944 when I went in a Flying Fortress from Foggia, in Italy, over much hostile territory to Bucharest, which had just been captured by the Russians. There, as I waited for liberated airmen of the United States and Britain who had been shot down while bombing Ploesti oilfields to be put aboard the Fortress, I had my first encounter with the Soviet Army. The Russian soldiers were stocky peasants who had motorcycled into Bucharest as an advance patrol of the main forces. Then, too, we exchanged jokes and congratulations and slapped each other's backs as we talked about the end of the fighting and the future amity of nations. Alas, both occasions were to be sterile. As with the Russians after 1944 so with the Cubans after 1959—misunderstandings, cleavage, bruising political warfare, and finally the settlement of the Cubans into the antiwestern camp in the classic ideological struggle of the 1960's. It all seems so juvenile and utterly unnecessary at this stage of human development, especially when the common man in both camps bears such instinctive goodwill for his fellow.

I must now record here, in fairness and because of all that has happened since 1959 in and to Cuba, that Fidel Castro's army of rebels was one of the best-behaved armies one could imagine. They were almost too good to be real. To a man, so far as I could determine during the first month of the occupation of Havana, they were dedicated to Fidel Castro. To a man, they behaved impeccably. There was no looting or licentiousness and there was hardly even any drinking. The bearded warriors would laugh as they told you they could not remember when they had last been paid. They had been living off the land and on the resources of willing peasants in the field, and they certainly had no need of money in these first rapturous days of victory in Havana, for the people felt they could not do enough to honor the men who had rescued them from the oppressions and cruelties of the regime of Batista. It was just as well that

people could not see the disillusionment and despair that lay
only three years ahead.

The rebels were well disciplined and efficient, surprisingly so
for Cubans. I had one remarkable example of their quality.
Two days after the flight of Batista, when it became evident
that Castro was in no haste whatever to come to Havana, I
despatched Robert Perez into the mountains with orders to
send me an account somehow of what was going on there and,
if possible, to have a talk with Castro. I had no great hope
that Perez would be able to achieve anything, since the whole
country seemed to be in confusion and communications were
especially unreliable, but I was in for a surprise. Two days
after Perez had gone, I had a telephone call from an officer at
rebel headquarters at Camp Columbia who said that he must
see me as soon as possible as he had a letter for me. He would
not say over the telephone what it was. I told him that I should
be out of my hotel for some hours and would be grateful if he
would send the letter there. No, that would not do. He had
orders "from the top" to hand over the letter to me. Puzzled,
I arranged a rendezvous. On the dot of the hour of the appointment the officer, who turned out to be a lieutenant in the rebel
air force, found me and, saluting most formally, produced the
letter. He asked me to sign a receipt for it. I did so and thanked
him for taking so much trouble to get it to me. I inquired,
diffidently, whether there had been any expense in its delivery
that I could repay. No, there had not, the young man said with
a smile. He had flown to Havana with the letter from Santa
Clara and, now that it was safely in my hands, his mission was
done. With a parting salute he was gone.

The letter contained what is commonly known as a scoop.
Castro had talked with Perez during one of the many halts
in the Caesarlike progress to Havana in a jeep. Perez had
written out his version of the interview in English and trans-
lated it back into Spanish so that Castro should know exactly
what was being attributed to him. He had approved the script

and then, in one of those grand gestures so characteristic of this flamboyant man, he had ordered that the letter be flown to me. His orders had been scrupulously carried out.

The interview obtained by Perez was not sensational by international standards, but since it was the first Castro had given for foreign edification it had certain historical significance. Since he was representing a London newspaper, Perez had sagely asked Castro to talk about his intentions concerning Cuban-British relations now that he was in charge of his country. This was a matter of special interest because there had been friction between Castro and the British government, which had sold naval airplanes (Sea Furies) and tanks to Batista only a little while before he had capitulated and fled. This sale was later to be a subject for some bitter questions and answers in the House of Commons when opposition M.P.'s asked, with justification, why the government had not been better informed about the wobbling dictator's plight. While still fighting in the Sierra Maestra, Castro had issued an edict ordering the confiscation of any British property that might fall into the hands of his forces.

Perez started by asking Castro about this edict and inviting him to say what he intended to do further about the ill-timed deal with Batista. Castro promptly showed skill at making statements that sound important but boil down to very little when analyzed. He was to display this confusing quality many times in the long and rambling television discourses that he made in Havana in the next few years. "Our sentiments toward Britain are of sympathy and friendship," he opened, smoothly. "We watched attentively when the British fought in the difficult days of the World War. But our relations with Britain will now have to be carefully reviewed." He added that the law of confiscation of British goods passed in the field had not been implemented. "It will be reviewed," he conceded, thereby cancelling much of the menace of his remark about future Cuban-British relations. Then he renewed the menace.

"We are going to ask some straight questions and we shall expect some straight answers in writing from them. The Sea Furies and the tanks were sold to Batista to kill rebels and innocent people. We shall have to study how these shipments came about, who allowed them and why they were made." He ended by announcing what was apparently a decision made at that very moment, that the tanks for a ceremonial parade to be held in Havana when he reached there would be manned by his own troops.

In the outcome, for all his fine words, he did nothing about reviewing his relationship with the British. For the next two years the countries became more friendly in direct proportion to the cooling of relations between Cuba and the United States, as Cuba found increasing use for British exports. Eventually, as the communists took charge of Cuba and the country slid into the ranks of the Soviet bloc, the British were cold-shouldered in their turn, until by the end of 1962 the small British diplomatic colony in Havana was almost out of contact with official Cubans.

I recall two incidents concerning Castro's international relationships that illustrate some of the oddities in his character. After Castro had at last reached Havana and installed his first makeshift regime, the British Ambassador, A. S. Fordham, tried to see him to try and straighten out Cuban-British affairs. Fordham was just as much out of luck as so many other people, including even members of Castro's own cabinet, who tried the same difficult feat. Castro just spent most of his waking hours roaming around Havana in a jeep or car, going where the fancy took him, or fluttering to and from Varadero, the Cuban resort that has the most wonderful beaches in the world, by helicopter. Either he ignored appointments altogether or arrived hours late for them. When in Havana he lived mostly in a suite on the top floor of the Havana Hilton Hotel, and there he was guarded day and night by a fanatically faithful and watchful bodyguard of bearded rebels.

nobody listening to him that afternoon and it added its mite
to the growing mistrust of him. For the most part, however,
he charmed his foreign questioners. He certainly charmed me
in answering one of my questions.

I went back to the topic he had discussed with Robert Perez
and asked him if he could yet say just what attitude his government intended to take toward Britain. Castro looked across at
me with those extraordinary black-depthed eyes of his. He
stroked his long black beard contemplatively. Then, with arms
outspread, he began, "There are, of course, many things to be
considered in connection with . . ." He stopped. With a beaming smile, he then added, "I just don't know." He joined merrily
in the laughter that his admission evoked. How could one possibly not be disarmed by such a man? But these were the early
days, the very early days, when he was still on a fairy-tale holiday with Cuba and most of the rest of the world, and everybody
concerned could still manage to laugh at and with him.

2 ◆ *Stumbling Hero*

I TRIED during the seven years following Fidel Castro's astonishing victory, and his even more astonishing physical and political survival, to keep a close eye upon the Cuban revolution by making as frequent visits to Havana as I could. I had stayed there continuously for the first three chaotic months of 1959 and regularly read and analyzed every scrap of written or spoken information that came my way. The visits were illuminating and exciting enough, for each one had its individual flavor and yielded its own crop of impressions and trends. Often these contradicted in more than one respect what had seemed to be indicated by the previous visit, but this was not surprising; the revolution, while it was from its beginning set on a general leftward course of anti-Americanism and procommunism, was forever making unexpected lurches into sideroads.

The apparent reason for the anfractuous course of events was the inability of Fidel Castro to stay for very long on one tack or to keep his mind occupied for any worthwhile period on a particular topic or goal. At one period he would be obsessed by grandiose plans to teach every Cuban to read; at another, his enthusiasm for that would have died down and he would talk and think of nothing but, say, importing some of the world's finest and most expensive bulls, so that Cuba should have a magnificent cattle industry; at yet another he would simply not be visible for days on end because he was down at Varadero or elsewhere venting a transient passion for spearfishing. One of the first characteristics about him that I noted in 1959 was that even while conversing with anybody he could not keep still but forever fidgeted, scratched, swayed from side to side, or otherwise betrayed his inner restlessness and impulsiveness. A Cuban once explained Fidel Castro to me by saying that as a young man he was thrown off a motorcycle and dashed into an unconsciousness that lasted for several days. "He was," said the Cuban, "never normal again."

I must say that learning about the revolution at second hand through other people's writings and observations has always been confusing to me, and it has often also been highly discouraging. Few have seemed able to think dispassionately about it. Those who have been bowled over by the magnetism of Fidel Castro or have welcomed with glowing political fervor the piloting of Cuba into the communist fold have seen no flaw whatever in the revolutionary jewel. Those impelled by the very opposite sentiments have been guilty of equally distasteful bias. Of all the political developments that have unsettled the North and South American world in the past twenty years, the Castro revolution has provoked by far the most harrowing impact. Most people have talked and written about it from pure emotion, not with logic or even common sense. Yet I can sympathize

with, even if I cannot excuse, all those Americans who cannot
bear to hear a word that conflicts with their passionate certainty that Castro is just as terrible a villain as most of the
caricaturists depict him. It was a shattering setback indeed
when a communist crab could attach itself to the Florida big
toe of Uncle Sam, and the dilemma of how to get rid of it
seemed insoluble as one year followed another.

One trouble is, of course, that it was always really impossible
for anybody outside the hierarchy of the Castro regime to
know all that was going on after January, 1959. I am positive
that only those persons permanently close to the three chief
actors—Fidel Castro, Raul Castro, and Ernesto ("Che")
Guevara—know anything approaching the real, full story of
the revolution, and they are not many who managed to stay
the course. Painstaking inquirers like the American scholar
Theodore Draper have shown admirable zeal in collating information, assessing statements and facts, and presenting be-
lievable surmises of what could have happened, but I do not
imagine they can have gathered all the consequences of the
whims of the wayward Fidel, and many events have never been
confirmed by a written record. Analysts have also had to rely
quite strongly upon statements by Cubans, and Cuba has impressed me as being one place in the world where torrents of
words are spoken or written and little is really said or revealed.
Furthermore, most foreigners, myself included, have tended to
confer upon the volatile Cubans a talent for organization that
many of them simply do not possess. I am tempted to say, and
will, that if any person can mismanage a scheme, plan, or event
of any kind, it is the Cuban. In my contacts with Cubans I
have had to note their habit of pretending many times to know
more than they do, considering it demeaning to have to confess
ignorance. Most of us outside observers have rated the revolution at far higher than its real level as a planned entity. Much
that has happened was never planned at all from within. Only
after the fall of 1961, when Moscow-trained communists took

administrative charge of the creaking revolutionary organization, did there come regimentation, long-overdue rationing,
political marshaling, and the many other distasteful but seemingly inevitable aspects of a communist police state. Before
then, it seemed to me, only Ernesto Guevara, the Argentine
politician-soldier of fortune, knew where he was going and
where he was trying to take the revolution.

I do not propose in this work to try to give an account of
my interpretation of the course of the Castro revolution, for
the reasons that have been indicated. I think the most valuable
contribution I can make to knowledge about it is to relate what
I saw and heard for myself, or feel within me to be probably
true. In estimating truth, I shall rely on some thirty-five years'
experience as a journalist and foreign correspondent in trying,
not always successfully, to find the facts.

My first serious assertion, then, is that I have never believed
for a moment that Fidel Castro was a communist, a disguised
one even, when he went into Havana as a conqueror in January,
1959. I believe he was then too immature politically to be able
to dissemble convincingly. In other words, he was exactly what
he said he was, first and foremost a Cuban patriot who had
dedicated himself to ridding his country once and for all of
corrupt dictatorship tied with economic bondage to the United
States and, second, a visionary seeking to give his people a new
life of independence and emancipation through his creed of
Humanism. By "Humanism" I believe he meant, as nearly as
his imprecise and apolitical mind would allow, a leveling policy
of do-good socialism that would take from over-rich Cubans
and their foreign abettors and would give to too-poor Cubans
for whom his heart bled. He felt that these unfortunates had
been exploited and oppressed far too long, and he wanted to
lift them out of bondage. That is what he said he wanted to do,
and I believe he meant it. He did not then know or care if the
communists were going to join him. If they joined with him and
helped him in his idealistic crusade, so much the better for him

and them; if they did not, then let them go hang. He was in the
unassailable position of a country's deliverer and idol. He just
did not care who was with him or against him in those heady
days of early 1959. Unhappily, there went with this wholly
admirable inspiration from within a fatal weakness founded
upon political immaturity and fertilized by a streak of flamboy-
ancy and theatricality. That streak was to betray him time
and again in his dealings with friend and enemy. The weakness
first let him down decisively quite early in the spring of 1959.
It led him into alienating the United States long before it was
politically necessary for him to do so, at a time when there
was a strong popular feeling that, in spite of the uncertainty
about him aroused by his refusal to stop summary executions
of so-called traitors, and his already plain incapacity both as
politician and administrator, he should still be given help and
encouragement by the United States.

The circumstances of his crazy, unnecessary self-betrayal
were memorable. One day in January, 1959, he ambled into the
Havana Hilton Hotel to find, as usual, a mob of Cuban Castro-
worshippers awaiting him in the main vestibule. To his people
at this time he was a savior, a kind of god, and Fidel Castro
would have had indeed to be of godlike substance to resist erosion of character promoted by such adulation. In fact, so far
as I could ever tell from watching him, he loved it all. This day
he was particularly relaxed and beneficent. He put his arms
around the nearest members of the crowd swarming around
him and, with a beatific smile lighting his swarthy and black-
bearded face, he talked with them. "People! People! Let the
people see me—let me talk with them!" I had heard him say.
Now he was doing just that, day in and day out; he would stop
anywhere and at any time. He cared nothing for the day-to-day
government of the country or for fulfilling even the broadest
outlines of a personal program of engagements and obligations.

That day's audience in the vestibule of the Havana Hilton
was a particularly appealing one. There were the usual bearded

rebels and their friends, families, and followers always to be
seen milling around the hotel, savoring the delights of victory
without a thought for the morrow. There were, too, a number
of well-rounded and full-bosomed young Cuban girls who had
put on the olive-green uniform of the revolution, although they
had probably never even seen the Sierra Maestra, and had
added the feminine touch to their garb with sexy-looking high-
heeled boots. Most of them had completed the picture of alluring
banditry by thrusting tiny silvered pistols into their black
belts.

I do not know how the topic of possible American interference in the revolution came up, for the hubbub around the
Maximum Leader as he talked and stroked his beard was so
intense that only those very close to him could possibly have
heard what was being said. But I do know that in an excess of
verbal intoxication, Fidel blurted out in his hoarse Spanish,
"Yes, I tell you, two hundred thousand gringos will die if the
United States send the marines to Cuba!" It was a preposterous
outburst, only understandable when one takes account of the
childlike trust and hero-worship his people were lavishing upon
him, and also when one remembers that the welling, flamboyant,
and extravagant mind of Fidel Castro had not yet been curbed
by sobering events or responsibilities.

The impulsive, senseless remark haunted and harmed him.
He thought he was talking in rhetorical rhapsody to only a
group of his devoted followers. Alas for him, his words were
caught clearly by others, including the journalist Robert Perez,
who had managed to get within a few feet of Castro. Perez is of
Puerto Rican origin but was brought up in Ohio and is impeccably bilingual in English and Spanish. He told me later that
there was no possible chance of any misunderstanding of what
Castro said, as the embarrassed Leader was to claim sheepishly
afterward. The impact of the grandiose remark upon the
United States was disastrous to the Cuban revolutionary cause.

It came at a critical moment so far as American opinion was concerned.

At the beginning of the year Americans had been captivated by the bearded leader and his startling total triumph. He was a man who had never managed to catch their attention or their favor during the two years of his apparently profitless efforts in the mountains. But Americans love a winner, and particularly a handsome and rather mysterious one. When later they learned of many executions up and down the island by firing squads acting after hurried and possibly perfunctory trials, their first doubts about him arose. Most Americans, however, were still disposed to trust Castro when he made that chilling remark, for, as I and other observers on the spot had pointed out in our despatches, Batista's men had committed some abominable crimes, and there was at least some justification for the rebel argument that if they did not deal out swift justice by court-martial the people would take the law into their own hands. This had in fact been happening before rebel troops gained control in some areas. I had heard of one man being hanged from a bridge outside Matanzas because a frenzied mob had seized him as an agent of Batista, and I heard of another man being hunted down like an animal outside Varadero and shot down instantly when cornered.

So Fidel Castro's extravaganza did more than any other single factor to turn the American tide against him. Nobody was even thinking vaguely then of invading Cuba or of interfering in its affairs. Castro's senseless utterance gave substance to suggestions that had already been made by a few American commentators that this man was no friend of the United States. It was enough in the political climate of the cold war and not-yet-forgotten McCarthyism to make him a communist to some Americans.

To be sure, the anti-Americanism of some elements within the Cuban revolution was bound sooner or later to make itself

felt, but it need never have become decisive and landed Cuba
into the Soviet bloc; and many Americans say that the policy
of the State Department toward Fidel Castro in the critical
two years after his victory did as much as anything else to
help Cuban communists to take her there. My own suggestion
here is that if Fidel Castro could have been persuaded to stop
making speeches and giving out ill-calculated boasts such as
the one about the gringos he could have obtained Cuban emancipation and a new and more equitable relationship with the
United States without all the difficulties, clashes, and venom
that followed. If my contention that Castro was not a communist (a matter that I propose to discuss in more detail later)
is accepted, there is some room for a belief that if he had been
capable of navigating his revolution more deftly and quietly
he could have avoided getting it and himself sucked into the
communistic morass. The general political climate in the hemisphere favored him. Awakened to danger by increasing Soviet,
communistic, and even Chinese penetration of Latin and South
America, the United States was reviewing the situation within
its so-called sphere of influence and was taking note of growing
political awareness and education in many countries. Only three
dictators of the detestable established type now survived, and
even they were living on borrowed time.

As I had found in a journalistic tour in 1958, states such as
Brazil, Chile, Peru and, in a more woolly and disappointing
way, the post-Perónist Argentina were making stumbling but
sometimes upward steps toward political adulthood. In the
world as a whole other shifts were taking place of which the
United States had to take note. Former British and other
colonies were gaining independence, and the balance of power
within the United Nations was changing to the temporary
disadvantage of the United States. One result was, as I found in
talks with Americans not wholly occupied with their own affairs
and finances, a spreading willingness to debate the point that
perhaps the United States had been since the start of the cen-

tury too materialistic and commercial in its dealings with Cuba
and that new arrangements might be possible. One could hardly
expect Americans to go further than that, as one should hardly
have expected Britons in their heyday of imperialism to admit
exploitation of colonial possessions.

Had he but realized it, Fidel Castro had an unprecedented
opportunity in the history of Cuba. He could have secured
most of what he wanted for his country from the United States,
certainly all that he needed to be getting on with as a first instalment, without forfeiting the profitable side of the working
arrangement that existed between the two countries and without ruining, as he did, his own political future and liberty and
the well-being of his country. He muffed his chance by sheer
political inexperience and incapacity and because he relied on
his vanity and emotions instead of his brain.

I was appalled as I watched him behave like an irresponsible
adolescent in the spring of 1959. He used to carry a checkbook
tucked in the breast pocket of his creased green fatigue jacket
as he flitted from place to place on his daily meanderings around
Havana, and sometimes, I heard, he would write out a check for
a plan or project that particularly appealed to him when it
was mentioned by devoted Cubans pressing upon him from morn
till night. One evening I heard him addressing a meeting of
sports officials and organizers. He told them he was not satisfied with Cuba's lowly place among the sporting nations of the
world and he said, with grand gestures, that he would provide
all the sports arenas and training grounds needed to take her
close to the top. It was another revelation of the man—a wonderfully intentioned but impractical and histrionic simpleton.
It simply did not occur to him that his splendid words and
promises would cost a fantastic amount of money if put into
effect, and he assuredly had not given a thought to wondering
where this would come from, since it would be far more than
Cuba could afford while she was repairing the dislocations of
the civil war and was being put on the adventurous new course

he had in store for her. He was also forgetting that while he
had just appointed a cabinet to run the country and did not
himself even have an official post of any kind with the government, he was committing his administration to an enormous and
costly scheme about which it had not been told a word. Of
course, no deeds followed his speech. His promises to the sports-
men were forgotten, as were to be so many other promises of
Fidel Castro. It was all extremely sad and disappointing—so
soon.

Even sadder, and certainly more ghastly, was his floundering
in the matter of executions of so-called war criminals. These
created immediate revulsion in the United States, but Castro
did nothing for some weeks to abate the resulting criticism in
the newspapers and elsewhere. At one of his impromptu meetings with foreign correspondents he was asked for his reaction
to the American protests against the daily shootings and he
answered, curtly for him, "They will go on until justice has
been done." Ernesto Guevara gibed, "Before the United States
starts complaining about what is going on here let her stop
all the murders and rapes and lynchings on her own territory."
Guevara was already disclosing his antagonism to the United
States. It must be said for him that he never tried to hide it
from the start.

Fidel Castro was so full of anger at the crimes he knew
Batista's soldiers, police, and thugs had committed that he simply could not think coolly about the matter. He argued that
since he and others around him in his regime knew these men
were guilty there was no need to waste time in proving them
so. He would not see that since the rest of the world did not
have the knowledge and proof that he professed to have it was
bound to be disturbed about what was being done. Its unsatis-
fied sense of justice was affronted by the daily reports of men
being given only the most perfunctory trials before being led
out to some squalid place, offered a last cigarette and the con-
solation of the church if they wanted it, and then shot. Eventu-

ally, some kind of light dawned in Castro's mind, but all it did
was to stimulate him to another kind of wild immoderacy.

I could scarcely believe it when I heard that, as the world
wanted to see justice being done, trials in Havana would be
held in the full beam of publicity—inside a vast sports palace.
It was the building in Havana most like a modern version of
the Colosseum in Rome. It had been built at great cost and with
many scandals during the regime of Batista and it was a perfect
setting for a spectacle of any kind, except a murder trial. It
had a big circular arena at ground level, with an amphitheater
of tiers of seats rising far into the heights of the building. It
was, of course, about the last place Fidel Castro should have
chosen for a trial in which Cuban life was the stake.

Some seventeen thousand persons were in this great hall
during the twelve-hour trial, lasting all night, of the first victim
of the show trials. He was Major Jesus Sosa Blanco, a swarthy,
low-browed man of fifty-one years who had been in charge of a
military district some distance from Havana. I did not doubt
that he was a murderer, for Castro would not otherwise have
chosen him for the role of villain in the first spectacle-trial of
all, but I felt pity for him as he cringed and grimaced during
his ordeal.

As usual with anything arranged by Cubans, the event was
hours late in starting. Sosa Blanco was eventually brought into
the arena three and a half hours after the time of starting
announced in the newspapers and over Radio Havana. In the
period of waiting, the crowd had been eating ice cream, peanuts,
and chunks of fat pork hawked round on skewers by vendors,
and as time went on it vented its annoyance at the delay with
increasingly frequent rounds of slow hand-clapping and derisive
whistling. The people had been promised a circus and they
wanted to get on with enjoying it. I reflected as I, too, waited
that human nature had not changed much since Roman days.
The only significant difference that I could see between games
in the Colosseum two thousand years earlier and the present

show was that the inevitable end, the human sacrifice, would take place later in private. At least there would be no blood spilled in the amphitheater that day, unless a riot happened.

Sosa Blanco played his role at first with spirit. Before his nerve went, he was snarling and defiant. He glared as he was hustled into the arena, manacled, by an armed guard of half a dozen rebels. As soon as the crowd spotted him there many shouted, howled, whistled, and spat down upon him. He looked up at them and smiled an awful smile, brazen and contemptuous. His guards thrust him into a chair on one side of a roped square about the size of a boxing ring and then sat down themselves on each side of him and behind him, with their guns between their knees. I remember seeing their captain bring out a cigar from the pocket of his tunic and start smoking. Sosa Blanco, sitting there with his manacled hands upon his lap, reminded me of one of those inmates of the Belsen concentration camp I had seen in Germany in 1945, even to the striped, pajamalike costume he was wearing.

Facing him only a few yards away were his three judges, all rebel officers, who glared at him with appropriate, impressive authority. Immediately on his left and just in front of him sat his lawyer, another officer, who to his credit tried hard with legal arguments and challenges to preserve his man, although he must have known as well as everybody else that the task was hopeless. Most extraordinary sight of all was provided by some twenty to thirty Cuban and American photographers who were squatted right in front of Sosa Blanco, some of them little more than two yards from him. These professionals worked with cold efficiency. To them, of course, Sosa Blanco had to be a subject and not a doomed man whose hours of life were swiftly closing. They watched him intently, lifting their cameras and pressing their shutter buttons whenever he made the slightest movement of interest or changed expression as one emotion chased another through his brain. He was an intensely interesting study and I was hypnotized by the changing picture he presented. Sometimes when his lawyer earnestly made a point that seemed to be in his favor he would smile, not now in defiance but pathetically, in a manner that seemed to indicate that momentarily he was deluding himself, in spite of his forebodings of doom, that perhaps there was just a chance for him. At other times the fear of death seemed to surge strongly within him and would be transmuted into trembling hands, shaking knees, and involuntary grimaces.

Sosa Blanco would sweat as this fear gripped him, and when he lifted one hand to wipe away the moisture from his forehead the other was dragged up with it by his handcuffs, adding another element of grotesque pantomime to the pitiable picture. All was noted by Cuban and foreign reporters as they sat just outside the roped arena in an enclosure filled with long trestle tables and hard benches for seats. Sometimes reporters would join the photographers and watch the accused at close range as they sprawled or lay on the dusty floor in front of him. He occasionally exchanged words with them. They told me that mostly he was cursing Batista for leaving him thus in the lurch or muttering protestations of innocence. He would say, "There might have been one or two things—but murders? No, no, no! . . ." Witness after witness was brought into the place to give evidence against him. Whenever some bewildered or ignorant peasant was asked by one of the judges to identify Major Sosa Blanco and could not do so, he or she would be prompted by shouts, howls, and pointing fingers from the uncontrolled crowd in the balconies on high.

Most of the evidence given was either being retailed at second-hand by the witnesses or was dragged out by ludicrously weighted questions from the bearded prosecutor. Yet I could not help feeling that for all the offenses against the basic concept of justice, for all the abominable shrieks for vengeance by the crowd, that a groping effort was being made to produce, before the victim was despatched, a show of fairer legal process than the earlier court-martial. It would have been unjust to have expected from so young and inexperienced a people as the Cubans a demonstration of the administration of justice as decorous and profound as comes from other nations that have had centuries of practice at the art.

The presiding judge was Dr. Humberto Sori Marin, who held the two dissociated posts of Minister of Agriculture and Attorney-General of the Rebel Forces. He was a wiry, intelligent man of about forty who wore enormous horn-rimmed spectacles that gave him the look of an owl. He tried to conduct the unique proceedings with as much decorum as could be managed in adverse circumstances. He went at the task nonstop during the night except for one recess of a quarter of an hour. He used the break to enjoy an ice cream that he bought from a vendor who roamed freely around the roped enclosure while the trial was halted.

I talked with Sori Marin as he enjoyed his ice cream. One remark he made—halfway through the trial, let it be noted—astonished me: "Yes, this chap here is only the first of many who will pay for their crimes." I looked across at Sosa Blanco as I listened to his chief judge. The photographers were swarming all round him now, talking with him and inducing him to pose this way, that way, with this expression, with that expression . . . He seemed to be cooperating, not minding at all. Perhaps their attentions were giving him temporary respite and comfort. He would have needed more solid comfort if he had heard what Sori Marin was saying to me.

At last, long after dawn had broken, the spectacle drew to an end. All the witnesses had told their tales, the long speeches had been made with fiery Latin fervor for and against the prisoner. Now Sori Marin pronounced sentence. He did so in ringing voice, obviously conscious that the eyes of everybody within the sports palace were upon him. He was shouting as he ended by declaring that Sosa Blanco was condemned to death by shooting.

The prisoner showed little evidence of impact. He did not flinch at the words, possibly in no condition to understand them after what he had gone through that night, and he quietly allowed himself to be led away by the six guards clustered around him. But gangs of young Cubans who had been watching the trial all night raced down from the galleries to line the passages through which the doomed prisoner was being taken to an army lorry in which he was to be driven back to his cell in La Cabaña where he would await death. The youths hissed, screamed, and yelled as he was whisked past them, and some of the more foolish among them even tried to rush the guards escorting Sosa Blanco. They were roughly thrust aside, some of them landing with thumps on the dusty road.

Sori Marin, his duty done, gathered his papers from the judges' bench at which he had sat for so many hours and made ready to go home. He walked over and shook hands with me, smiling, before he left the sports palace. Neither of us had an inkling of what was in store for him. In less than two years from the day when, full of revolutionary fervor, he had condemned Sosa Blanco in such resounding tones, fate was to play a tragic, ironic trick upon him. He slowly became disillusioned with Fidel Castro. Angered by the betrayal of what he considered to be the glorious revolution that he had served, he joined a band of secret plotters against the regime who decided in a fatal error that the time to move against Fidel Castro had come when the invasion on the Bay of Pigs was made in April, 1961. Havana was closed from the rest of the world except by wireless while the invasion was being met and overcome and few know exactly what happened to Sori Marin and his fellow-conspirators. All that emerged at the time was an announcement over Radio Havana that he had been wounded "while trying to evade capture." Later came another brief announcement that he had been executed for crimes against the revolution.

Once again, in the case of the trial of Sosa Blanco, the effect
of an impulsive tactic on the part of Castro was exactly opposite to what he had expected and intended. It ought to have
been obvious to him beforehand that the reaction in the United
States and in many other countries to a spectacle-trial held
in the garish and wholly unsuitable setting of a sports palace
would be one of revulsion and contempt for those who had
organized it. Reports and photographs of the trial, including
especially lurid pictures of Sosa Blanco grimacing and shaking
in front of his judges and the crowd, caused almost as much
disgust as the earlier ones of men being shot by firing squads.
Dismayed by this boomerang in propaganda, Castro impetuously made another serious mistake. He announced that the
verdict at the trial would be set aside because of the criticism
of the manner in which it had been reached, and a new trial
would be held in quieter and more decorous surroundings. It
was a ridiculous thing to do. He was saying, in effect, "All
right, we found him guilty in one way that you didn't like, and
now we'll find him guilty in another that we hope will suit you."

Clearly, nothing would or could upset the first verdict in
reality, and all that happened was that Sosa Blanco was
brought out again from the condemned cell and put through
another ordeal that could bring no profit to him or anybody
else. A ritual trial was staged in a small room in a suite at
Camp Columbia, the sprawling military headquarters on the
fringe of the city. This time a few chosen spectators were allowed to be present on behalf of "the people," and the proceedings were short, proper, and wholly anticlimactic. This was
inevitable because all they could achieve was confirmation of
the message of the first trial, death for Sosa Blanco.

One hoped that this was to be the end of the doleful story,
but there was one last exhibition of bad taste before the affair
was finished by a volley. It was a demonstration of the Cuban
fascination for pathos and was to add its small quota to the

feelings of dismay in the United States at the antics of the
Castro regime.

Being a Roman Catholic, Sosa Blanco turned to his church
for solace and absolution in the last hours of his life. Nobody
would quarrel with that. But the rebels, still making propagan-
dic melodrama, allowed one of their photographers to attend
and take a series of pictures showing the wretched man lying
prostrate at the foot of an altar, on his knees in tearful com-
munion with a priest, and in a last reunion with his wife.

Sosa Blanco, an ill-equipped and guilty man but in the end a
brave one as well, died with dignity. When at last he was taken
from his cell to ride the bumpy road with his firing squad to a
bloodied spot against a pitted wall lining the moat to the citadel, near Morro Castle, he found unexpected reserves of calm
and courage, according to the accounts which came to me later.
He was the hundred and third recorded victim of official revolutionary vengeance, and he was one of the first—if not the
first—to set the fashion among the condemned men of giving
an execution squad the final order to fire. Before doing so, I
heard, he directed the young men to aim at his heart and not
his head, and he told them, "I forgive you, *muchachos* [lads],
and I hope you forgive me."

Executions went on night after night in 1959 against the
wall near that moat. Only a few independent witnesses ever
attended any of them, and one of these men told me they were
a sickening sight. They were often bungled, mostly because of
the inexperience of the young riflemen concerned, but partly
through the fault (if one should apply the word here) of the
condemned.

The fashion of giving the order to fire had to be followed
carefully if you, as the victim, were not to suffer more than the
instant pangs of death. If you told the officer in charge of your
execution that you wished to give that final order he explained
the routine. After ordering the squad to bring their rifles to

shoulder and take aim, you must allow a few moments before going on to cry, "Fire." Many of the condemned men did not do this. In haste to have the whole thing done with, they gave the fatal order only an instant after ordering the squad to take aim. The men had no time to take accurate aim at the heart, and the result was often awful. Usually, the victim was felled but only superficially wounded by the volley and would be fully conscious as the officer in charge came to give the *coup de grâce*. Men would shriek: "Don't! Don't do it!" as the officer pointed his pistol to the side of the head, and a man died with the screaming words still coming from his mouth. Other men just could not bring their courage to the sticking point to go through with the intended gesture of ordering their own death. They would be able to get as far as the command to take aim and would then stand, pitifully speechless, with the guns pointing at them. Their executioner had to speak for them.

3 ❖ "Paredón!"
Roared the Crowd

AS THE outcry against the ghastly blood-lettings became louder in the United States, and even in comparatively distant and detached Europe, Fidel Castro became even more determined to go on with them. A week after he had swept into Havana like a triumphant Caesar, I encountered Castro as he shouldered his way through the inevitable mob of adulatory Cubans packing the spacious vestibule of the Havana Hilton Hotel, and asked if it were true, as had been rumored that day, that an order had been given to suspend executions because of the impact abroad. He answered brusquely, "What order? There has not been any such order. On the contrary, we shall punish every one of these murderers." He was not going to be moved by foreign reactions. "You may take it," he went on, "that even if we have to battle world opinion to give these people the penalty they deserve, we are ready to do so. The time for Americans to start worrying about this sort of thing was when Batista and his crew were killing innocent people."

Raul Castro, the younger brother, showed by deeds rather than words that he cared even less what anybody thought. This young man of twenty-eight—a ruthless soldier, a procommunist extremist if not yet an avowed communist, and a person without a vestige of the magnetism or the humor of Fidel—had been appointed Military Commandant of Oriente Province, and the reports coming from there supported by photographs indicated that he was taking vengeance wholesale. Nobody believed at first a report that somebody from Oriente brought into Havana on January 13, but it later turned out to be perfectly true, and it showed that, since the eyes of the world were upon Havana and Raul was hundreds of miles away to the east, at the far eastern end of the island, he was not being hampered as yet by any awkward publicity about his orders and methods. The story was that he had superintended the execution in one day of seventy-one Cubans who had worked in one way or another against the rebel forces before victory, or at least were accused of having done so. These men had been given hurried trials during the night by a revolutionary tribunal set up by Raul Castro and had been taken at dawn to a place used ordinarily for target practice. They had been felled in batches by squads using rifles and other arms. The bodies had collapsed into a long trench hacked out earlier to a depth of ten feet by bulldozers, and they had then been covered by earth. The executions had occupied three and a half hours, and Raul Castro was believed to have watched them for some time. A newspaper in Havana, *El Mundo*, reported that one batch of executions had been postponed for a little while for the light to improve so that photographers making a film to be called "Revolutionary Justice" could get good pictures.

I cannot say, of course, how solidly the Cuban people were backing the Castros in this wave of savage vengeance, but the impression was certainly propagated by the regime that people did not want the shootings to stop. Union leaders in Manzanillo, a port in eastern Cuba, called a general strike to protest against leniency being shown to "war criminals" who, they said, were being sent to prison instead of being shot, as they deserved. In Havana I saw a procession of men and women school teachers on one of the streets off La Rampa leading school children behind banners saying: "We demand justice against the assassins" and "Execute the murderers." I reflected as I watched that Cuba had a long way to go before she could expect the world to take her seriously if her teachers, the persons supposed to be spreading enlightenment among her future citizens, could spend their time in calling for blood in this fashion. I was even more dismayed when I heard the boys and girls behind them chanting the slogans on the banners, presumably having been schooled to do so, even though many of them could scarcely have understood the grim meaning of the big words they were chanting.

The strains of keeping up a senseless, and self-imposed, pace of being on duty and on display almost round-the-clock first laid Fidel Castro low before his revolution was a month old. He had to go to bed in his quarters on the top floor of the Havana Hilton Hotel and stay there until an enforced rest and some much-needed sleep cured him of a severe chill. The man had scarcely been to bed at all since New Year's Day, and it seemed like a miracle to me that this abuse of his physique, plus the enormous mental pressures of leading a revolution that (probably to his astonishment) was not only undergoing racking internal convulsions but had aroused the hostility of much of the world from the moment of its triumph, might have been expected to cause him to break down altogether. Fidel Castro, however, had been very obviously in magnificent physical condition when he came into Havana after two years of rigorous but healthy life in the mountains. He bounced back in three days to resume the old merry-go-round. He turned with characteristic impulsiveness and flamboyance to the urgent task of trying to redress the harm done by the continuing executions, which he still insisted were necessary and just, and by what he considered to be the unfounded hostility being shown him by the United States.

It surprised me then, and it continued to surprise me for years afterward, that Castro and those around him could forever be talking about killing twenty thousand Yankees, crying that American companies were fleecing people, flinging out accusations against the crimes of Yankee imperialism, and the rest, and become hurt when these same Yankees ceased to look kindly upon them. No matter what the Yankees had done or had not done in the fifty years of Cuban sovereignty and before, there was no logic about believing that you could now give them a verbal and political beating and expect them still to be your friends. I can only offer a suggestion that there must be in the character of many Latin Americans an element that causes them to argue thus: "Well, he is so powerful and wealthy and he has done so well out of dealing with us that he cannot blame us for taking it out on him sometimes."

Fidel Castro's way of trying hastily to turn back the tide of international disfavor that had been created by the executions and the overt anti-American trend of his revolution was characteristically extravagant and unorthodox. He telegraphed invitations to hundreds of newspapers, television and radio stations and networks, and other branches of public information throughout North and South America asking each to send a representative to Havana, with all travel and other expenses paid, to see for himself what was really happening in Cuba. He gave his venture the literal but still symbolic quasi-military name of Operation Truth. His spokesmen explained to me that he was incensed because he considered the relatively few American reporters based in Havana biassed against him because they had been operating comfortably under Batista and had never been sympathetic toward him while he had been struggling in the mountains. He also believed, they explained, that capitalistic institutions in the United States, alarmed at the thought of what his revolution might do to their Cuban interests, were spreading falsehoods about him.

There was possibly something in these charges, but I had to point out that a person would have had to be insensitive indeed to be unaffected by the relentlessness of revolutionary retribution, the fantastic chaos in Havana since January 1, and the hollow sound of Fidel Castro's professions of goodwill toward the United States when these were compared with his other utterances and threats against it. Above all, I conveyed the doubts one could not now help feeling about his capacity to resist the communist pressures that were already growing within his army and his so-called administrative machine. I had already seen and read some unjustified exaggerations and plain untruths disseminated about him and the revolution, but all that I had seen for myself, as a neutral in this purely inter-American drama, had caused me to write doubtfully about him on January 18, "Is he really as pure, politically and morally, as he has seemed in these glamorous days of victory? Is he really equipped for the role that lies ahead? Is he, in fact, just a little too good to be true?"

One facet of the role ahead of him would clearly need the talents of a statesman of the highest order. As I saw it, Castro was committed to attaining emancipation and true independence for Cuba; that was the very theme of his revolution. To reach that goal he would have to remove the U. S. investment and power in the country. How could he arrange to enjoy the friendship of the United States and a blessing on his revolution while taking away everything the United States had acquired in Cuba? The process would have to be carried out very slowly, very cautiously, and eventually with the understanding and cooperation of the United States. I was doubtful at the

time that, for all his charisma and blarney, he was wizard
enough to perform such a near miracle, but I was still willing
to give him a chance to prove me wrong; I could not forget—
and I still cannot—how like a Messiah he had seemed when he
entered Havana.

Castro had an excellent response to his mass invitation in
Operation Truth and, with the sweet-smelling and intoxicating
scents of victory still inflaming him, he put on an exciting
personal show. Over 380 journalistic representatives from organizations in twenty countries came into Havana in the planes
chartered by the rebel government. There were about a hundred
of them from the United States, three from Britain, and one
from France. Most of them were given quarters in the gaudy,
opulent, and unlucky Havana Riviera Hotel, which had been
built with American money during the Batista era to outclass
rivals such as the Havana Hilton and the Nacional but was
doomed because of the revolution never to gather the golden
harvest that its promoters had expected. Each guest was given
a badge of identification proclaiming association with Operation Truth. The badge opened all doors and, with luck, guaranteed protection against arrest, robbery, accidental shooting,
and other hazards of existence in the jumpy Havana of the
period. Since I was already operating in the city under my own
power, as it were, I enjoyed none of the hospitality or other
benefits of Operation Truth, but I had the advantage of watching with some detachment as it unfolded.

The main event was an appearance by Fidel Castro before
his guests in the luxurious dining and cabaret room of the
hotel. A big stage, enormous mirrors, and glittering chandeliers
set off tables and rows of seats. Bearded rebel guards posted
at the entrance to the salon made sure that nobody brought a
bomb or other offensive weapon within range of the Leader.
Everybody entering was told to hold his hands above his head
and submit to a quick search. Then, as he walked to his seat,
he was given a folder containing some of the most revolting

photographs I have ever seen; they were said to represent murders and atrocities committed by Batista's men. The impact was softened by the daiquiris and other drinks proffered by Cuban maidens obviously chosen for their dark-haired beauty and, of course, their shapeliness. The guests had plenty of time to enjoy both drinks and beauty, for even on this critical occasion Fidel Castro was very late in appearing. I timed his tardiness at two hours and forty minutes, impressive even for him.

But he had had a crowded twenty-four hours indeed. The day before he had called a mass meeting around the Misiones Park in front of the Presidential Palace, and as this was the first of these phenomena which were to mark his reign of government by microphone and harangue, his men had made sure that it should be a truly tremendous affair. Its purpose was to give Cubans an opportunity to demonstrate to the world their solidarity with him in the matter of executions and defiance of United States susceptibilities. It was claimed afterward that a million people had jammed the area, but most qualified persons said this was nonsense and that there might have been up to half that number present. Flanked by Camilo Cienfuegos and other bearded idols from the Sierra, Fidel Castro had the crowds roaring and shouting as he declared frenziedly that Cuba had no need to apologize to the United States or anybody else because of the executions; only justice was being done to scum who had tortured and killed.

I was chilled as I heard Cubans about me shouting a word that I had not heard before but which I sensed was ominous as its three syllables were chanted relentlessly around me. It was *"paredón."* I asked one Cuban what it meant. "Send them all to the execution wall—that's what it means," he said, his eyes suddenly ablaze. I was sickened. Here was Fidel Castro using his heaven-sent gifts of oratory and natural leadership to incite the most brutal and savage instincts of the followers who adored him. Here was a massive crowd crying for blood, more and more blood. Here were the appalling banners proclaiming

in the beautiful winter sunshine of Havana: "Revolutionary
Justice for the Batista Murderers," "Extradite the War
Criminals," and (inevitably) "Away with Yankee Imperialism." I turned and elbowed my way through the monstrous
crowd. I wanted no more of it that day.

Yet Fidel Castro could count it as a day to live in his memory.
Never again would he have a crowd such as that from which to
draw revolutionary sustenance. He spoke for some hours, and
when he had finished he could not calm down or rest. He did
not lie down until an hour before he was due to appear before
his guests at the Riviera the next day. "I cannot sleep because
my blood is still on fire," he said, as I was told later, while he
and his intimates watched dawn break over the city.

He showed no signs of exhaustion or strain when eventually
he turned up at the hotel. His expression was alert and his
loping stride determined as, with an unlighted cigar jutting
à la Churchill from the right-hand side of his mouth, he marched
down an aisle to a dais on the stage of the salon. A phonograph
played a lively military tune as he did so.

He was relaxed and at his most charming to his guests. There
were many harmless jokes to lighten the expounding of the
Castro doctrine of the moment as he answered questions. Some
of his hearers applauded softly and, I thought, sycophantly,
from time to time, but the North Americans were not among
them. He made one point again and again. It was that vested
interests had been trying to drive a wedge between him and
friendly peoples outside Cuba. "The American government has
not been hostile to us but has recognized us," he said, suavely.
"But powerful interests have been trying to influence the American government against us . . . I ask you friendly journalists
to tell the truth about us."

Did he really mean or want that? I did not think so. What
he wanted was that the friendly journalists write only the
nice things about him and his revolution. His thinking was all

lopsided, like Hitler's had been. A dictator's has to be so, or he
ceases to be one.

It was quite impossible in these hectic early days to keep
abreast of everything that was happening within, and to, the
revolution. One reason for this was that too much was happening all at once for anything like a clear picture to be delineated.
Many events happened behind the scenes and did not become
known for months and even years afterward. But some trends
and developments did become obvious. One was a brief but
bitter struggle for political power in the new Cuba between
the various groups that had fought alongside Fidel Castro in
the long campaign from east to west of the island. These groups
included the *Directorio Revolucionario* (mainly composed of
university students), the Second Front of Escambray (bureaucrats, clerks, and a proportion of members of the bourgeoisie),
and the 26th of July Movement (Castro's original revolutionary corps).

The first two organizations had been at odds with each other
for a long time in the field, but I knew nothing definite about
this. Certainly when members of the *Directorio* reached Havana
they went straight to the university and occupied it, and others
also helped to put this section of the bearded rebel force into a
strong strategic position by occupying the Presidential Palace.
The Second Front, appropriately in view of its name and its
comparative weakness, took second place by setting up its quarters in hotels and in offices and buildings abandoned by the
Batista regime. The two organizations then set about issuing
statements and appeals and calling press conferences to emphasize their claims. They might just as well have saved all
their effort, for the communists were already mobilizing for a
campaign that in the end sent not only the *Directorio* and the
Second Front into oblivion but the 26th of July Movement as
well. Communist leaders who had been in exile for some years

came back to Havana and took over the control of lesser communists who had been among the squabbling minorities in the capital since January 1.

Among those who now returned was Blas Roca, the Moscow-trained agitator and organizer who was to become one of the most powerful figures in Cuba in the following six years. Indeed, this skilled organizer and unquestioning communist theoretician might have remained at the top of the party pyramid for much longer than six years but for a decline in health. He began to show visible effects of some serious malady by 1964, and thereafter less and less was seen or heard of him. I last saw him for myself in the summer of 1964, at a public meeting at which he was a principal speaker. As he sat awaiting introduction he seemed to be enveloped by a slight but persistent shake. His head wobbled minutely but regularly, and even though he rested his hands on a table in front of him these, too, exhibited the tremor. While he was addressing the meeting, animatedly and with his notably powerful voice, the symptom was not apparent. But it was there again when he sat down.

One wished for long after 1959 that it had been possible to catch up with the ever-moving Fidel Castro and find out what guidance he was giving, what part he was playing, in these desperate and decisive maneuverings between the communists and the others. Was he already abandoning his former comrades-in-arms and nursing the communists into power under him? Or was he just letting the situation sort itself out according to the strengths and weaknesses of those involved? To know the answers to questions such as these would be to settle once and for all the still unsolved riddle of whether Fidel Castro's revolution was a communist one from the very beginnings.

My own impression at that time was that he was having very little association indeed with the political scramble. Either by intent or from inexperience, or because of the consuming demands of his supreme position as the leader, figurehead, and very essence of a victorious revolution, he was just not in-

volved. Far too many other preoccupations were chasing each
other through his head, I felt, for him to have the time—even
if he had the talent and the inclination—to take a hand in the
political machinations.

There was one piece of evidence that showed that he was
not yet favoring the communists. On the contrary, it implied
that the political course of the revolution was to be only moderately to the left. It was that his first cabinet and administration did not include one man identified as a communist, but it
did include men who were ardently anticommunist. Castro, who
at thirty-three was two years below the age that would qualify
him to become President, appointed Dr. Manuel Urrutia, a
respectable and moderate man indeed, to the post. Dr. Urrutia
had been for a long time a judge of the Court of Appeals. The
Prime Minister was Dr. Jose Miro Cardona, a leading lawyer
and a prominent member of the Havana Bar Association; the
Minister of the Treasury was Rufo Lopez Fresquet, an economist with an American wife and a man who for years had
had the trust of various American companies with interests
in Cuba; and the Minister of Agriculture was Dr. Humberto
Sori Marin. Sori Marin, as I have described, served as presiding judge at some of the trials of accused Batista criminals,
later joined a plot against Castro because of disillusionment at
the annexation of the revolution by the communists, and eventually was shot in mysterious circumstances after being arrested.

To be sure, this first administration did not last long. It
quickly began to fall apart under the strain of trying to keep
up with Fidel Castro, who was an administration all to himself.
The very first rupture came, most surprisingly, at the beginning of February, on the unlikely topic of gambling. When a
Cuban informant came to me on January 30 and told me most
soberly that it looked as if not only the President but the Prime
Minister and one or two of the ministers in the cabinet wanted
to resign because they disagreed with Fidel Castro about the

reopening of casinos in Havana, I thought my leg was being pulled. Here we were all agitated about whether communists or noncommunists were going to seize control of Cuba, and now the cabinet was supposed to be in turmoil about whether roulette wheels should spin, and whether people should be allowed to test their luck at vingt-et-un and on the slot machines.

When I made my own inquiries I found that the report was substantially true. I soon perceived also that the question—gambling or no gambling?—was no incidental matter but had implications in Cuba at least as critical as, say, the abolition or continuance of taxation on liquor or tobacco in the United States, Great Britain, or any other big country. Gambling had been for a long time an important factor not only in the Cuban character but in the country's economy. Almost every Cuban was addicted to gambling in one form or another. The poorest people were often the most deeply involved, and many of them inevitably became poorer as they indulged in the legal and the various illegal lotteries, risked their pesos on the slot machines in the casinos and elsewhere, or diced and drank in the back rooms of the dimly lit bars that stood almost side by side in some of the more popular tourist sections of midtown and downtown Havana. And, of course, the gambling tables of the sumptuous casinos not only represented a livelihood for many thousands of Cubans but actually went a long way toward keeping the country going, since they were an attraction to hordes of rich American tourists who mostly expected to leave behind some of their dollars in the casinos when they went back home. You could gamble round the clock in prerevolutionary Havana.

But when the rebels occupied the city they shut down the casinos as part of the brief general strike that Castro ordered as a mark of confidence in him. The casinos had stayed shut after the strike was over, and the lotteries were still banned. There had been evidence of the public discontent at the deprivation and hardships that the closure had caused, but it had been expressed most deferentially and, sometimes, pathetically. I had seen pickets parading one day round the Presidential Palace, carrying placards, some of which said, "President Urrutia, we are behind you, but please let lotteries be restored. Over 10,000 ticket sellers and their families are almost starving."

President Urrutia and Premier Cardona had said publicly that they opposed the resumption of gambling in any form whatever. Fidel Castro had promised that the casinos would be reopened, but only to foreign tourists. There had thus been a difference between Castro and his two chief administrators, but I had scarcely believed that it was of sufficient seriousness to cause a split in the cabinet. In the end, President Urrutia decided to stay on, and so did the cabinet ministers who had threatened to go with him. But Dr. Cardona would not give way on his principles, and he resigned. So Fidel Castro became Premier in just over a month after his conquest, and he was to stay in that post for year after year, through all the vicissitudes and startling and dangerous crises that he and his revolution—and the world—were to endure.

The casinos were opened under close governmental supervision, but the American tourists never came, of course, and in the end all the places were closed down and put to other uses. The casino at the Havana Hilton was stripped of all its luxurious and glittering fittings and turned into a kind of exhibition hall in the service of the revolution. Drab charts and propaganda posters followed each other in dreary succession on its walls. Students and prorevolutionary visitors from Latin America used it for a meeting place and conference hall. One would never have dreamed in the end that it had once echoed the click of the roulette balls, the discreet and soft announcements of the croupiers, the swish of silken gowns, the clink of glasses, the slowing tick-tock of the wheel of fortune, and the staccato whirs and clops of the slot machines standing against the richly decorated walls. Cuban casinos always fascinated me because, although they served one of the most inflaming passions in the human make-up, their atmosphere was always muted, bottled up. People used their eyes and their hands far more than they used their mouths while at the tables. I often wanted to hear a whoop of joy from some sudden big winner, or even a shriek of despair from a loser, but I never did, and now I suppose I never shall.

Although Dr. Urrutia stayed in office after the upheaval over gambling, he became steadily more out of sympathy with Fidel Castro and the revolution. He went eventually, in July, 1959. After rumors had been spreading for weeks that he was in disgrace because he would not do instantly and without question whatever Fidel Castro asked of him, he was edged out in circumstances of high drama. Fidel Castro suddenly plunged the capital into turmoil by resigning his position as Premier. In answer to the intense public clamor that, I feel sure, he had deliberately provoked so that he could do as he wished with President Urrutia, he agreed to address the nation by radio and television. When he did so he rambled on for a long time in generalities about the aims and problems of the revolution. At last, he turned upon President Urrutia and in doing so he included one remark that, I suggest, must be noted by anybody interested in solving the communistic conundrum of Castro and the revolution. On this evening (July 16, 1959) Fidel Castro said in his speech that he was not a communist and that his revolutionary movement was not communistic. And he added: "But we do not have to say that we are anticommunists."

This was a cue for him to turn upon President Urrutia, whom he accused of displaying himself as a champion of anticommunism, refusing to sign ordinances into law, and generally behaving as a traitor. Even while Fidel Castro was still attacking his President, crowds began gathering outside the Presidential Palace, perhaps because they had been ignited by the frenzy of their Premier at the microphones, and perhaps because they had been told to go there. "Out with Urrutia," they chanted. He had resigned even before Castro had finished dealing with him on the airwaves. The cabinet was convened hurriedly and it chose Dr. Osvaldo Dorticos, then serving as Minister of Revolutionary Laws, to succeed him. Dr. Dorticos was a lawyer from the province of Las Villas and had the reputation of being far to the left in his thinking, if not a thoroughgoing communist.

One by one, members of that first revolutionary cabinet went with Urrutia, either into oblivion or into passive or active opposition to the revolution. But after almost seven years there was still one original minister in his original post. This was Dr. Armando Hart, the Minister of Education. He managed to keep himself clear of all the perils besetting anybody associated with the revolution and its mercurial leader. I shall want to read his reminiscences, if and when he ever writes them.

At least three tourists spent a holiday in Cuba during that turbulent spring of 1959. They were my wife, my son, and myself—and what a checkered time the three of us had. Some of it was so enjoyable as to give us the happiest memories. Some of it was so ludicrous as to make us wonder whether Cubans ever would grow up and organize themselves. Fidel Castro's revolution was beginning to achieve a few changes, but many of the simple and carefree customs and habits of island life were still being followed as strongly as ever, and certainly the peculiar Cuban talent for producing a muddle, if one is ever possible, had not diminished.

After spending almost three months trying to follow the twists and turns and mysteries of Fidel Castro's revolution, I felt I needed both a change and a rest. I went back briefly to New York—to find only a small minority of Americans still cherishing some of the first idealism about him and his product—and then undertook a real change by going down to Cape Canaveral, as it was then called. There I was to await the spectacular launch or depressing fizzle of another of the early space rockets devised by United States technicians and scientists, including many who had come from Germany after the Second World War, trying to catch up with other Germans who were putting the Soviet Union ahead in this new field of international rivalry. I was then to take a holiday—and as I would be within little more than half an hour's flight of the beach resort at Varadero, why not spend some of it there? I suppose really the lure of watching the new Cuban drama develop was becoming too strong for me to resist. . . .

While I waited in the cosy comfort of the Starlite Motel at Cocoa Beach for the expected launching attempt, my wife and son drove by easy stages from New York to Key West and took themselves and our Chevrolet station wagon across to Havana aboard the car ferry still plying two or three times a week between Cuba and the American mainland. The strategy was that they would spend a day or so in Havana and then drive the eighty miles to Varadero, where we were to occupy a house close to the beach which we had rented from members of a local family. I was to make the easy flight from Florida as soon as my mission at Cape Canaveral was over. It was as neat a piece of planning as you could imagine.

But the Cubans managed to wreck it. On the evening of the Friday when my wife had crossed to Havana, I had a telephone call from her. She was speaking from the Zarragozana Restaurant, which the revolution had not yet ravished as one of the finest eating places in the whole of Spanish America, and to which she had gone to compensate herself for the disaster that had befallen her. The Cuban immigration authorities had simply impounded our car—locked it up in a compound surrounded by barbed wire and gone off for the weekend with the key. They had done so, as far as she could understand, on two preposterous grounds. Firstly, they said that as the car documents were in my name and I was not there, she was probably trying to run away from me, taking our son with her. Secondly, in case that were not so, she was importing the

car into Cuba either to sell it in toto or as spare parts at a
vast profit on the black market.

I almost went into elliptical orbit as I listened to the
incredible story in my quarters on Cape Canaveral. Recovering,
I dashed off feverish cables to the British and American
Embassies and to the Cuban Department of Immigration,
pleading for something to be done to prevent the holiday of
about the only foreign tourists going to Cuba that spring from
being totally ruined before it began. The British Embassy
worked hard and effectively and on Saturday morning induced
the Cubans to agree that my wife really was a genuine holiday-
maker and could have her car back. The snag was that the
man with the keys both to the compound and the car just
could not be found. He had gone off for the weekend, probably
to Varadero. My wife eventually got the car on Monday, after
waiting hours on the steamy quay in Havana's dockland, and
established our residence in Varadero that evening.

Thereafter, the holiday was wholly an education and mostly
a delight. To be sure, there were oddities about the house that
took a little absorbing. Some of the rooms provided homes for
myriads of sand flies, which seemed to be equipped with dog's
teeth, judging by the pangs caused by their incessant bites.
And we found we had a well-nourished toad as a resident of one
of the toilets. I think he spent most of his time in the sewage
pipes, but he was visible quite often, with his head and un-
blinking eyes poised just above the water level whenever one
of us went into that bathroom. I tried flushing him away once
or twice, but he always managed to bob back.

The flies and the toad were as nothing compared with the
pure joys that Varadero could still offer before it was utterly
ruined as a choice resort by the revolution. Its clean sandy
beach stretched literally for miles. The water was warm and
wonderfully clear, and there was every kind of roller for every
kind of swimmer. It drew us like a magnet, and we would stay in

it or close to it for hours at a time, until hunger called us away. Then we could have the delight of a rum cocktail, flavored by the juice of limes that we simply plucked off the trees in our garden, followed by platefuls of tiny delectable oysters brought to us at the rate of six or seven dozen at a time by a smiling little man on a bicycle equipped with boxes just to carry them behind his saddle. At other times his boxes would be filled with Morro crabs, so full of life that one of them once snapped two claws in a vice around one of my wife's fingers. It clung there immovably for many minutes of pain and anxiety before suddenly becoming bored and letting go.

The shops on the long main street of Varadero were not yet feeling the pinch of the revolution. The bowling alley and the clubs and relaxing open-air refreshment gardens were still well filled with Cubans who were behind Fidel Castro to a man. Sotero, the hard-working proprietor of the old provision store near the Yacht Club, was feeling no shortage of the multitude of goods that he had been accustomed for years to offer to friends and tourists alike. He had many shelves lined with bottles of rum that he dispensed at the rate of eighty-five cents for the common white Bacardi and $1.25 and upward for the dark and the *Anejo* Bacardi. He would cash checks, lend money, do anything for you if he liked you, and I am happy that, almost uniquely and perhaps because Fidel Castro had a soft spot for Varadero, he had still not been wiped out by nationalization several years later.

Yet the revolution *had* made its mark on the town. Many of the homes of the wealthy folk in the area of the Kwama Club were empty or emptying while we were there. Other homes standing within a few feet of that magnificent beach were locked and shuttered; they had belonged to cronies of Batista who were either dead or safely away in the United States or some other haven out of the Castro reach. Bridges and road junctions at the approaches to Varadero were manned day and night by young bearded rebels who methodically stopped every car. They became most friendly and perhaps fond of us when they devotedly stopped us day after day and asked to see our papers as we made our holiday jaunts down the roads flanked by sisal fields and sugar plantations. Most of the time we were on the way to the lively shopping towns of Matanzas and Cárdenas or to use our snorkels in the teeming waters of Bocas de Camarioca, where the fishermen's sons played baseball near the beach for many hours on end each day, and where cockfights were still held every Tuesday at 3 P.M.: admission one dollar. Quite often we would have a great stretch of Varadero beach to ourselves for most of a day, and the only people we would see would be two or three rebel soldiers, in olive-green fatigues despite the heat, strolling past us as they took an hour or two off from their duties as members of the local garrison. And one day we heard only the merest details of the exciting story of the *Teniente* (Lieutenant) in the Rebel Army who had been unmasked as a former Batista agent and had been hunted high and low throughout the town. One household we knew had given him brief shelter, and he had had to flee from them, leaving his cap, when his rebel pursuers closed in on him. We never learned of his fate, but we regarded it as certain that he was captured and had to take the gloomiest view of his chances of survival. Only his cap remained in the possession of our acquaintances as a relic of the episode.

Varadero worked its beneficent magic not only on us but on a friend from upstate New York who had been laid low by the rigors of a cold and snowy winter. By the time she flew back to the mainland, after only a brief dalliance in the sun by those magnificent waters of the western Atlantic, she was restored. One could not help feeling regret, as the recuperative miracle happened, that the convulsions, stupidities, and hardships of a politico-military revolution were inevitably going to deny places such as Varadero to the world for a long time to come. I was to go again briefly to the place a year or two later, as I shall relate, and I was to thank my stars that I had the fortune to get out of it without being arrested as a spy. It was then by no means the Varadero of 1959.

We wound up our Cuban vacation by making a week's motoring tour of the extreme western province of Pinar del Río. This was no luxury tour of the kind where all the details are arranged beforehand and one knows where the weary but satiated head will lie from night to night. As far as we could ascertain before we left Varadero, there would be scarcely more than a handful of hotels or other resting-places worthy of the name along our whole route. We were to travel several hundreds of miles along the coast and in the hilly interior of the province. With a revolution already exerting its unsettling influences, we might easily find ourselves without a roof at all. So we took our roof with us. We put a mattress in the station wagon and borrowed all the other necessities not only for sleeping but for eating as well. We got one of those inflatable mattresses for our son, so that he could sleep under the stars whenever it was clear and along the front seat of the car when it was not. We had a fine tour, revolution notwithstanding.

We saw the Cuban countryside at close quarters indeed. We lived in it and mostly off it for a week. We would buy simple foods from peasant farmers or at one of the few stores we passed in villages and small towns as we made our unhurried way through the province, and each evening we would pull off the rough and rocky road and park our mobile car-hotel on a track or in a meadow—anywhere that suited the purpose. The few Cubans we met who were willing or, to be frank, bright enough to exchange some words with us seemed to know little of the revolution that had turned Havana and the other big cities upside down, but they had all heard of Fidel Castro and were for him. Their eyes lit up and their faces broke into smiles at mention of his name, although their knowledge of him seemed not to go much further than the judgment, "He is a good man" or "He will do much for Cuba." It struck me that they were usually much too preoccupied with trying to drag a meager existence out of their pieces of land and their few pigs, cows, and other animals to have either time or inclination to bother their heads about the revolution.

Many of these Cubans lived extremely primitively. Sometimes as we camped out and surveyed what was going on around us we could imagine ourselves back in biblical times. There would be a man ploughing but a foot at a time with a skinny ox dragging several pieces of wood and a blade held together here with a nail or wooden bolt, there a leather thong or piece of rope. His progress would be so dismally slow as to be almost painful to watch, for the makeshift nature of the implement he was using was matched by the blundering lethargy of the ox. This picture of primitivity was completed by other details. The man's home would be a tumbledown shack with perhaps two rooms and an outbuilding or so to serve for everything—people and animals alike. From time to time his wife or one of his daughters would appear from the doorless opening to gather water from a stream in the meadow or to perform some other chore. The languid ritual of life ended early in the day, for often enough we should see nothing more of our remote acquaintances once plough and ox had been put away. But in the early morning we should be awakened by a strange grunting and shuffling around our car; one of the man's sons was taking a pig along the track. Why or where we could not tell, for not a word could be coaxed from the lad, although he would smile shyly as he prodded the pig along past us.

Such people as these seemed to take us altogether for granted, as if foreign tourists taking an alfresco holiday in their midst were a commonplace. It might well have been courtesy that prompted them to show such little interest in us and not to stare at or interfere with us in any way, for I have found Cubans to be notably considerate of other people, especially foreigners, even in circumstances of stress. I reflected as I watched these humble people in the valleys and on the rounded hills of Pinar del Río that Fidel Castro could, and would, claim that they were the ones to whom his heart went out; they were the ones his revolution would benefit, because they were the most exploited victims of an economic and political system that he intended to uproot. Quite so, and if he could better their existence—in education, standard of living, health, and all—without making Cuba an outcast among her neighbors, all would be well. I still felt, late in that unforgettable spring of 1959, that he could yet pull it all off by learning from the early errors of immaturity that he had committed and was still committing how to ensure the good will of the United States, the one country that could do everything for him.

4 ◆ *Left Turn*

IT BECAME clearer and clearer, as the first summer of the revolution advanced, that Fidel Castro was not going to fulfill my hope; he was not to learn how to exploit his chance of achieving Cuban emancipation almost painlessly through shrewd and skillful diplomacy. One oratorical, political, and economic item after another showed that, instead of untying quietly and slowly the bonds which held the two countries together, he was going to hack a violent way to independence. Some people contend that he chose the brutal method because he was a communist all along, and that his ultimate goal was not only to turn Cuba into a communist state but to set up a communistic empire throughout Latin America. Others believe

65

that skilled and determined communist zealots saw him as a perfect dupe and used him with the purpose of achieving that goal for them. Still other people feel that he was forced to turn to the communists because the more moderate of his supporters were not strong or clever enough to capture him for themselves and were let down anyhow by the feebleness of the official American reaction to the unfettered defiance from Havana. It is a puzzle that will probably not be resolved for a very long time. My own opinion was, and still is, that the truth lies not in the proposition that Fidel Castro was always a communist but in the third alternative I have outlined. In any case, if the United States did not like what was happening, it should have acted early and effectively to stop it. The Johnson administration was to do so, without paying too much attention to the clatter of criticism that followed, in Santo Domingo six years later.

The catalog of events during the first nine months of 1959 illustrated the reformist trend. On the home front the new brush swept mostly clean. No corruption was evident anywhere within the regime and everybody felt that Fidel Castro meant it when he said in March that anybody appropriating government funds would be shot. Prostitution was not, of course, eradicated, but it was curtailed and made less brazen than it had been in the gay old decades now but a memory. Although trade was still plied more discreetly in the bars and quasi-clubs that had not yet felt the constrictions of revolution, brothels were raided and removed, and girls with establishments in the ground-floor apartments on some of the narrow streets in midtown and downtown Havana were forbidden to parade in their customary brightly colored and ultratight pants or even to sit at their open windows and try to cajole the passer-by into joining them. Rufo Lopez Fresquet, not yet disenchanted with Castro, did surprisingly well in conjuring tax payments out of people who either had never paid them at all or had grossly underpaid. One of his successful stratagems was to make deals with delinquent taxpayers. Instead of rigidly enforcing the law with heavy fines and imprisonment he arranged for offenders to pay on the instalment plan.

But it was in the revolution's dealings with, and treatment of, American interests that it showed its teeth. On March 4 the Cuban Telephone Company, which was mainly American-owned and was a subsidiary of the International Telephone and Telegraph Company, was seized, and Castro announced that as of April 1 the price of a local call would be reduced from ten cents to five. (You could still make a call at this half-price years later, but your chances of completing it were nowhere as good as they had been.) A little later in the year the Cuban Electric Company was likewise seized and rates were drastically cut. Even Americans and other foreigners living as permanent residents in Cuba felt the sting of the revolution. An announcement was made on June 16 that all such foreigners must get a government permit to leave the island and, of course, a similar permit to come back. Hitherto there had never been any restriction whatever on the movement of foreigners in and out of Cuba. Americans had not had to have visas but along with other foreign visitors had paid a modest toll to the Cuban exchequer before flying or sailing to Havana by forking out $2.50 for a so-called tourist card.

The pace of annexation and expropriation quickened as the Agrarian Reform Law went into effect in the first week of June and other independent seizures were made. The recompense offered to dispossessed owners was in the form of twenty-year bonds bearing interest at 4.5 percent and repayable only in pesos. The protests about this treatment were so loud that the State Department made its first formal complaint to Fidel Castro. In a note despatched on June 11 it reminded him that while confiscation might be admissible under international law, there was an accompanying obligation on the part of the confiscator to pay "prompt, adequate, and effective compensa-

tion." Not even Castro could claim that the twenty-year bonds
fulfilled this obligation, but mere words in a diplomatic note
meant almost nothing in the circumstances and, as was to be
expected, they were brusquely turned aside by Castro. Severe
action was obviously necessary here and, if the United States
government had meant business in coping with Castro they
would have taken it. I felt that the first critical opportunity
of checking him had been missed; he would now be encouraged
to go on and on.

In fact, while the cat and mouse game was continuing between him and Washington, Castro was still under the spell of
two delusions that tended to confirm my impression of him at
that time as an unrealistic political amateur. One delusion was
that American tourists would still be eager to come to Cuba in
spite of the savagery of the blood revenge that had been taken
by his revolution and in spite of all his violent words and
actions against their country since January. The other delusion, which must have been associated in his mind with the first,
was that the American people and the American government
were separate entities and could be detached from each other.
I was staggered when I saw in American magazines and other
publications whole pages of advertisements alluringly illustrated and phrased to spread the message of, "Come to Cuba,
the pearl of the Caribbean, for the most wonderful vacation
you ever had." Varadero, Havana, and choice spots in the
mountains were used as magnets. An enviable fortune must
have been spent on these advertisements; and all to no purpose
whatever, for the last thing any Americans I knew wanted to
do was to go to Cuba for any reason whatever. They would
regard a Cuban holiday almost as an un-American activity.

Fidel Castro's visit to the United States in April was used,
and it might well have been inspired, to explore his other
delusion that he could split the country into two halves—the
government, which was now his enemy, and the people, who
might very well be won over into becoming his friends. The

visit turned out to be a spectacular personal success but a
total political loss. As so often happens with Americans, they
were bowled over by the physical magnetism of a visitor who
had provoked their deep curiosity and interest, but once they
withdrew outside the scope of his personal influence, having
sated their curiosity about him, they went back to their original suspicions and abhorrences of his deeds.

Castro had magnificent moments of stardom as he traveled—
with an entourage that often numbered one hundred—from
Havana to Washington, Princeton, New York, Boston and on
to Canada and thence to Argentina. The one occasion when I
came within range of him was when he spoke at a luncheon
given at the Astor Hotel in New York by the Overseas Press
Club. The crush to see and hear him was so immense that,
arriving a little late, I never got any lunch and had to stand
on the fringe of the crowd when he spoke. I had to smile
admiringly at his performance after he had had a good lunch.
He oozed sentiments of peace and friendship toward the great
American people. He used all the actor's tricks of gesture and
histrionic appeal that he knew (and they were many) and his
command of English was appealingly awful. It became worse
than ever when he was dealing with awkward subjects, such as
those continuing executions and American fears of communist
influence upon him, so much so that one could not really understand what he was trying to say, or maybe trying not to say.
I thoroughly enjoyed his performance that day, savoring the
adroitness. This was a Castro brilliantly using all the talents
he had to beguile an audience whom he felt he might be able to
win over to his side, against their political leaders. He was an
artist here, whereas on his appearances before the microphones
in Havana—speaking to the mostly converted—he used harsh
or humorous oratory, forcefulness, and rarely turned on the
great reserves of charm that he had at command because there
was no need to do so. As I watched him in New York I realized
once again that in him the world was having to deal with a

man of extreme versatility and quick if not profound mental agility. In other words, I felt that Fidel Castro was emerging as a man who, if he found he could not get his will by one approach, would rarely be at a loss for using another, without too much regard for truth, ethics, or consistency.

But he was really wasting his time on that visit to the United States. The soft words he used often during the summer did not offset the impact of one slash after another at American interests and influences in Cuba. The seizures of property, use of agrarian reform as an anti-American weapon and, in September, the raising of excise duties on imports by up to 100 percent virtually to cut off supplies from American traders and manufacturers, made the people of the United States well aware that, for all the soft soap and play-acting, Fidel Castro meant them no good.

Yet they were still not ready to take him seriously as anything like a permanent menace. In a despatch from New York on November 16, I wrote: "It is hard to find an American nowadays who does not believe that Dr. Fidel Castro is on the edge of economic and political collapse and, thank goodness, will soon be gone as a nuisance who had broken the peace of the Caribbean and grown far too big for his boots as the leader of a little republic owing all it has to the grace and favor of the United States." That, surprising now as one reads it so long after the time it was written, was an accurate summing-up of the attitude toward Castro less than a year after he had seized power in Havana. It was a grossly mistaken one, of course, and I think that the feeling in the United States that he was only a passing irritation was due mostly to the absence of vigorous reaction to him and his policies by the Eisenhower administration. There had been only that one note of protest in June against the terms of compensation for confiscation of property, and that had not been followed up by action when it was ignored in Havana. If the State Department apparently was willing to allow Fidel Castro to use

enough rope to hang himself with sooner or later, who were
ordinary Americans, without any inside knowledge of what
was going on, to think otherwise? Besides, many of the newspaper and magazine reports and articles about him were depicting him as a kind of clown with an obsession, and these
did not encourage anybody to take him over-seriously. The
feeling in the United States at that time was that he was
careering toward bankruptcy because of his irresponsible policy vis-à-vis the country that really supported Cuba.

But I had just been to Havana again at the end of October,
and I had found the truth to be quite different. The discernible facts showed clearly that the running-down process
had not gone anything like so far as wishful thinking within
the United States imagined, and the American and British
and other observing diplomats in Havana knew this. I did
not find one who believed that the end of the Castro era was even
within remote sight. Firstly, there were intangible but quite
important assets operating in his favor. He still had the almost worshipful devotion of most of the masses of Cubans—
those who had started the great Cuban exodus were the very
rich and the very vulnerable, who had perceived from the
beginning that they would be the first to be hurt by the
revolution—and I thought it important to note that half a
million Cubans were still ready and even eager to turn out in
front of the Presidential Palace to hang on to every word he
spoke.

Castro's hold over the masses was exerting one incidental
effect that was helping to stave off trouble for the revolution.
He had inherited from Batista about six hundred thousand
unemployed, equal to about one in ten of the population, and
he had been able so far to do very little indeed to help them
because of all the besetting difficulties that fulfillment of the
revolution had brought. These people were not, however, as a
whole, pestering and agitating him to do something for them.
Somehow or other they were managing to scrape up a few

pesos here and there and, without receiving a dole or any other
handout, were waiting patiently for him to help them. I remember vividly talking to one of them soon after I had landed in
Havana, one time in 1959. He had said with impressive gravity: "If you criticize Fidel Castro you are like somebody
who would have criticized Winston Churchill when he was
winning the war for you." I could find no ready answer to that.

Yet Castro's revolution was being propped up by others, in
spite of all he seemed to be doing by diplomatic amateurism,
emotionalism, and histrionics to discredit it in the eyes of the
world. The foreign diplomats gave most of their praise for the
way any looming fiscal disaster was being staved off to Dr.
Felipe Pazos, then serving as president of the National Bank
of Cuba. Pazos had had for many years a high reputation
within the hemisphere as an orthodox economist of great efficiency, and he seemed to be showing his gifts to telling effect
in directing Lopez Fresquet, the Minister of the Treasury, and
the other governmental administrators who were running the
financial affairs of the country. So, while Fidel Castro was
ranting against foreign interference with his revolution and
cutting off Cuba from the United States, the men working behind him were doing their level best to repair the resulting
economic damage. They had courted Britain and had so built
up trade with her that by October Cuba had become Britain's
third best market in Latin America, after Argentina and Ven-
ezuela. It struck me as bizarre that, on the very day I was
being given this enlightening information from the British Embassy, the Cuban newspapers were trumpeting a statement on
behalf of Fidel Castro that if Britain did not give Cuba the
airplanes and other arms it was seeking to defend itself against
aggression from any quarter, Britain would eventually lose all
its holdings and markets throughout Latin America.

Nobody could pretend, of course, that Cuba's financial position in the late fall of 1959 was in any way rosy; but the
figures that foreign commercial attachés were able to deduce

about the fluctuating state of her dollar reserves, using their
own well-tried sources and not taking account of suspect trading figures issued by the Cubans, confirmed that erosion was
taking place at a much less frightening rate than a year
earlier under the regime of Batista. According to these independent estimates given to me, Cuba's reserve of free dollars
stood at about $110 million when Batista went. They had
been built up steadily in the early months of 1959 by proceeds
from the sugar harvest, which as I knew had been enthu-
siastically gathered in early revolutionary fervor, and had
stood at $141 million in June. Then they had slowly fallen
until they were at $110 million again at the end of August
and at about $113 million at the end of September. The down-
ward trend had then been resumed, but at a markedly lower
pace compared with what had happened during the same period
a year earlier under Batista, and it was estimated that by
the end of the year they would stand at something between $70
million and $80 million.

Thus there would be a loss over the year of between $30 mil-
lion and $40 million—compared with a corresponding loss of
$220 million under Batista the year before. The current loss
was serious enough, for it brought the dollar reserves far
below the level of past standards, if one could apply these to
the new Cuba that Fidel Castro was creating. Yet I felt that
the record was an astonishing one considering the temporary
chaos that had followed his succession to power. It was one of
the factors that caused me to realize that most people in the
United States had been paying too much attention to the adverse developments during the year—Castro's anti-American
shouts and deeds, crises in the cabinet, reports of communist
infiltration (not necessarily harmful, after all, to the physical
internal running of the country), defections—and not enough
to the retrieving ones. Few had wanted to hear about the temporary benefits gained by strict control over foreign currency
exchanges, the reduction of imports, and unheard-of honesty

in government and the bureaucracy as a whole. Cubans had responded to Castro's magic and to the appeals of his ministers by paying their taxes in unprecedented volume as a mark of their faith and hope in the revolution. Tax returns up to the end of September had amounted to $329 million, compared with $281 million for the whole of the last year.

There had certainly been a steady leftward drift within the regime since January. Even at the top the moderate Urrutia had been replaced as President by the extremist Dorticos. Outspoken officers had complained openly about the infiltration of communists into the armed forces as well as the administration. One was Major Pedro Diaz Lanz, chief of the Rebel Air Force, who wrote a letter to President Urrutia expressing alarm at efforts to impose communist indoctrination upon officers in training; he soon saw that his letter had placed him in physical jeopardy and escaped in time with his wife in a small boat to Florida. Another was Major Huber Matos, the military chief of the province of Camagüey, who was not so lucky after he had protested about the appointment of communists to positions of authority within I. N. R. A. (Institute of Agrarian Reform). Fidel Castro went to Camagüey to deal with him personally, with the usual theatrical fanfare, only to find that thirty-eight officers under Major Matos expressed full support of him and resigned with him. All were arrested. Eventually Fidel Castro managed to turn the Matos protest into an act of treason, no mean achievement, and this valiant officer, who had served brilliantly in the Sierra Maestra, was sentenced to twenty years' imprisonment.

Clearly, therefore, the communists were advancing within the regime. My difficulty was to find out just how far they had gotten in less than a year, and to determine what open or covert support and encouragement were being given them by Castro, if indeed he was having anything to do at all with such developments. Nobody would speak out, particularly to a foreigner, and officials in positions of responsibility in Havana would sometimes put on a display of double talk to avoid compromising themselves.

I went downtown one day to the Ministry of Finance to see Rufo Lopez Fresquet, the minister, whom I had met socially once or twice and had found to be a most reasonable and likable person. This day the only place where we could talk was not in the quietude of a corner at some diplomatic cocktail party but in a big office, being used by several members of his staff. And the Lopez Fresquet now with me was by no means the same man I had known, with all those big ears listening. He was vehemently anti-American, whereas earlier he had acknowledged that the United States had a point of view that he could understand. "We should have told them to go to hell in the first place," he said, loudly enough. "There is a deliberate campaign to intimidate and starve us. And we should never hear a word about communism here from the Americans if we weren't going to expropriate their sugar interests." Oh, well. I sensed his situation that day, and lost none of my liking for him. Within three months he had left the government, pleading serious ill-health, and he had gone into retirement in Florida. After seeing him that day I was entertained at a leisurely lunch by one of his chief subordinates, whose name I do not think I should disclose even at this late stage in view of what has already happened to him and his family. He loyally treated me to an uncompromising exposition of the case for the revolution and only late in the conversation did he cautiously concede that there were two factions striving for power within the administration. This man later resigned with his chief, but he did not manage to reach sanctuary in New York and Florida for a long time. His brother was arrested and given a long term of imprisonment for "antirevolutionary activities," and my acquaintance risked his own safety by doing what he could for his brother before he had to flee to avoid involvement. Serving in a position of any importance within Fidel Castro's revolution was becoming less and less attractive and more and more hazardous for anybody unwilling to push the policy of anti-Americanism and leftwing extremism that was stamping the revolution steadily more deeply; and when a man found it all just too hard to bear he had to play his cards very skillfully indeed to back out without suffering vindictive revenge in one form or another.

The violent death of Camilo Cienfuegos, by far the most romantic of the original desperadoes of the revolution, brought the deepest grief to the Cuban masses while I was in Havana that October. Cienfuegos was unmistakable because of his wide-brimmed Buffalo Bill type of hat and luxuriant buzz-fuzz of long black whiskers. The beard obscured much of his face, except, notably, his twinkling eyes. One just had to guess what the face was like beneath the foliage—he could easily have been a chinless wonder, for all the viewer could tell—but he undoubtedly had an aura of gaiety and charisma that made him from the beginning of the year second only to Fidel Castro as a popular idol. He had only to appear on, say, the balcony of the Presidential Palace for the crowds to start screaming his name in ecstatic welcome until he took off that wonderful hat to wave it to them—revealing another thick thatch of unkempt hair. I have emphasized the worship that Cubans lavished upon him because, according to some people, it explains his sudden and mysterious death in an airplane on October 28.

Cienfuegos took off from Camagüey in a small army plane for Havana on the afternoon of that day, after fulfilling some mission as part of his duties as Chief of Staff of the Army. With him were the pilot and one other soldier. The plane never reached Havana and nobody has ever disclosed, or maybe even found out, what happened to it. All manner of wild stories spread after the government belatedly announced that it was missing three days after its last flight—that Cienfuegos had defected, had been shot down, that he was still alive in the United States minus his whiskers. One likely explanation that came my way was that Cienfuegos, in his carefree way, had just sauntered over to the plane at the airport at Camagüey and told the pilot to take off, without bothering to see whether there was enough fuel in the tanks for the journey, and that the plane had simply crashed in some remote area as a result of this improvidence.

The United States was asked by the Cuban government to send out military planes to look for the missing plane and did so, and scores of volunteer searchers also looked for it from the air and by sea. Nothing was ever found. One afternoon in the first week of November I was sitting in my room in the Hotel Riviera when I heard a loud hubbub from the street below. There had been a report over the wireless that Cienfuegos had been found alive and well, either in the province of Las Villas or just off the coast. The report started rejoicings all over Havana, and the gloom was correspondingly great when, after only a few hours, the report was denied as totally untrue.

It has always seemed to me that there is only one acceptable alternative to the theory that the plane crashed for lack of fuel. It is that somebody wanted to get rid of Cienfuegos and had him shot down—his plane was only an unarmed Cessna— at a chosen point between Camagüey and Havana. This theory has been widely discussed, and it has been usually Raul Castro rather than Fidel who has been accused. There could have been a disagreement, military or political, between the top members of the revolutionary organism. Cienfuegos might have become disaffected, like so many others. He would most certainly have been a contender for the succession if anything ever happened to Fidel Castro, whereas the sour Raul was never popular. I can say that for years after the disappearance of Camilo Cienfuegos, up to the last time I was in Havana, his photograph was still to be seen on the wall of many a Cuban home and displayed in a number of shop windows in the capital and other towns and cities. He is now a legend.

The revolutionary regime rounded off its first hectic year of existence by firing a long and, I must say, impressively eloquent barrage of words against the United States government. Its first assault was to distribute thousands of copies of a pamphlet showing photographs of people supposed to have been killed and wounded in a hit-and-run bombing attack by Major Diaz Lanz, now a counterrevolutionary, and violently criticizing the United States, not only for harboring Major Diaz Lanz, but for doing nothing to stop him from raiding Havana. (The truth of this affair is obscure, as usual in such politico-military forays, but it seems more than likely that the two dead and forty-eight wounded were the victims of notoriously wild Cuban antiaircraft fire and equally wild shooting by two Cuban planes when these went up to try to intercept the intruder.) The United States rejected the charges made as "inaccurate, malicious, and misleading," and in an audience with President Dorticos the American Ambassador, Philip W. Bonsal, formally complained of "deliberate and concerted efforts in Cuba to replace the traditional friendship between the Cuban and the North American peoples with distrust and hostility."

This was a cue to the Castro regime to go to remarkable lengths to compile and distribute its response. It produced a document of well over sixty-five hundred words, in both Spanish and English, well printed and enclosed in a stiff cover, which it distributed as widely as it possibly could. It made sure that I, for one, received a copy, for a Cuban emissary brought it into my office in New York and left it with me. It was called, on its colored cover, *In Defense of National Sovereignty*, and it comprised the full text of a reply made by Dr. Raul Roa, the Minister of State, to Bonsal. Naturally, the Diaz Lanz affair was only incidental to its theme, which was a review of Cuban-American political and economic relations over a period of fifty years. It struck me as I read it that this was a document of some historic importance, and I preserved it carefully. I knew that one day it would be useful in giving a clear picture of what the regime was thinking, where it thought it was going, and how it was reacting to suspicions of communist infiltration, one year after it had come to power. I think it will be appropriate and enlightening now to quote some of its passages verbatim:

The Cuban people always made a clear distinction between Official Spain and the Real Spain; that is why they never confused the Spanish people with the Government structure which deprived them of their most elemental rights and liberties. And, likewise, they have always been prompt to discern between Cutting's United States and Lincoln's United States; and so they have never confused the North American people with the power structure that attempted to annex, acquire or enfeoff Cuba, and finally, in open violation of the spirit as well as the letter of the Joint Resolution, imposed the Platt Amendment on our country, under the protective pall of which banquers [sic] and enterprising business promoters secured privileges and special prerogatives much to the detriment of our economic development, our social advancement and our democratic stability.

The Revolutionary Government of Cuba believes it of utmost importance, if it is desired to improve the relations between our two countries and achieve some sort of trade equilibrium, to change things so that our sugar trade with the United States will be governed by a bilateral agreement which cannot be modified by any unilateral decision of Your Excellency's Government. The privilege with which the United States Government has vested itself has made and is making it possible for American senators, press services and certain interests opposed to the self-government and economic development of Cuba to make use of the threat to reduce the sugar quota as an intolerable instrument of undue pressure. The United States have always been the most favored party in their trade relations with Cuba. In the last ten years the balance of payments has been adverse to Cuba by more than a billion dollars, of which 506 millions represent our trade balance deficits, and the rest represent Cuban tourist expenses, freight charges and capital investment returns. Such unbalanced situation is an unquestionable proof of the fact that the economic relations between Cuba and the United States of North America must be peremptorily revised. At a recent press conference

President Dwight D. Eisenhower voiced his surprise at the possibility that the Cuban people might have forgotten that the United States are Cuba's best customer. It is unquestionable that your country is a particularly good client of Cuba but it is none the less unquestionable that Cuba is a much better client of the United States. It is no wonder that, despite her small size, during the last ten years Cuba has been forced to search everywhere for dollar exchange to cover the continued deficits of her balance of trade with the great neighboring power which has received from Cuba much more dollars exchange than vice-versa. In this case, the alleged reciprocity operates to the obvious detriment and disadvantage of Cuba's interests.

The Revolutionary Government admits that North American capital investments have positively contributed to the material advancement of our country but it cannot help pointing out that those investments have also contributed to give the Cuban economy a semi-colonial character evidenced by its absolute subordination to our sugar productions, the insufficiency of the agricultural production to fill our own consumption requirements, and by the advantageous position of many foreign industrial products when they compete with their Cuban counterparts.

We neither practice international spying nor interfere with the internal affairs of other nations, nor do we expect to be authorized to investigate criminal events taking place beyond our coasts. The Revolutionary Government, which affirms the national sovereignty in the same measure that it is exercised—with a strict sense of duty and responsibility—believes and preaches that the internal affairs of each country are within the exclusive competence of its authorities and of their people and that each country, unless it violates human rights and international agreements, is under the obligation to prevent the execution of acts which jeopardize the security of its neighbors.

The United States Government has the right to deny licenses to export arms and other war implements to whom it likes. But what it can not do is to exert its influence with other governments, using as a pretext that it does so to contribute to the maintenance of peace in the Caribbean area, in order to prevent a friendly government from providing itself for simple defensive reasons with the planes it needs to replace obsolete equipment with adequate new planes.

The United States Government efforts towards the British Government to block such an exchange coincided unfortunately with the air aggressions against Cuba and they were continued, notwithstanding the fact that Your Excellency was notified that they constituted an unfriendly act, inasmuch as the Cuban Government and people were left at the mercy of an international pirate and a gang of criminals [the Trujillo regime in the Dominican Republic]. The Revolutionary Government is in possession of trustworthy information that the United States Embassy in Belgium insistently tried to secure from the Belgian Government the cancellation of our orders for small weapons. It has no information, however, that similar efforts have been made with the Governments of Belgium, France, Great Britain, Holland and West Germany to demand the cancellation of numerous orders from Trujillo in spite of the fact that he is the only true disturber of peace in the Caribbean.

These steps notwithstanding, the Revolutionary Government will acquire the aircraft, arms, and ammunition required for its country's protection and defense from whomsoever may be willing to supply them, inasmuch as our orders for that necessary equipment are not only not filled but are prevented from being filled by the same Government that furnished the former dictator Batista with all the aircraft, arms, bombs and other weapons with which his troops spread terror and death, desperation and ruin, in a friendly nation populated by friendly people.

The Government of the United States "cherishes and takes pride in the independence and objectivity of the Press and wire services of the country" and refutes in a sharp tone, considering it untrue, the accusation of having engaged "in a deliberate campaign to give a mistaken impression of, and utterly discredit, the Cuban Government." Really, this is not the time to argue the so-called independence of certain North American Press media; however, it is timely to point out the great moral responsibilities assumed by the Government of Your Excellency by expressing its pride in those wire and Press services which have propagated, and are still propagating, the most flagrant falsehoods and the most humiliating insults against the Revolutionary Government and its foremost figures. Is it by any chance a proof of objectivity to instigate the assassination of Dr. Fidel Castro, to present traitors as heroes, to publish insidious re-

ports, to foster rebellion, to brand as Communist the first really
Cuban government we have ever had here, to promote economic
strangulation, to circulate all manner of rumors which are as false
as they are villainous?

The Revolutionary Government is unaware of the real intentions
of the Government of the United States of North America when it
refers through Your Excellency to the topic of Communism at your
conference with the President of the Republic; however, the truth is
that the so-called "Communist infiltration" in official circles is the
same old song record, unpacked and dusted once again, which has
been maliciously and constantly played by our internal and external
enemies in order to promote the conditions they consider propitious
to create distortions and encourage a foreign intervention. The nature, structure and objectives of the Revolutionary Government are
reflected by its actions and accomplishments and not by the labels
and the clothing so maliciously ascribed to it. Only those who want
to be misled and confused are actually misled and confused.

The Cuban Revolution does not fear ghosts. It knows where it
came from, what it wants, and where it is going. It sails on pure,
clear waters, and flies the flag with the lone star at the top of its
mainmast.

So ran the more striking passages of this remarkable note.
It was spirited, defiant, and sufficiently weighted to give the
impression that the Castro regime had all the right on its
side—which is the basic purpose of any such diplomatic note.
It also showed how far apart the two countries had drifted in
such a short time. The United States was now suddenly in the
position of, say, the proprietor of an industrial concern with
a number of branches who is confronted unexpectedly by the
manager of one of these branches. The manager explodes, saying he refuses to go on being "exploited" and proposes to set
up shop on his own—using the proprietor's premises and equipment. Naturally the owner is shocked and needs time to work
out what to do next to protect his interests, such a remarkable
thing never having happened to him before.

5 ◆ Breaking Point

THE SECOND year of the revolution, 1960, was even more
critical and decisive both for Cuba and the rest of the world
than the first. This was the year in which the revolution—an
irritating and unwanted phenomenon in the eyes of millions of
Americans who just wished and hoped that it would collapse
or go away—not only survived but began visibly to take on
the ominous shape of an extremist, alien element in the Latin
American organism. For this reason alone the second year
should have had much more attention than the first, when all
had been in flux, but in the event it had much less.

There were several good reasons for this. For one thing,
Cuba in 1959 had given the United States, and others, such a

violent succession of shocks, disappointments, surprises, and confusions, that time was needed for absorption; people could take no more of it for the time being, and so they were disposed to avert their eyes and ears whenever they saw or heard the words Cuba and Castro. Another reason was that this was an election year in the United States, not one in which the incumbent president was likely to be re-elected but one in which two new contestants were going to slug away at each other for the victory. America's friends as well as its enemies know from experience how preoccupied with internal affairs it becomes in such a year; friends despair of getting anything like full attention, and enemies rejoice that they can take all manner of liberties and do America grave harm at a time when it is like a boxer fighting with one arm tied behind his back or, perhaps more pointedly, a general engaged in a worldwide struggle who has temporarily to turn away from his great atlases and pore over his domestic maps.

Some of the events and developments in Cuba during this year become more understandable when one takes into account that it was an election year in the United States. The most important development of all was the open, physical advance into Cuba by the Soviet Union. The strategists in Moscow evidently decided that Fidel Castro was now ripe for exploitation. Their communist crusaders on the spot had permeated the revolution deeply enough, and Castro's position vis-à-vis the United States was now independent and strong enough, for them to make their own physical probe into territory that until only a year earlier had been the enemy's. They sent Anastas Mikoyan, the First Deputy Premier of the Soviet Union, to make the first open contact with Fidel Castro and to inaugurate a Soviet exhibition in the Palace of Fine Arts in midtown Havana. About a hundred Russian specialists, supported by several hundred Cubans, put up the exhibition during January, and Mikoyan arrived to a full ceremonial welcome on February 4.

Mikoyan's visit was a success, if only for the smarting affront it presented to the United States. The fact that a high Soviet official could now go to Havana, lead an impressive propaganda demonstration, announce a deal whereby the Soviet Union would not only buy a million tons of Cuban sugar every year but would grant her credits of many millions of dollars for industrialization showed glaringly just how far Fidel Castro and his revolution had wheeled to the left. This was indeed a slap in the face for the United States. I was surprised that this taunting and ominous venture by the Russians into the Caribbean aroused comparatively mild protests in the United States. But it was an election year and, as I have suggested, nobody is *too* venturesome at such times—as both the Russians and Cubans well knew. There were some protests by students in Havana and there was even some shooting off-stage when Mikoyan was about to open the Soviet Exhibition there, but such demonstrations were too fleeting and too minor to take much of the shine off the visit. I have always felt that the incursion did more than any other single event to cause the American military and political planners within the administration to decide, notwithstanding an intervening election, to sponsor an invasion of Cuba before everything was lost.

An immediate American effort to offset the impact of the Mikoyan visit upon the rest of the hemisphere was to despatch President Eisenhower on a spectacular "goodwill tour" to Puerto Rico, Brazil, Chile, Argentina, and Uruguay between February 22 and March 7. I went with him as one of the hundred or so international chroniclers of the mission. The one fact about it which impressed me above all others was that it had been badly needed. To be blunt, the President's reception was by no means a unanimously friendly one. At the very first short halt at San Juan, Puerto Rico, one section of crowds of demonstrators who were kept out of his sight during the airport ceremonies were shouting loudly for independence from the United States and waving little banners on which were written, *"Viva* Fidel !" There were even more determined demonstrations later in Montevideo and Santiago. Police had to use hoses and tear gas against students in Montevideo who suddenly appeared at windows of the university with banners saying, "Fidel *Sí,* Eisenhower *No,"* and other unflattering slogans. I do not know to what extent the Cubans had been actively promoting such anti-American manifestations, but I do know that their leader and his revolt were providing the theme for them. Fidel Castro had obviously kindled a Latin spark, and he was thus early being used to effect by extremists in Uruguay and Chile.

It was in Santiago that the most striking of all the events associated with the Cuban revolution occurred. It came about two-thirds of the way through the tour, when President Eisenhower was showing some worrying signs of fatigue from the nonstop traveling he had been doing and was also clearly upset by the unevenness of the reception his mission had had. It was the moment when the Federation of the Students of Chile chose to submit to their country's illustrious and long-suffering, but tired, visitor a windy letter of some fifteen hundred words. The document was written most courteously and respectfully but bluntly reminded the President of the so-called mistakes, misdeeds, and exploitations perpetrated by United States policies toward South America and warned him that if these continued for very much longer the continent would be lost to democracy and would turn inevitably toward communism.

Since the letter had clearly been drafted in all sincerity by the representatives of some twenty-five thousand students at seven universities in Chile, and since it equally clearly gave warning that Castroist complaints against past American policies in Latin America were not limited to Cuba, I think it deserves some elaboration here. Its principal points were these:

The Inter-American system is the most complete of the many international arrangements in which the United States takes part. But it is equally true that in no other does the United States obtain more advantages, at the same time acquiring fewer obligations in respect of its associates.

The Inter-American system has been up to the present time a regime of obligations accepted by the weak in favour of the strong and the poor in favour of the rich. Reciprocity and not aid should be the moral basis of the Inter-American System.

Has the United States become a "satisfied nation," one which fights for the maintenance of the prevailing order in the world and Latin America? This dangerous image is becoming more accepted each day. In Latin America to defend the prevailing order means maintaining the privilege of a thin layer of the population which controls the power and the wealth, surrounded by an ocean of poor people to whom the social order means little or literally nothing.

Two-thirds of the population live in a chronic state of malnutrition; two out of five Latin Americans are illiterate; Latin America has the lowest rate of economic development in the Western world and an average income of only 275 dollars per annum. If trees are known by their fruit, it is a mockery to pretend that this situation reflects the Christian or the Democratic order for which the immense mass of starved, illiterate and uncultured people, as well as those lacking rights, freedom and poverty, populating the majority of Latin America, could hope. It is a crime against the spirit. If the injustices of today are all that Christianity or democracy can offer this continent, nobody should be surprised if the best children of these nations turn towards Communism, seeking these elementary needs which they lack and which are the essentials to morality and civilisation: food, shelter and education.

Beware! These anguished nations are much closer to the limit of their resistance and to the rupture point than the satisfied of this world think.

There was a good deal more of the same in the letter, of course, and there was the predictable warning to the President against any intervention in Cuba by armed force, economic reprisals, or press attacks. As had happened all through the Presidential tour, Castro was being used as a handy emblem, and warning, of Latin American emergence.

The letter jerked President Eisenhower out of his fatigue in a most remarkable manner. The morning after it had reached him he went to the small Windsor Theatre in Santiago to meet and greet members of the American community in the city. As he walked down the center aisle to the platform that had been rigged up, I was quite shocked by his appearance. Although his face bore a superficial tan from a broiling sun that had burned him while he was golfing and trout fishing two days earlier in Southern Argentina, it also had an underlying grayness. The muscles were slack, and somehow there was about him that morning the aspect of a man, an old man, of whom too much had been asked. He was making a trip in which in one week he would pay ceremonial visits to four countries and, according to calculations made by his press secretary, James Hagerty, would be flying over fifteen thousand miles by jet and propeller aircraft, 225 miles by helicopter, and traveling 325 miles by car. My concern about him became greater than ever as he spoke his short set speech. His voice was weak and he slurred words like "exist" and "interest." He misread "North America" for "South America" and said "production" at one point instead of "protection." I even wondered as I listened whether he would get through the day without some form of breakdown, and I certainly doubted whether he could carry out the rest of the trip to Buenos Aires, Puerto Rico, and back to Washington in just over four days.

But Eisenhower showed that morning that he had all the instincts and qualifications of a champion. He suddenly cast off his fatigue as if it were a disposable burden. He became all fire, indignation, and eloquence. He laid down his prepared script to deal with the letter from the students. He spoke without notes, from his heart, and he framed glowing sentences. They made such an impression on me, coming from a man who only a few moments earlier had been fluffing his lines, slurring simple words, and seeming to be so very close to exhaustion, that I began taking shorthand notes of them and have kept the record ever since:

Surely no nation loves liberty more, or more sincerely prays that its benefits and deep human satisfactions may come to all peoples, than does the United States. We *do* adhere to a policy of self-determination of peoples. We subscribe to and observe with constancy the cardinal principles of inter-American life; the policy of nonintervention. We repudiate dictatorship in any form, right or left. Our role in the United Nations and in the Organization of American States, in two world wars and in Korea, stands as a beacon to all who love freedom.

It was not, of course, even an outline of an answer to the accusations of the students—he said he would write to them in detail when he got back to Washington—but it was a moving brief performance. He was putting forth a kind of personal credo, in the simple words of a simple man. I thought as I listened of the inspiration that Americans would get from their public and political figures if only the ritual of the set text, the careful conformity to avoid making even the slightest indiscretion, and the demands of the deadline and the time-table, were cast aside.

But the President was too tired to make more than a brief effort that day. He paused for a moment after the few sentences, spoken with passion, had gone from him. Then he picked up his prepared text again and, once more the jaded traveler, finished it.

Soon after getting back to New York from South America I went again to Cuba, in May, 1960, on another of my keeping-in-touch visits. This time I took an artist with me—Brian Davis, whose work over the signature "ffolkes" is as well known and liked on one side of the Atlantic as the other.

Our mission was not to collect the heavy facts of economics
and politics but to try and find enough material for a des-
cription of the lighter side, if any, of life in Cuba in this
second year of revolution. We managed to do so, even though
in the process ffolkes was taken briefly into custody after
somebody had reported to the police that a foreigner was
behaving suspiciously by making sketches in the streets. But
I found very little to inspire levity. I could not smile when, as
I strolled around a Peoples' Fair in one of the squares in the
formerly chic area of Vedado, I saw a shooting gallery seeking
to attract customers with the following legend: "Learn to
shoot; then, when Fidel calls, you will be ready."

Learning to shoot, march, drill, and play the soldier seemed
to be the spare-time craze of most young Cubans. Fidel Castro
had started forming the Peoples' Militia. Every evening the
squads of recruits formed up in the streets for their training,
given usually by a soldier of the regular Rebel Army. The
majority of the recruits were teenagers, of both sexes, but I
also saw enthusiastic squads of very young boys and girls,
some not more than seven years old, frowning hard as they
tried to follow and obey the drill-master's commands. I saw,
too, lots of well-built Cuban girls giving a coquettish air of
unreality to a drill as with their rifles at the ready they swung
and turned with such grace and gaiety that one felt sure they
were doing it to some mystic Cuban music. Brightly colored,
wide skirts positively flashed in the evening sunlight as the
girls minced and pivoted. I reflected that there is after all more
than one way of stopping an invader in his tracks.

I watched them with enjoyment. This was how the drill—
far more like a performance by a chorus line than anything
else—went: One, two, stamp, turn; one, two, swing to the left;
three, four, turn about. Now start all over again. . . . These
girls might have been training seriously to defend the revolution, but they were having a glorious time while doing so.

They cheered up the rather lonely foreign visitor, compensating him for the air of debilitation that he detected in Havana for the first time since 1959. Traffic was no longer swirling with the old mad intensity—with devil-may-care Cuban drivers hooting, tooting, and outsmarting each other—along the Malecon. Restaurants, night clubs, places of entertainment of all kinds, were suffering ruinously from lack of business, but the government would not let them close. Instead, it was taking them over one by one and letting the Treasury absorb the losses until, vain hope, trade became better. The Monseigneur, which had been one of the smartest and liveliest restaurants in town in the old days, had been taken over by the state, and looked it. It had lost not only its customers but all its gloss and sharpness. The night I was there no other table was occupied and the three-man orchestra and the big staff of cooks and waiters were all congregated in one corner, enjoying their leisure in gossiping and joking. There were only three people at the bar and they were the very three I had seen earlier at another place. The same anaemia was afflicting the casinos that were still open. Rarely did one see more than a handful of people using the tables, and they were all Cubans playing not with American dollars but Cuban pesos, now worth only a fraction of their former par value with the dollar, even though the fiction of parity was still being maintained by the regime.

While schooling the people to be ready to sacrifice themselves however uselessly if the United States Marines should come, the regime also tried now to show the peasants from the sugar fields of Oriente and the other provinces that the revolution really had increased their equity in the assets of Cuba. Peasants who had distinguished themselves during the harvest that had just been gathered were brought by the busload to Havana to view and stay (at the rate of about six to a room) in the palatial hotels that in the pre-Castro era had been the haunts of rich American tourists. I watched some of these parties inspecting the communal property of the Havana Hilton Hotel—now renamed more or less appropriately the *Libre*

(Free), since rooms which used to cost $30.00 and more a day were now available to the proletariat at a mere peso or two. They made a rather touching sight as they shuffled reverentially through the Antilles Bar on the mezzanine and then took the still-smooth American-made lifts to the top story to admire the wonderful view of Havana from the Sugar Bar. They all wore their Sunday-best whites, with a tiny Cuban flag pinned to the upturned corner of their broad-brimmed hats. Their seamed faces and hands glowed like well-polished tan leather. Their machetes, symbol of their service to King Sugar, dangled from their belts. They either did not talk at all or murmured only in shy whispers as they followed their government guide around. I cannot think that they believed that all this really belonged to them. They were just as much out of place as would be an American tourist with his multicolored Florida shirt and his many cameras in a sugar field in Oriente. But they made a good propaganda picture for the Cuban newspapers and television cameras, and they would most certainly talk about the splendors they had seen when they got back among the folks at home.

Fidel Castro was still trying hard to lure some of those American tourists to Havana. The daily plane from Miami was met by members of a three-piece band that stood at the foot of the landing stairs and strummed a few bars of Cuban jazz as the visitors, mostly nontourists, descended. The music, plus a daiquiri served with it, did something I suppose to offset the rather chilling wording on the enormous banner fastened across the front of the airport building: *"Patria o Muerte; Venceremos"* and *"Cuba, Territorio Libre de América."* ("Fatherland or death; we shall conquer" and "Cuba, the Free Territory of America.")

This strange duality of the Cuban attitude, this shaking of a defiant fist at the United States balanced by a genuine friendliness for the individual American, could lead to some odd situations. One evening that spring I went with three

American friends to dinner at one of the downtown restaurants that was at one time a retreat of the late Ernest Hemingway. We were the only diners in the place for a long time, until two Cuban young men with their girl friends came in and sat at another table a few yards away. It was Saturday night and they were enjoying themselves. Out of high spirits and not, I am quite sure, to show off or be unpleasant in any way, they started singing a popular revolutionary song that had the words *"Cuba sí, Yanqui no"* as its refrain. It was a catching song and as the tuneful quartette fluted it out with abandon we joined in. It was a moment of unreality somehow appropriate to postrevolutionary Havana. The Cubans sang until their meal was prepared. When they had eaten it and as they drifted out into the evening they gave us a "good night" and a courteous nod of farewell. They had seen nothing incongruous in the episode.

In matters of official diplomacy, however, the two countries were moving swiftly toward the ultimate break. There could be no avoiding it. As the year progressed and Cuba's attitude of "You must give us everything we ask and we will give nothing" became clearer and more permanent, the question one asked was not whether relations would be broken but how soon. Really there had been no hope of avoiding rupture after the Cuban communists had opened the door to the Soviet Union and Mikoyan had walked in. Cuba resumed diplomatic relations with Russia on May 7, 1960. Just over a month later the Cubans arrested two American attachés and declared them to be no longer acceptable because they had been having "conspiratorial" conversations with disaffected Cubans. Two days later the United States retaliated by expelling three Cuban diplomats for spying, agitating, and otherwise behaving improperly. The game of diplomatic fisticuffs was on.

Next, as the U. S. Congress prepared to give President Eisenhower a free hand in deciding how severely to punish Cuba by interfering with her sugar quota, Fidel Castro got in a sharp blow by seizing the Texaco refinery in Santiago de Cuba because its officials had refused to refine Russian oil. He followed this by seizing the refineries and other properties of the Esso and Shell companies. Now it was the turn of the United States to deliver a punch. The President said that Cuba would not be allowed to send the rest of its deliveries under its sugar quota for 1960. This would cost Cuba about one hundred million dollars in a lost sale. Although Fidel Castro sought to minimize the effect by asserting that it would give Cuba a freer hand in disposing of its sugar, there was no doubt that this was a shock to the Cuban people, who were still not yet ready to accept the loss of American friendship and patronage. The third party in the deadly political battle, the Soviet Union, now tried to quiet Cuban anxieties by offering itself as a substitute friend and protector. Nikita Khrushchev said that Russia would help Cuba to resist any economic blockade and would support the island with rockets if the United States attacked. (Some months later Khrushchev had belated second thoughts about this pledge and pointed out that it had been meant "symbolically.")

American counterpunches became fewer and fewer as the presidential election campaign absorbed more and more of the nation's attention and administrators became less inclined to take political action of any kind. As the world was to learn *after* the election, the administration was preparing what it hoped would be the final answer of all—invasion—and that was to turn out to be one of the worst disasters in all of American politico-military history. In the meantime, America's enemies were having a fine old time plucking the eagle's feathers. One American property after another in Cuba was seized without compensation, and occasionally even without a receipt, until by the end of October there was scarcely anything left untouched. President Dorticos went around Latin America delivering such foaming attacks against American dollar imperialism that the State Department made formal protest, without

any effect upon the Cubans and not very much on opinion at
home. Cuba made barter deals not only with the Soviet Union
but with Communist China, Poland, Czechoslovakia, East
Germany and other European countries. To cap all, Fidel
Castro journeyed with a rag, tag, and bobtail entourage of
about fifty persons to join Khrushchev on a marauding sortie
into the enemy's camp in New York, just when that enemy was
in the process of changing generals or, accurately, a general
for a senator.

I watched much of this squalid political maneuvering by
Khrushchev and Castro in and about the General Assembly of
the United Nations with distaste. Sometimes I felt I was
watching a couple of imitators of Messrs. Laurel and Hardy,
as when Fidel Castro extravagantly applauded Khrushchev
making an exhibition of himself in trying to shout down
Macmillan, the British Prime Minister, or some other speaker.
I also began to perceive for the first time since I had started
observing the Cuban drama that Fidel Castro was being
manipulated—albeit docilely enough now, for his own grandiose
nationalism was being well served in the bargain—by men
cleverer than he. It dawned on me that his revolution was no
longer his. It had been neatly taken from him by the organizers
of international communism, who had seen that in him they
had been presented with a unique tool to forge a hole in the
wall that the United States had built around Latin and South
America after the Spaniards had gone from there. I recall that
remarkable photograph of Castro being given a bear hug in
New York by Khrushchev. I thought it told much of the story
graphically enough—the senior and junior bandit, the old and
the juvenile political prankster, playing their saucy parts
right in the enemy's citadel. For effrontery and opportunism
that episode late in 1960 took some matching.

But the revolutionary regime was not having everything its
own way at home. An underground movement in Havana kept
reminding it of persisting opposition by letting off bombs,

starting fires in department stores and elsewhere, and organizing anticommunist demonstrations. Life was becoming occasionally hazardous for the foreigner, and at the end of September the U. S. State Department recommended that American businessmen and others still resident in Cuba send their families home. Three weeks later it prohibited all exports to Cuba except food and medicine. Castro turned to new friends to fill the void. His regime established diplomatic relations with such remote countries as North Vietnam, Albania, Outer Mongolia, and Hungary—places that had never before seemed to have much in common with tropical Cuba here in the Caribbean.

The revolution had turned everything topsy-turvy, including Christmas. This year it perpetrated one of the most childish, not to say sacrilegious, crudities it has ever been my misfortune to observe. Men rigged up a painted version of the Nativity in the street outside the central television and radio headquarters in Vedado in which, incredibly, the three Wise Men hovering around the infant Jesus in a Cuban peasant home were Fidel Castro, Ernesto Guevara, and the ranking Negro officer in the Rebel Army. One of the angels looking down benignly upon the scene was the vanished warrior Camilo Cienfuegos. The gifts brought to the newborn Saviour bore the labels of Agrarian Reform, Urban Reform, and (a real bonbon) the 1961 Year of Education. Long after Christmas had come and gone this awful hodgepodge was still to be seen aloft in the street, getting steadily more tattered until it either fell apart or had to be torn down.

The long-expected final rupture with the United States came at the turn of the year. For the benefit of visitors who had come to celebrate with him the second anniversary of his triumph, Fidel Castro organized a New Year parade at which he showed off the weapons he had acquired to strengthen his defenses against any intruder from overseas. There were many tanks, guns, mortars, antiaircraft artillery, and other weapons from the Soviet Union, Czechoslovakia, and Belgium, as well as a few leftovers from the United States and Britain. That evening he repeated the prophecy that he and Dr. Roa, his Foreign Minister, and other Cuban spokesmen had made that Cuba would be invaded before President Kennedy was inaugurated. Then, declaring that the United States Embassy was nothing but a nest of American and Cuban agitators and spies, he demanded that its staff of some three hundred be reduced to a skeleton one of eight persons within forty-eight hours. This was another example of his method of what one might call instant diplomacy. It was one of those outbursts, typical of him, that he would blurt out toward the end of a long speech, leaving his hearers to guess whether he had thought it all out carefully beforehand or had just manufactured it out of impetuosity and the inspiration of his own rhetoric. Sometimes it would be one, sometimes the other. My opinion is that this demand had indeed been thought out in advance, and that it was made with the thought that the long-suffering United States might even swallow this indignity.

It did not. In just over twelve hours the State Department announced that there was now no alternative but to break off diplomatic relations with Cuba, if only because of the fact that the embassy simply could not be maintained physically by eight people. In a few days the handsome white building off the Malecon was boarded up and empty, except for caretakers and one or two Swiss officials keeping an eye upon it as part of their country's new task of acting on behalf of the United States in relations with Cuba, such as there might now be. The queues of Cubans that had been forming daily outside the visa section of the embassy disappeared. Many who had wanted to get away from it all were now prisoners on the island.

6 ✦ *Communist Captive*

I HAVE said that I do not believe that Fidel Castro ever really was, or ever could be, a conforming communist. I shall now go further and say that judging by everything I have seen or heard on reliable authority about the man, he has never had it within him to conform to anything for a moment longer than the impulses of his variable and emotional mind have prompted him or, once his early principles had been blunted by megalomania, political necessities demanded. I do not believe that Fidel Castro ever grew up fully; I have never known him to display that kind of emotional stability we attribute to the mature adult. But perhaps he was just being Cuban.

On the night of December 2, 1961, Fidel Castro took his

favorite position—in front of the microphones and television cameras—and made a speech lasting about five hours. In it he tried, most unconvincingly as it appears when one probes the record of what he said, to explain his association with communism. As he did so often in these inordinately long verbal meanderings, he did not make one clearly stated explanation of his position but touched time and again on the theme of the evening, thereby creating a general impression more than anything else. As had happened many times since 1959, this led inevitably to some misrepresentation and excusable misreporting by those journalists who listened to the speech by radio in Miami and sent out the first news interpretations in English of what he had seemed to say in Spanish. Some of those who did so were Cuban exiles—anti-Castroites—and they would scarcely have been human had they not let their feelings about him influence their assessment of what he had said, or had seemed to be trying to say. He was always an infuriating speaker to follow during a harangue, partly because he spoke for so long that the listener's mind became saturated and dulled, and partly because through his incapacity or by his intent, it was often very difficult to perceive his meaning.

Unfortunately, the first reports of the crucial speech on December 2 gave an entirely wrong rendering of what on reflection most knowledgeable analysts believe he was trying to say, and that first false interpretation was never wholly set aside. One of the first reports to catch the headlines and the news bulletins in the United States was to the effect that he had said he was a Marxist-Leninist and had been one since the start of his revolutionary movement in 1953. Now, this is what a lot of people in America and elsewhere had always wanted to believe about Fidel Castro, and it was consequently just what they wanted to hear him confirm. Alas, he never actually did so in that speech. What he indicated, according to the later analysts, was that he had not been a communist before he entered Havana as its conqueror in 1959, although he had had leanings toward communism ever since 1953. He explained his tardiness in embracing communism by saying that he had been misled between 1953 and 1959 by "imperialist propaganda"; and he said that the change in his political thinking had begun after he had taken over control of Cuba.

That has since been accepted as a more or less accurate interpretation of the message he was delivering in the speech. If so, it was one of the most revealing declarations he ever made, and not only on account of its transparent importance in confirming the belief held by so many, non-Cubans as well as Cubans, that he is a conscripted and not a volunteer communist. It is equally revealing in its timing and in what I believe to have been his personal position when he made it. I had been in Havana only one month before he made the speech, and I had come away feeling very strongly that the communists around him had simply taken him over and were at last in effective control of the revolution and the country.

Castro was very quiet during the ten days I was there, and I do not believe he was even in Havana. He was thought to be in seclusion somewhere in the Sierra Maestra, where he invariably went whenever he had a problem on his mind. Everything I heard from the resident diplomats and the handful of journalists still stationed in the capital strengthened the probability that, at the very least, he was in one of his low periods in his seesaw struggle with the influences around him, and some of my informants and friends said they were wondering whether he could ever restore his position. As usual, it was impossible to find out anything certain about what was going on within the revolution. In Cuba, the flow of information has been particularly sparse and sporadic because the supporting cast has mostly stayed in the drama very briefly before either defecting or being despatched out of it, and the small band of permanent players have really given away very little at any time, for all the windy harangues of Fidel Castro, the snarls of his brother, and the controlled bluntness of Che Guevara. The outside ob-

servers have had to become very adroit in reading between the
lines of the Havana newspapers, noting hints and innuendos
in the speeches, exchanging and sifting the gossip at cocktail
parties and receptions, and in many other ways building up
an assessment. Many of the diplomats have been extraordinarily
successful at this strange game—and here I must pay tribute
to the talents of the cool-headed British—and time and again I
have found since 1959 that my own deductions based on what
the diplomats and others told me they believed to be happening
have been later proved accurate by events.

Perhaps one day it will be shown that Fidel Castro spoke as
he did on December 2, 1961, because he had concluded that to
do so represented his only way out of an awkward and even
dangerous personal situation. In the meantime, a case may be
made in favor of the theory. After two years his political and
diplomatic naivety and his administrative sloppiness and in-
competence had got him into a corner. He had so frittered away
the early reverence and hopeful loyalty of his people that the
careful diplomatic observers in Havana were estimating when
I was there in the November of the year that he then had the
useful support of no more than about 30 percent of the population. (The proportion was later to go much lower, for all his
maneuvering and cajoling.) Worse still, he had let the communists, whom he had gathered within his revolutionary fold
in the first place because he could use them, turn the tables on
him. Step by step, they had taken charge of his ministries,
the unions, the police and security organs, and were now running the country. Russians, Czechs, Poles, Chinese, were already
coming into Cuba and working closely with the Cuban communists on the task of turning the country into a Soviet-type
state. He was now perceiving belatedly that he was being used
increasingly as a mere figurehead and that his revolution was
being stolen from him.

What could he do in such a situation? According to the
theory I now tentatively advance, he decided that there was

only one solution—to bluster and bluff and fight his way out
of his self-made difficulty. He resolved to do this by making a
speech proclaiming that he had directed the great coup whereby
Cuba had been taken into the communist bloc and that he had
been the man who all the time had been guiding her along this
only road to political and economic emancipation. If he had
not spoken in this fashion, avowing by inference rather than
direct statement his allegiance to communism, he might not
have been able to continue to convince Cubans that he was
still the Maximum Leader, and once he had forfeited that claim
upon them he could easily have gone down at last for good. It
is quite possible that the counterattack he delivered on December 2 effectively, if temporarily, checked a communist clique
headed at that time by Blas Roca, the man trained and chosen
by Moscow to take him over. At any rate, despite many more
ups and downs that followed the speech, he was still there,
evidently again in charge of affairs, for a very long time after
December, 1961; whereas thereafter one heard less and less
of either Blas Roca or any other of the formerly powerful
Cuban communists.

Fidel Castro certainly proved for seven turbulent years after
the conquest of Havana that he had a phenomenal capacity
for personal survival. Right into 1966 he was still overcoming
crises, rebuffs, and challenges any one of which would have
doomed a man of lesser talents. One reason for his long in-
violability was his disregard of physical danger. Any leader
who gives no heed to the danger of attack or assassination is
obviously in a much stronger position than one who does. The
man who never cares about his personal safety, trusting to fortune and the zeal of those who guard him, spreads all the
wider aura of respect and admiration. I have always felt this
factor to have contributed to the Castro charisma, to the
spell he casts over those who come into close contact with him
for a while. I have seen Fidel Castro and been with him scores
of times when he could have been picked off like a sitting bird

by somebody with a pistol, and I have never seen him show the slightest concern on that account.

Another reason, perhaps an even more powerful one, for his long survival is his phenomenal mental resilience. Blows such as a diplomatic setback, a plot against his regime or himself, an unexpected and unwelcome defection, and even a cold-shouldering by Khrushchev (as happened in November, 1962) affect him temporarily, of course, but very soon he recovers his poise and confidence—either by sheer quickness of thought or by rationalization—and he is then able to go on more or less as if nothing had happened. There are other reasons, such as his ruthlessness and his hypnotic powers of persuasion, but I believe the two I have singled out are probably the most important.

By no means all who have observed and analyzed the Cuban revolution will agree with the interpretation I have advanced of the cause of Castro's announcement of his devotion to Marxism-Leninism. There are many respectable inquirers who have devoted much of their time since 1959 in trying to prove the exact contrary—that Castro has been a communist all his adult life. When one reads what they have to say the impact is strong, yet they are in exactly the same position as myself, for none of us can produce a single item of incontrovertible evidence to prove our case. Nobody has yet produced a party card made out in the name of Fidel Castro, nor even a written record of any kind to prove his affiliation or even association with the comrades. I am puzzled to know why all these scores of Cubans who joined Fidel Castro in the Sierra Maestra, fought with him there until the victory, worked for a while for him in Havana and elsewhere, and only then began defecting because the revolution had become a communistic one, never knew that their leader was a communist. I find it unthinkable that any man, even Fidel Castro, could pull the wool over the eyes of so many people for so long. To be sure, those who claim that he has really been a communist can produce many thousands of words of statements and interviews and speeches by loquacious Cubans, including Castro himself, which tend to show that they might be right, but my fairly considerable experience in the country, and indeed in almost every other one in Latin and South America, has taught me that it is unwise to place too much reliance on what one hears and reads in the absence of hard supporting evidence. A Latin will tell you something false or misleading for any one of a number of reasons unusual by Anglo-Saxon standards and when challenged later will often smile charmingly and pass on to the next business. There is above all no point in going by what Castro himself says about anything, for in the short time he has been in power in Cuba he has proved himself a masterly liar!

Since I do not believe that he was a communist when he was campaigning in the Sierra Maestra to oust Batista, I must also presume that his animosity toward the United States was not the product of any communistic or other doctrinal impulse. As I have described, he seemed to me to be inspired by an obsession in 1959 to liberate Cuba from the economic and political straitjacket in which he considered the United States to have placed the island, and his objective was accordingly to end once and for all the domestic dictatorship that had been practiced by corrupt tools of the United States. He was impelled by patriotic and nationalist zeal, not doctrinaire communism. I submit that at that time he would have attacked the Soviet Union with just the same heat and vigor and amoral opportunism if it had been in the position of the United States vis-à-vis Cuba. In other words, he would have gone for any power that he considered to be the oppressor of his country and his people.

It seems to me that with Che Guevara, his right-hand man (or perhaps more accurately his left-hand man!) the case was different. Here was a politico-military crusader and a believer in international communism. He was not even a Cuban until honorary citizenship was conferred upon him somewhere

around the end of 1959. Until then he was an Argentine, a man
who had already plotted and operated in Guatemala and elsewhere against the capitalist boss and had joined the Cuban
revolutionary movement because it offered still another opportunity to continue what he considered to be the great mission
of expanding the frontiers of communism. He, too, wanted to
liberate Cuba, but not from patriotic motives. His deep hatred
of the United States, which he never bothered to hide at any
time, did not spring from within him primarily because he
looked upon that country as the despoiler of Cuba. It sprang
from his realization that the United States was the one great
power that could thwart the fulfillment of communism across
the world and was doing everything it possibly could to that
end. So, for Guevara, there could never be any deal with the
United States unless by some unbelievable miracle it were to turn
communist, whereas I have always felt that some form of arrangement between Fidel Castro and the United States was a
possibility, at least until the catastrophic invasion of such
bitter memory; and another chance may yet come.

I have only a few comments to add to the millions of words
that have been written about that invasion. The first deep error
made by the United States was in allowing it to fail after it
had started. When it was seen to be faltering, no matter for
what reason, there should have been a decisive intervention to
make it succeed, even if this be interpreted not as causing the
immediate downfall of Fidel Castro but at least establishing
a firm lodgment within his territory to open a military operation that would eventually achieve that object. Use might even
have been made of the American forces close at hand at the
base at Guantanamo.

The essential point was that no matter what the cost diplomatically, morally, and militarily, the invasion should have
been sustained; the cost of failure—perpetuating and, indeed,
strengthening Fidel Castro and making it out of the question
to mount another invasion for many years—was far too high

from the point of view of the United States. I do not write this because I necessarily think that Fidel Castro should be flung out of Cuba. I say it pragmatically, feeling that avoidable failure in any such venture is deplorable and inexcusable. In the case of the Bay of Pigs invasion, it is specious to argue that since this was an affair in which Cubans were seeking to liberate their country the United States should have stayed out of it. If this was just an all-Cuban matter, why was all the planning done by the highest military and political authorities in Washington, and why did President Kennedy regard its failure as (according to Theodore C. Sorensen) "the worst defeat of his career"?

Four years after the invasion, Sorensen and Arthur Schlesinger, Jr., who were both close to President Kennedy while the invasion was being prepared and carried out, published their versions of what happened. The one impressive disclosure they made was that from beginning to end President Kennedy insisted that there should be no overt participation by the United States. Sorensen defends his chief with devotion and justification by emphasizing that Kennedy had inherited the plan for the invasion from his predecessor and was only just installed in office; and he claims that the President was misled and badly advised on the military aims and possibilities of the invasion. But the harsh fact remains that President Kennedy remained inflexible to the end on his insistence that Americans should not openly take part to save the invasion from utter disaster. His decision to cancel an air strike on the morning of the landing was made, according to Sorensen, on the advice of his advisers on foreign policy and without consultation with either the Central Intelligence Agency or his military advisers, who were headed by General Lyman Lemnitzer, Chairman of the Joint Chiefs of Staff. This was the critical expression of the policy of no open American involvement. So the invasion was doomed for political considerations—fears about retaliation by the Soviet Union and the damage that would be done to the American "image" in the world as a whole and in Latin America in particular if its own force were used to turn the invasion from a disaster into a triumph.

On the first count, there had been evidence in plenty since the death of Stalin that the Soviet Union was no more prepared than the United States to contemplate the risk of war. On the second, at least as much damage was done—and probably more—by failure as would have been done by triumph. The whole world knew that the United States was providing everything for the invasion except soldiers. It was never described afterward as a *Cuban* failure but as an American failure, and that is how it will be described in the history books. It might just as well have been turned into an American triumph. Fidel Castro certainly had no illusions about whose invasion it was, and there was evidence that he expected American troops to be taking part in it. I recall seeing the propaganda posters in Havana three months before it happened—luridly warning *los Yanquis* not to invade Cuba and advising them of the fate that awaited them if they did. One printed sign on the front fender of a Czech-made truck ran, "Let the Yankees make their wills before they come."

One further speculative thought may be considered. It is that if Richard Nixon instead of John F. Kennedy had won the election of 1960 and been in office in the White House when the invasion took place, the outcome would have been very different. I accompanied both candidates around the country during their grueling campaigns and thereby obtained a useful insight into their characters. From what I learned about Nixon I would say without hesitation that he would not, as President, have denied the invaders air support. On the contrary, he would have made absolutely sure that the invasion succeeded at no matter what cost or effort, for stubborn aggressiveness is one of the pronounced characteristics of that complicated man. But if he had thrust the invasion effort through to success and overthrown Fidel Castro would that

have been a desirable or permanently effective development? I
doubt that. A Republican President would have been under
considerable pressure from business interests to put Cuba back
into her old position, restoring the pre-Castro relationship between it and the United States, and might have felt obliged to
do so. I do not believe that re-established relationship could
have been maintained for very long. Whatever else Fidel Castro
might or might not have done, he has given Cubans a whiff of
the scent of independence, and sooner or later, probably sooner,
they would have found another leader to guide them to it or,
at the very least, to enforce a new arrangement with the United
States.

If, to use business terms, one sees Fidel Castro as the chairman of the board of the revolution for the first two years after
the occupation of Havana, Che Guevara was at first its general
manager and, for a period, its managing director. He was by
far the steadiest and coolest of the inner board of administration and while saying the least achieved the most. His executive
power and his international importance grew steadily after the
entry into Havana and, in spite of fluctuations in his public
authority, he seemed to be until his sudden disappearance early
in 1965 the one man to whom Fidel Castro always paid heed.
He was, as it happened, the first of the top revolutionary
leaders to reach the city in 1959. He acted as Castro's advance
man. I remember noting his gnomelike, bearded face—a very
youthful face—as he stood in the back of an American-made
jeep, clutching the side determinedly to keep his balance as he
was driven along the Malecon, while thousands of howling and
gesticulating Cubans lined both sides of that distinguished thor-
oughfare.

Guevara, who is a shrewd and able administrator, started
his career in the New Havana as commander of the city garrison, but as time went on he filled one high position after
another. He often stepped in to fill an executive hole caused by
a defection, a dismissal, or even a trial and execution. His

most spectacular post, which he filled in picturesque fashion by continuing to sport his beard and his loose-fitting and untidy olive-green fatigue uniform in quite palatial surroundings and by impishly using his nickname, "Che," for a signature, was President of the National Bank of Cuba. He took on this job after Felipe Pazos, one of the most skillful and respected economists in Latin America, had given up in despair at the unorthodox and disastrous ways of the revolution and its Maximum Leader in matters of finance.

One reason why Guevara gained authority so quickly was the failure of Raul Castro, the oriental-looking half brother of Fidel, to stand up to the role of being the younger brother of a temporary god. Although Cubans tried to make allowances for Raul and to make excuses for him, they could not come to love him. I saw him only two or three times, but the contact was enough to cause me to accept the verdict of others who knew more about him that he has an unpleasant personality— sly, calculating, and evasive—and there is a streak of cruelty within him.

A young Cuban who seemed to know something about the family background of the Castros told me in Havana in 1961 that Raul probably did have some Chinese blood in his veins. The story in Oriente was that at one time the father of Fidel and Raul had a relationship, maybe even a common-law marriage, with a Cuban woman of Chinese extraction, and Raul was their offspring. An alternative version I heard elsewhere was that it was their mother they shared. I do not offer either story as fact; I merely record it. The family story of the Castros has never been fully told and I have never heard or read any explanation, other than the ones I have just advanced, of the oft-stated fact that Fidel and Raul are half brothers. The father, Angel Castro, was a Spaniard who emigrated to Cuba from Galicia as a young man. By all accounts he was tough and licentious and there were many scandals about him. Probably that is why so little has been said or written about him since his son became a player of importance on the world stage.

As for Raul, he made a deplorable debut in the post-revolutionary era, as we have seen, by his inhuman lust for blood in Oriente. Nothing I have ever heard of him doing afterward has effaced that blot. He slowly lost his public prominence as Fidel Castro and Che Guevara drew closer to each other until, in 1962 and 1963, one rarely heard his name mentioned in Havana. From time to time he made a speech, usually more threatening and crude than anything his brother said, or he represented the regime at a funeral or a wedding or some other function, but he seemed no longer to have much influence in the conduct of the nation's affairs. Fidel Castro once made a revealing aside during one of his long speeches in Havana when he said, "If you think I'm an extremist, just you wait until you see what my brother is like." Incidentally, Fidel more than once indicated that he expected Raul to take over the leadership of Cuba if anything happened to him, but I for one do not believe that the Cubans would give Raul their support for very long.

The wide difference in character between Fidel and Raul—and between them and Juanita, the sister who after she defected sensationally in 1964 showed that she detested Fidel—is part of the family mystery. The one fact that stands out here is that Fidel was the only one out of six, maybe more, children who was given or insisted upon having the best available education in Cuba. And the story in this respect and in his general personal history goes a long way toward confirming that he was no communist until after he entered Havana in triumph in 1959. The evidence is rather sketchy, but there is significance in it because it does not contain one fact indicating the contrary.

As a boy Fidel went to expensive Roman Catholic schools in Santiago and Havana. He entered the law school of the University of Havana in 1945 and graduated in 1950. While at the university, and at the age of twenty-one, he married a fellow student belonging to one of the prominent families of Havana. She was Mirta Diaz Balart, daughter of a senior officer in the Cuban Army and the sister of an official in the Batista administration. She bore him a son in the year he graduated. Fidel was divorced by his wife in 1955 and thereafter the boy, Fidelito, is believed to have spent most of his childhood in the care of female members of the Castro family. Only very occasionally was he paraded publicly in the company of his father. But a year or two after the Russians had gone into Cuba he was given a trip to Moscow, where Khrushchev made a lot of him. After that he disappeared again into the background—another Cuban boy growing up and being educated under Marxist-Leninist auspices.

Fidel Castro was already mixed up in politics while studying for his law degree. He held various offices in student bodies and his already-violent spirit caused him to join an ill-organized expedition against the dictator Trujillo, which was squashed before it achieved anything, and he also joined demonstrations in Bogotá, Colombia, in which student blood was spilled. Nowhere in his record at the university is there a suggestion that he was either a communist or a fellow traveler.

His first plunge into national politics was also noncommunist. He stood as a candidate of the Orthodox Party in an election campaign in 1952. He never came to a test at the polls because of a coup by Batista that ousted President Prío Socarrás. His next exploit, the following year, was to organize a disastrous attack upon a military barracks (an affair to which I shall refer in some detail later) and again it was noncommunistic in spirit.

There were certainly communists around Castro in the Sierra Maestra, but they formed only a small minority in that otherwise bourgeois gang. Among them were his younger brother Raul, and Ernesto Guevara, who had joined him in 1955 while he was planning his revolution in Mexico. Guevara had fled from Guatemala to avoid the consequences of having supported the communistic government of President Jacob Arbenz, who was ousted in a revolt boldly and openly planned by the United States government. Nobody who visited the rebels in the mountains ever publicly suggested, so far as I have been able to discover, that either Raul or Guevara or anybody else was telling Fidel Castro what to do.

And nothing proclaimed by Fidel Castro from the Sierra Maestra bore any suggestion of communism. A manifesto he issued in July, 1957, promised general elections and guaranteed all individual and political rights mentioned in the Cuban Constitution of 1940. He was specific in suggesting similar undertakings in other declarations from the mountains, and in one manifesto issued only five months before he entered Havana he emphasized that after the fall of Batista he would guide the nation to normality by forming a brief provisional government that would pave the way to "full constitutional and democratic procedures." At about the same time he said scornfully, when questioned on his political beliefs, "I have never been a communist and am not one now. If I were I should have the courage to say so." I remember him saying with similar scorn early in 1959, "Yes, of course there are communists in my revolution. I use them like I use everybody else, because they are willing to work for me."

Perhaps the most conclusive evidence of all is provided by the failure of the general strike that Fidel Castro had called for in Havana from the Sierra Maestra in April, 1958. Here I accept without question the verdict of Theodore Draper, who has made a closer political study of the Castro revolution than anybody else. In his *Castro's Revolution: Myths and Realities* (1962), Draper writes:

It failed because the middle class could not carry off a general strike. Only the workers and trade unions could do so and they refused mainly for two reasons: They were doing too well under

Batista to take the risk, and the official Communists deliberately sabotaged the strike because they had not been consulted and no attempt was made to reach an agreement with them in advance.

Does that suggest that Fidel Castro was either a communist or a tool of the communists eight months before his victory?

But very soon after the failure of the strike the communists were making their bid for the soul of Fidel Castro. They sent to him Carlos Rafael Rodriguez, who was destined to become one of the communist leaders of the revolution after it had triumphed. They had decided at last in the summer of 1958 that Fidel Castro was going to defeat Batista and they hastened to join him. Carlos Rafael Rodriguez stayed with him until victory as an official representative of the party, and the process of attrition by which Castro's revolution was taken eventually from him had begun.

One question that remained unsolved for years afterward concerned the willingness with which Fidel Castro allowed himself to be politically seduced. Some believe that he always intended to "turn communist" and others that he fell eagerly enough during 1959 and 1960. I believe that anybody who, like myself, observed Fidel Castro's incapacity both as an administrator and a political strategist on the spot during that period would come to my conclusion that the communist coup was pulled on him before he was even aware that it was in existence. His ineptitude was certainly one of the reasons for the swift rise of the communist Ernesto Guevara within the revolutionary apparatus. Very soon after the regime was installed Guevara simply had to start taking charge because Castro not only did nothing toward running the country but got in the way of officials who were trying to run it for him. He either did not keep governmental appointments or was hours, even days, late in meeting them, and he was rarely at his desk to sign a document or make a decision. He was once again showing that he was an outsize Cuban personality by

outdoing everybody else in the fields of mismanagement, dila-
toriness, and incapacity to organize.

For a man not yet thirty, the non-Cuban Guevara performed
brilliantly. He built up the National Institute of Agrarian
Reform so that even though the inexperienced Cuban officials
working under him made some colossal blunders, the organization itself was sound and durable. Then, after directing the
National Bank until somebody had been trained to take over
from him, he took control of the whole state machine by which
the nationalized economy was being run, or at least being
kept from falling apart.

While he was thus Atlaslike propping up the revolution and
leaving the brassy trumpeting to Castro, Guevara was also
opening the door to international communism. He traveled a
lot behind the iron curtain, to Moscow and the other capitals,
and to the Middle East and Peking, and he negotiated most of
the politico-economic deals that had to be made with the
Russians to avert a Cuban collapse as the traditional two-way
traffic with the United States declined and eventually dried up
altogether.

There is evidence in plenty of the firm directional hand
toward the left that Guevara took once he and Raul, and other
communists who had been infiltrated into the revolution even
while it was still in the Sierra Maestra, saw that Fidel Castro
had neither the political wits nor the time and energy to stop
them. One authoritative witness is Sergio Rojas Santamarina,
who served in London as the revolution's first Ambassador to
the United Kingdom. He had been an agent of the revolution
before it succeeded and, like myself, believes that Castro was
not a communist when he took power. He related in an article
that appeared in the London *Daily Telegraph* on October 27,
1960, after he had resigned in disillusionment, that whereas
Guevara and his associates cold-shouldered the British and
other Western businessmen who went to Havana during 1959
to implement Castro's wish (expressed personally to Rojas)

for trade relationships with Western countries, they were warm indeed to East European business and economic commissions. Delegations from Czechoslovakia, Poland, Rumania, Bulgaria, and China had only to arrive in Havana to be received by Guevara, who would go personally to the airport to wait for them. A fleet of limousines was always put at their disposal, dinners and cocktail parties were arranged. After a couple of days, related Rojas, they usually managed to sign a big contract. Naturally enough, British businessmen kept waiting in the wings drew their own conclusions.

7 _Island Prison_

I CONFIRMED to my own satisfaction that Cuba had been delivered to communism when I went to Havana in January, 1961, to see just what had happened after the final diplomatic break with the United States. There were many telltale signs of the conversion. The economy had been transferred almost totally from free enterprise to state control. Communists were now in charge of all the big unions. Cubans whom I had known since 1959 complained to me, usually in whispers, that they were becoming aware of a growing furtive surveillance of them at their work and in the city by military and political agents. There was only one radio network and one television channel. All the independent newspapers had either been closed down or taken over and directed by the regime. Citizens were beginning to be schooled in the familiar totalitarian technique of spying upon and informing about each other; they were being given broad hints about this in leaflets such as one I saw being handed around one day: "We must always be on the watch for willing or unwilling enemies of the revolution."

The unfortunate Cubans were, in fact, beset by so many pressures, anxieties, and curbs, that I felt sorrier for them than at any time since the intoxications of January, 1959, had given way to disillusionment and dismay. First of all, they were now boxed in. After the break with the United States, the regime had cancelled the issue of exit permits to dam the flow of people who still had visas to the United States and were practically storming the Havana airport every day. The process of insulating Cuba from the rest of the hemisphere had begun. The rupture with the United States had struck deeply, I found, into the Cuban mind. Older people were especially depressed at the severance. For all that Fidel Castro and his fellow-revolutionaries had said about the Yankees and their so-called crimes, Cubans still felt friendship and even kinship with their great neighbor to the north, and they could not yet imagine how the void would be filled—perhaps that was just as well for those with no love for communism.

As if this were not enough, the wracked minds of the Cubans had now to face another scarcely tolerable strain. Adding to the confusion, excitement, and plain depression caused by the diplomatic breach was the exploitation of an invasion scare by the regime. I still do not know whether this scare was fomented to give the revolutionary leaders scope for imposing a firm hold upon the country during the crisis caused by the break with the United States or whether it was founded upon intelligence reports from Castroite agents in Florida and elsewhere. I am inclined toward the latter explanation, for events were to prove within four months that an invasion was indeed being prepared.

Perhaps the agents, excitable and impatient as only Cubans can be, had merely been premature in their warnings. Perhaps Castro really thought an invasion was coming within days. The pressure upon the nerves of a person coming from even the hubbub of New York was maddening. One could not move anywhere, even inside the Havana Libre Hotel, without some form of inflammatory propaganda assailing the eyes and ears. Revolutionary fervor was being kept in full fever by the playing of patriotic and military tunes and rebel anthems all day long, and for most of the night, from amplifiers in the streets and inside buildings. Radio, television, and the newspapers were full of provocative and mostly lying reports and accusations indicating that the invasion would certainly happen before January 18, that is within ten days of the first time I heard the hullabaloo.

Teenage Cuban soldiers and militiamen manned Czech-made antitank guns at positions all over the capital, notably in sandbagged emplacements along the sea wall of the Malecon and elsewhere so that their barrels quickly became ruined by cascading seawater. Hotels and buildings, including the American Embassy, were under the tender guard of handsome young militiawomen wearing black berets and olive-green uniforms. They were armed with rifles and machine pistols as they sat or stood at their posts at entrances and on rooftops. I marveled at the military reasoning that presumably inferred that these dark-haired and gay Cuban maidens could fight off the invaders who were expected to be pouring ashore at any moment. Once again I surmised that perhaps there is more than one way of stopping a U. S. Marine in his tracks; the test may yet come in Havana.

The incredibly noisy and wearing hubbub went on unabated until January 12, by which time I felt like tearing down every loudspeaker and other demoniac device that was assailing me with its deadly repetitive jargon and battle cries. Then it suddenly subsided. Some praiseworthy individual, perhaps Che Guevara, called the whole appalling fantasy off.

Perhaps the regime suddenly realized what a spectacle it was making of itself and, more importantly, that it was rapidly driving the population crazy. The martial and propaganda songs gave way to the gay jazz for which Cuba is, or used to be, renowned. Fidel Castro stopped issuing leaflets and posters proclaiming in pseudo-Churchillian grandeur, "We will defend every house from rooftop to cellar and when there is nothing else left we shall defend the ruins." The strident voices of announcers, actors and actresses and others, bawling their parrot cries of *"Patria o Muerte; Venceremos!"* night and day became silenced, and the air was now filled at intervals with more measured propaganda than the outrageous nonsense—including a story that the Marines in Guantanamo Bay had tortured and beaten a Cuban worker there—that had been pouring from the regime's propaganda factories. The soldiers and militia-women left the guardpoints they had been manning for days and nights and, perhaps after a brief rest, some of them answered Fidel Castro's appeals for volunteers to go into the fields to cut the neglected sugar cane. The capital slowly simmered down.

But Fidel Castro had gone a little too far with his people this time. The appalling assaults upon their minds since the New Year had numbed them into an apathetic daze, so that they did not now respond even to the oratorical magic of their leader. He called one of his periodic mass meetings for a Friday night in the square by the Presidential Palace, and less than thirty thousand of the faithful turned up. This was one of the thinnest attendances he had drawn since 1959, compared with turnouts of up to a quarter of a million on many similar evenings. Cubans had clearly had more than they could digest for the time being, and Fidel Castro showed that he knew this. He started his address cosily enough, as he usually did, but

like the first-class actor he is he soon sensed that he did not
have his audience with him. People listened apathetically and
applauded lazily. Soon they even began to drift away while he
was still talking. I could almost feel the heart going out of
him. Eventually he gave up altogether. It was all over within
two hours, a phenomenally curt period for a Castro occasion.
But if he had gone on much longer that cool evening he would
have had nobody at all listening.

While Fidel Castro was thus representing the public front
of the revolution, without much success, the real work of
sustaining it was still being done at this time by Che Guevara.
Behind the scenes he was working with zeal and determination
to complete the enormous task of dismantling a semicolonial
economy operating on a base of limited free enterprise and
putting in its place a communistic one. The talk I heard that
January was that he was courting the Chinese. The emissaries
of this mysterious and distant land were now in Havana in
considerable strength, surveying the possibilities of the new
political and economic field that the revolution had opened to
them. They were less obtrusive than the Eastern Europeans and
the Russians, but they were sometimes to be seen padding their
mysterious way across the city, or even disporting with their
wives and families, in mass and seemingly under the leadership
of one of their number, at the swimming pools at the hotels
and sequestered clubs.

The Chinese influence in Cuba was about at its greatest at
this period and so also, as matters later showed, was Guevara's,
for he was never to be quite so prominent later. There might be
a connection between these facts. To be sure, Guevara's ideological conviction is the same as that of the Chinese—a fight
to the finish with the United States and all who stand with it,
and no evasions and prevarications about peaceful coexistence,
victory without war, and the rest. There was also one unusual
bond between Mao Tse-tung and Guevara; both had made
themselves expert in guerilla warfare. This was a military link

that reinforced the political one. The affinity was so pronounced that, at about the period I am describing, a book containing translations of their writings on the subject of hitting and running was produced as a military treatise in America and in Europe. It showed that they thought in very similar terms—about the military aspect of revolution at any rate.

The invasion, which had been advertised in advance in a manner usually reserved for a Broadway musical, duly happened on April 17, 1961. It was a far more tragic flop than any musical ever produced on Broadway or anywhere else. As a non-American onlooker, I was surprised that the nation did not demand somebody's head for such a phenomenal disaster, worse by far than the failure of the hobbled British at Suez five years earlier. But the only head, the ultimate head, that could have been sacrificed was Kennedy's and his still had a postinaugural halo about it that made it untouchable. Also, he had inherited the invasion and had scarcely found his way around the White House by the time it took place. One wonders what would have followed if the disaster had beset him at any period other than during the flush days of a president's accession, when his popularity, almost his sanctity, is at its strongest. The most likely answer to the question is that there would not have been any such disaster for, after this one pristine and searing setback, Kennedy showed admirable courage and judgment during the rest of his senselessly curtailed occupancy of the White House. The failure of the invasion of Cuba is a blemish on his record that he was not enabled to erase, because of a maniacal deed which must stand for a long time as a reproach to the American attitude toward law and order and authority.

Some months after the dust and fuss kicked up by the abortive invasion had settled down, I went to Havana to see what effects it had had within the island. By this time the Cubans had ordered, for the first time during the relationship between the two countries, that Americans seeking to visit Cuba would have to obtain visas, and these were technically available through the Czechoslovakian Embassy in Washington. The State Department, wishing to make sure that communists and left-wingers and others of whom it disapproved did not go to Cuba, ruled that any person in the United States who wanted to go to Havana would have to have permission through the Department of Immigration and Naturalization. In practice, the effect of this arbitrary and controversial regulation was to limit travel to Cuba to American correspondents and a few other persons with special reasons for going there. Since only a handful of American correspondents were ever able to get a visa from the Czechs and the necessary approval by the State Department, the United States was becoming starved indeed of news from Havana.

As an Englishman I did not need a visa for Cuba because of reciprocal arrangements between the United Kingdom and Cuba, but as a resident alien in the United States I did need the permission of the State Department to make a visit and return to my place of domicile. I wish now to record my appreciation of the speed, efficiency, and courtesy with which the department always granted my applications. I tried to reciprocate by writing articles for magazines and newspapers and broadcasting by radio and television whenever invited to do so. I also gave lectures from time to time about what I had learned during my visits.

It was now November, 1961. One Pan American plane per day was still making the return trip between Miami and Havana. When it left Miami in the early morning it rarely carried more than half a dozen passengers. "Sometimes we do not have anybody at all," confided the stewardess as she sat beside me during part of the short hop over the Florida Strait. "But you should see us on the trip back. We are jammed to the limit with Cubans getting out—the backlog of lucky ones with visas they got months and months ago. They usually start singing and dancing—and weeping—once they are sure we have really left Havana—but only when they *are* sure."

Well under an hour after leaving Miami we had landed in Havana and I was walking in the blazing sunshine across the tarmac to the immigration building of the airport. I felt uncomfortable and exposed as I did so, for I was the only passenger that morning. Away to the left, a couple of Cuban mechanics were tinkering lazily with a grounded plane, one of the few still owned by Cubana Airlines. Behind them three other workers were putting up a sign over a hangar. On it was written, in big red letters, in Spanish, "This we shall defend to the death." The airport was eerily silent and it took me a moment or two to realize why. The sky was empty of planes. It was a reminder of the isolation of Cuba. It was also a sign, perhaps, of the truth of the story one had heard in New York that the regime could not now trust its military pilots to come home again after taking off. And there was now the sheer need to save gasoline.

It did not take long for the one visitor from the United States to enter Cuba. The only new ritual since I was last there was that I was required politely to go to a microscopic branch of the National Bank of Cuba located in a walled-off partition of the customs shed and there surrender every dollar and cent I had. The amount was methodically counted by a young clerk, recounted, and the figure entered on a piece of yellow paper. This was then handed to me with the warning that I must keep it carefully until I left Cuba, and with it I received the equivalent amount of new Cuban currency calculated exactly at par, dollar for peso. The process was obviously devised to stop me, or anybody else, from selling dollars at a fat profit on the black market, where dollars were now going against pesos at a rate of about one to six. The new paper money, which had been issued some months earlier to render valueless the millions of pesos that were thought to have been smuggled out of the country soon after the revolution, was stylish stuff indeed. It had been printed in Czechoslovakia and the designs on notes of different denominations depicted revolutionary victory in the field (bandaged men holding the victorious banner aloft, etc.), revolutionary progress in agrarian reform, and Fidel Castro talking. The notes were fancy and newly printed but they were tokens of a totally two-faced currency. The new peso was as solid within Cuba as is the American dollar within the United States, and its domestic purchasing power was only between 10 and 12 percent lower than had been the original peso in the gay old days of tourism and free trading for all. Outside Cuba it was utterly valueless.

An illusion of normalcy persisted for some time after one had left the airport and been driven at a cost of six of the new pesos into the city, fifteen miles away. Street traffic was orderly and quiet, even allowing that it was nothing like so great as in the noisy, haphazard old days. People seemed to be going about their daily affairs with a new seriousness, and, for Cubans, silently. There was none of the incessant tooting of automobile horns at every street corner, as of old; none of the insidious jazz from radios everywhere; none of that wholly Cuban slap-and-clap of leathern dice boxes being banged on the counters of bars with their doors open to the hot breeze and with their interiors mysteriously dim. Havana, in short, was just not at all like the old Havana. One slowly perceived that it was a new place altogether.

Therein lay the clue to the enormity of what the revolution had already done, and what it promised to do in the years ahead, unless, from one cause or another, it were checked before it ran its course. It had imposed many of the dreary trappings of a state believing itself to be struggling toward the millennium of socialization, but enduring the shortages, regimentation, tale-telling, jail-filling, lying propaganda, and the rest in the interim. Life was not yet as drab as in, say, East Germany or Estonia because you simply cannot do that sort of thing in a space of three or four years with a people as ebullient, life-

loving, and opportunistic as Cubans. But the revolution had
taken away most of the old vitality of Havana, and it had not
yet done anything noticeable to replace the loss. "We shall
have to be patient before we get the benefits of the revolution,"
observed one shopkeeper, obviously still with the regime, as he
apologized for the lack of toothpaste and other articles on his
shelves.

As for Fidel Castro himself, I was quite surprised to find
that, in spite of his triumph in fending off the invasion, he had
not been able to restore in his people the revolutionary fervor
that had already been so notably lackluster at the beginning of
1961. He had enjoyed an appetizing tonic in the rout of the invasion, and he had made the most of the victory immediately
afterward by bragging loudly about it, but I was now told that
the effect had been purely temporary and that the realities of
the imposition of a communist system in what was virtually an
island prison had taken the spirit out of most of the people. Incidentally, Fidel Castro was by no means as confident and cocky
a commander in the field while the dismal scuffle of the Bay of
Pigs was taking place as he was later on the speaking platform.
I have since seen a propaganda film issued by the revolutionary
regime about the defeat of the invasion. It had all the predictable shots of doughty rebel defenders at their guns, prisoners
trailing along the dusty roads, and piles of captured equipment, but it also had most enlightening studies of Fidel
Castro during the fighting. He was in full field array, complete
with side arms and battle-dress, but all his movements were
jerky and highly nervous, and there was a frown on his face
in every shot I noticed. He looked most apprehensive; and, as
a former war correspondent who saw a good deal of action in
the Second World War, I was by no means impressed by the
demeanor of his young Cuban troops while the action was on.
Many of them seemed to be jumping about like frightened
rabbits and hopping in quite a panic for cover at times. I
think they were the reason for Fidel's obvious anxiety; perhaps

he felt they might not stand up to any resolute attack made upon them.

Castro's confident and staunch support during this bleak period when at least three out of four Cubans had lost their original glowing faith in him and he was surrounded politically by dominant communists was Che Guevara. This cool-headed young man was one of the communists determinedly turning Cuba into a communistic state, and using Fidel Castro to that end, but he was unswerving in his personal loyalty to and, I feel sure, his affection for his nominal leader. One of the threads that remained unbroken throughout all the vicissitudes of the revolution—until 1965—was the trust and comradeship between these two, and I imagine that it was sustained at least partly because of their regard for each other as soldiers and comrades during the long and sometimes heartbreaking campaign in the Sierra Maestra. Fidel Castro never had a more loyal supporter than Guevara. Not once in the first six years of the revolution did I hear a whisper about Guevara turning upon Castro in any way, betraying him, or seeking to usurp the leadership. In fact, I have seen public evidence of their comradeship. Even in late 1961, when Castro was no longer the Cuban idol and Guevara must have seen how other communists trained in Moscow were elbowing him aside and systematically taking charge of the revolution and preparing to deliver Cuba to the Soviet Union, they were as gay and friendly as ever in front of the crowds.

One Friday evening Castro appeared on television for one of his regular marathon speeches, and his speech that night dealt mostly with an explanation of the national economic goals for the next year. He made an awful hash of the speech. He was holding a large sheet of paper on which, obviously, were written the facts and figures he was to use. He had either not read the paper beforehand or, if he had, its contents had not sunk in—which would not be surprising in view of his known allergy to mathematics and the like. Behind him as he floundered, garbled, and misquoted sat Che Guevara. He was holding his head in his hands in mock horror as one mistake followed another. In the end Castro gave up. With a comical gesture and amid a roar of laughter from the platform he turned and said, "Here, Che, you do it." And Guevara, also laughing, strode up to the microphones and finished the job. He stayed only long enough to explain the figures and then unquestioningly he yielded again to his chief.

But behind such public scenes as this lay the reality that Fidel Castro had by this time lost the personal control of the revolution he had enjoyed in 1959. He was never to regain it, for the Russians took over once the Cuban communists had thrust him aside and taken local charge. Those communists were already in a strong position at the time of the invasion. They had infiltrated most of the ministries and, in particular, they were running the Ministry of State Security. Their man, Major Ramiro Valdez, was in charge of this vital branch of government and their other man, Augusto Martinez Sanchez, was master of the influential labor unions.

I now learned that when the well-advertised invasion happened at last the secret police and other agents of Martinez Sanchez made a pounce upon suspects that was talked about with awe for long afterward by those who watched it go on. Waiters, craftsmen, women, insignificant Cubans who must have thought they were far too petty to matter, were all taken into custody. A cautious British estimate, or deliberate underestimate, was that over a hundred thousand people in Havana were arrested. They were packed into abandoned houses, government warehouses, and other property, as well as into the already well-filled prisons. It seemed as if the loathed and feared men of the G2 Intelligence Division had known all along what was going on in the hearts as well as the homes of so many Cubans.

After the invasion had been crushed, people were released slowly, after long and deliberately tantalizing inquiries and questionings. In the end over 80 percent of the suspects were freed, but at least sixty of the men caught in the roundup were shot. Some months after the invasion the process of sifting prisoners was quickened and releases came in batches, probably because manpower was so badly needed by the faltering economy, and late in the year four tribunals were often sitting at a time in La Cabaña prison, adjudging up to eighty persons in mass hearings.

The rout of the invasion certainly hastened the establishment of the Moscow-communist police state within Cuba. It frightened thousands of wavering and disillusioned Cubans into silent impotence. It all but destroyed the underground movement built up so painstakingly and against so many difficulties by Manolo Antonio Ray. That devastating sweep by G2, followed by all the questionings and inquiries, betrayed many who had been working alongside Ray's organization, as well as those within it.

Once imposed, the political and police grip upon the people was there of course to stay for as long as the revolution lasted, and it had to be continually tightened as living conditions worsened, with food becoming ever scarcer and money meaning less and less because there was so little to buy. The plan that emerged very clearly after the invasion debacle was to turn Cuba into as close a totalitarian state of the East European satellite type as could possibly be made out of the rather unreliable material available in the form of individualistic, volatile, and generally easy-going Latins. There were those who simply did not believe it could be done successfully and made to last, but done it was. In the second half of 1961 a single political party was flourishing, and the composition of its directorate showed which way the wind had blown.

Of the fifteen men known to be running the party, thirteen were old chieftains of the P. S. P. (communist) Party of Cuba. The 26th of July Movement upon which Castro had mounted his revolution had been thrust aside, the contemptuous communists allotting it only two seats on the directorate. The man

in charge (if it were conceded, as seemed unavoidable now, that
Fidel Castro was merely the figurehead through whom the communists were working) was Blas Roca, a politician now in his
fifties who had first caught notice as a Cuban communist as
long ago as 1950. Within two years he had become Secretary-
General of the Popular Socialist Party and seemed well set
for a lively career in the island when Batista, seeing that the
communists were becoming dangerous to him, declared their
party illegal. Blas Roca eventually realized that he would be
wasting his time if he tried to go on operating within Cuba, and
he left the country. It has never been known for certain how
and where he spent his exile, but it is sure that he spent some
of the intervening years in Moscow before hastening back into
Cuba in the wake of the Castro victory. He reached Havana
late in 1959 or in early 1960, and there has never been much
doubt that he went into Cuba thoroughly briefed by the Kremlin on his role of creating the foundations of a Soviet satellite
in the Caribbean—fastening a Soviet crab, as I have put it, to
the American big toe. When the single political party was
created in 1961 this man, who always looked to me very like a
younger Joseph Stalin, became its Secretary-General and its
boss.

One could not help noting at this time, toward the end of
1961, how he had stolen political prominence from Che Guevara,
in spite of the close association between Fidel Castro and
Guevara. One heard and read now the names only of Blas Roca
and his first lieutenant, Anibal Escalante (a very brief star,
this one, in the Cuban political firmament, for after a month or
two of extraordinary prominence he was suddenly ousted for
"deviations"). Once again the odd link between the fortunes in
Cuba of Guevara and the Communist Chinese was to be noted.
He was now in charge of all the nation's industry, trying to
fulfill the appalling task of making its branches work efficiently
and profitably under the new communistic impulse, but his
purely political influence within the revolution seemed to have

all but gone; the Chinese, too, had lost ground heavily in the ideological struggle for Cuba's soul. I was assured that there were still hordes of Chinese in the city, but throughout a full week I did not see one. They were working in their own strange way from within their embassy, behind a kind of Chinese wall. The embassy compound had been extended during the previous year to cover one whole block between two of the formerly fashionable avenues of the suburb of Vedado. The gaze of the curious onlooker was thwarted by a mass of bushes, fences, walls, and high trees and, although I passed the place several times, I never saw anybody going in or coming out. In fact, the Chinese seemed to be represented in Havana by proxy, in the form of tins of Chinese food, such as precooked pork, on the shelves of the nationalized food stores and in Chinese propaganda booklets lying alongside the periodicals from Moscow in the bookshops. There were also quotations from speeches and proclamations by Mao in the placards pasted on walls in the streets, together with fragments of the wisdom of Lenin and Castro. But it was quite apparent that both the political and economic influence of Communist China had been eroded during the year. Cuba was one area in which Soviet communism was gaining a victory over the Chinese brand in the ideological war then being fought between the two.

Penetration on behalf of the Soviet bloc in the form of technological instruction and the supply of civilian and military equipment was being done mostly by Czechs, probably the most capable, assiduous, and trustworthy of all the peoples within the eastern fold. They were to be seen by the score in Havana. More than seventy of them were staying at the fraying Hotel Libre, formerly the Hilton, while I was there. They were unmistakable as they moved in and out of the hotel in sizable groups, all wearing the orthodox uniform of white shirts, nondescript lightweight trousers, no hats, and carrying slender briefcases. I did not see them talking to Cubans or, indeed, anybody outside their own ranks. They never spoke a word to each other when they were in an elevator in the Libre, obviously having been warned not to do so there or, I imagine, anywhere else where they might be overheard by a Czech-speaking foreigner.

Most of my friends among the resident diplomats in Havana estimated that Fidel Castro now had the active support of only about 30 percent of the Cuban population, and it was felt that the great majority of these faithful adherents were young people. This was not surprising because the eager young Cubans were obviously attracted to him and his Juvenile Rebel Movement in the same fashion that the young everywhere are attracted to anything that gives them parades, a uniform, parties, and other outlets for blowing off steam. But adult discontent was growing. People queueing for eggs and milk in the steaming downtown streets made a lot of noise and indirect protest as they pushed their way to the counters. The talk in the buses—and these became fewer by the day as one after another broke down and could not be repaired—was occasionally defiant. I always was a constant patron of the buses in Havana, for I found that rides in them gave a flavor and insight not to be found elsewhere. Now I began to hear the muttering of Cubans who after a lifetime of soft living were finding the going rough. I recall one man in a bus in 1961 ending an argument that had been carried out in low tones by commenting disgustedly, with a spit, as he left the bus, "*Patria o muerte —pah!*"

But what could people do from within Cuba to get back their freedom? The militia, over one million strong, was being kept permanently mobilized in shifts of fifty thousand trained or half-trained young men and women. This militia was the open, naked force keeping Cuba docile, no matter what the regime said about it being maintained to meet the invader. Membership of the militia was induced by the bribery of extra rations and clothes, propaganda, and by the other odious pressures of a communist authority. Hundreds of thousands of so-called Committees for the Defense of the Revolution had been set up across the whole island. They were to be identified by small initialled flags placed over front doors and in the hallways of blocks of apartments. They were manned by about three hundred thousand petty watchdogs—time-servers who were the detestable symbols of dictatorship and oppression, spying upon their fellow-citizens as did the Blockwart in Germany in the days of Hitler. It meant that about one in every twelve Cubans was spying upon his friends and neighbors and even his own family. The task of the informer and the watcher was made easier because, thanks to revolutionary "reforms" and the spread of pettifogging and inefficient bureaucracy, it was almost impossible for a family to change its home. There was little scope for dodging the spies.

I decided on an impulse that before I left Cuba this time I would make a pilgrimage to Varadero. As a visiting correspondent I was not supposed to leave Havana without telling the Ministry of Foreign Affairs, but I decided that the chance was worth taking one sunny Sunday when the ministry was closed anyhow and, I hoped, I might be less conspicuous among the crowds making their excursions on a day off than on a working day. I went from the Libre to the bus station near the Principe Prison, noting sadly as I passed that formidable-looking citadel the little groups of Cubans waiting patiently to be admitted in their turn to visit a hapless friend or relative held inside as a captive of the invasion or for some crime proven or otherwise against the revolution. I paid my three or four pesos for my ticket inside the bustling long-distance terminal and took a seat near the back of the American-made bus. Surprisingly, we were away on time and were soon speeding at a lively Cuban clip over the narrow and occasionally bumpy roads to Varadero, some seventy miles away.

When I got there I found there had been changes indeed in the place since we were there in 1959. Blocks of flats to ac-

commodate holiday-making workers and members of the many
organs of the revolution had been built near the International
Hotel, which had been one of the haunts of the rich in the old
days, and the center of Varadero itself had been transformed
by the construction of a Peoples' Recreational Park just off
the sea front. I wandered round this rather severe addition to
the scenery, noting that very few people were tasting its amenities this Sunday at any rate, and finally came to rest at the
counter of a snack bar, where I ordered a Cristal beer. A
yard or two away to my right were four Czechs also out for
a day by the sea, and to my left were a young Cuban couple
taking a modest lunch.

The Czechs took not the slightest notice of me or the Cubans
but munched and drank solemnly as if nobody else was within
miles of them. When they had finished they went off still not
having said one word to my knowledge. Now came an overture
from the two Cubans. The woman—in my possibly limited experience the female is ever more adventurous than the male—
made the approach by looking across at me from a seat on the
other side of her husband (as he turned out to be) and asked,
in English, if I would please pass the sugar. So the contact was
made. I told them who I was. The man explained that at the
time of the revolution he had owned a small but thriving export
business that had taken him on many travels to the United
States and Europe and was now, of course, extinct. He was now
working in a nationalized store. He suddenly asked me if he
might speak in French, giving a meaning look at the man behind the counter who was the only person within earshot. Freed
from the risk of being overheard, he spoke his mind. Havana had
been turned into a veritable cemetery as far as business was
concerned, he said, and it was absolutely clear that the whole
island was being systematically handed over to the Soviet Union. "What I do not understand is why Fidel should think he
would get a better deal from them, with their record, than Cuba
had from the United States," he said. Then he added, with vehe-

mence, "Now I know for the first time in my life what it is
like to lose all liberty. . . . It is killing. I cannot tell you
what a relief it is to be able to talk to you like this. I look
at those Czechs and the other foreigners from communist countries who come here and I wonder how many of them perceive
all the natural bounty that this country has and think to themselves what idiots we are to have anything to do with communism. They cannot be all that dumb, can they?"

The young man went on thus for many minutes, until I
noticed that the man behind the counter was looking hard and
curiously at him. It was time to stop. I interrupted and said
I must go. The three of us shook hands, and I left them. The
last thing I wanted was to become involved in any incident. I
was lucky that I did not know what this strange day had in
store for me.

I ambled leisurely about the center of the little town and
looked again at the landmarks I remembered—the "bowling
alley," the Fisiatria shop where we had bought snorkel masks,
the unpretentious but pleasant little restaurants we had enjoyed, and finally Sotero's provision shop. I found Sotero too.
He was sorting boxes of vegetables near the side door of his
store as I walked up. "Remember me, Sotero?" I asked quietly.
I have rarely seen a man so startled. I might have been a
ghost, as in a sense I was. For once, this friendly and humorous
Cuban could find no words to speak, although his eyes widened
and gleamed in recognition. "How are things, friend?" I asked.
Sotero found speech at last as he recovered his poise. "Good,"
he said warily and he did not elaborate. I deduced that he also
had changed. He dared not trust me, for I might now be a spy
or an agent out to trap him. He muttered two or three words
to himself and turned and went indoors. Not the hearty Sotero
of old, but it was good to see that he and his modest monument
to private enterprise had survived, so far.

Now I found a small open-air restaurant that also had
survived the revolution, in the sense that it had not been

taken over, as had happened to all restaurants in Havana, and offered a choice of two or three dishes of meat and fish. I was attracted to it because a party of ten Cubans, men and women, were seated at one long table and were eating and talking with some enjoyment—a rarity indeed in the Cuba of 1961. As I took my seat I fished out of my briefcase one of the packs of American cigarettes that I had brought from the United States, as I always did, intending to offer a couple of smokes to the waiter when he took my order. I had already found that a Camel or a Chesterfield or other well-known cigarette had become like treasure since American imports had been cut off. Neither Cuban cigarettes nor the weedy objects from Eastern Europe could take the place of the favorites with the Cubans. Even so I was not prepared for what happened next.

One of the men at the big table turned around and saw me. He must have reported back that I was an "Americano," for all his friends now turned and looked at me. They all smiled. And before I quite realized what was going on, the men were coming over to my table, one after the other, and asking if they might have not one but several cigarettes. They all thanked me profusely and one, more daring than the rest, murmured hurriedly, "Tell them when you get back, señor, that we are still with America."

Luncheon over, there was one thing more to do before I walked to the bus stop for the journey back to Havana. I had not come prepared, but I wanted to have a swim on the beach in that incomparable water we had enjoyed so much two years earlier. I let my lunch digest and then I strolled over to the beach. There I stripped down to a pair of underpants and waded in. Yes, the water was just as caressing as I had remembered. I struck out and swam exuberantly away from the beach. And suddenly, to my horror, I found I was being carried swiftly out to sea far beyond my depth. I had chosen the one small stretch of water where, as I should have remem-

bered, there was a powerful undertow because of an undulation
in the shore. I must confess that for a moment or two I
thought I was a goner. There was nobody anywhere near to
offer help. Instinct impelled me to make one last fight for my
life. I turned face toward the shore and struck out with a
breast stroke. At first I made no headway and I had the awful
sensation of feeling the water thrusting me slowly backward.
The instinct for self-preservation again rose to my help. I
swam harder, harder, and harder and, blessed reward, I
began to make a slow gain toward the beach. I think I knew
then that I should survive. I swam on and finally came the first
touch of one foot on the sand. I was safe, although I still had
to thrust with all my strength against the pressure of the
water rolling away from the beach.

Drained, I plodded back to the spot at the foot of some
stone steps leading down from an abandoned house where I had
left my things. As I sat on the bottom stone, slowly getting
back my breath and my strength, I thought of the hubbub and
the mystery that would have been created if I had disappeared.
On the beach would be found my clothes and my briefcase—my
notebooks filled with a mixture of Pitman's shorthand and
other hieroglyphics that I used deliberately when on a mission
in Cuba to confuse any prying eyes—my underpants as the
only missing piece of clothing. I had slipped out of Havana
without telling anybody I was going to Varadero, or why. It
really would have been a first-class mystery worthy of revolutionary Cuba, but, I reflected, I should not have been there to
enjoy it.

The day was not yet done with me. There was one last
unnerving adventure in store to make me remember this return
to Varadero as long as I live. When at last I had recovered
from my fight against the sea and had been warmed and soothed
by the strong winter sunshine, I slowly dressed and then made
my way back to catch the 4 P.M. bus to Havana. The little
terminal was a long, narrow hut on one of the avenues just

beyond the Peoples' Park. I sat down on a bench, the only obvious foreigner in a crowd of about a score of Cubans also waiting for the bus. I leaned back and relaxed, reflecting on the very narrow squeak I had had such a little while ago. And then I became aware by some sixth sense that I was being watched. Surely enough, the burly Cuban sitting at the ticket desk at the far end of the waiting room was weighing me up intently. After one glance at him I pretended I had noticed nothing. At length he slowly got up and walked down the room, right past me and into the street. Now I knew what was afoot. He was going to report me to the militia as a suspicious foreigner and a possible spy.

There was nothing much I could do. If I got up and tried to make a bolt for it I stood a very good chance of being shot at. Why should I try to escape anyhow? But even as I debated this thought I realized the discomfort and danger that would come if I were indeed arrested. My friends at the Havana Libre and the British Embassy might miss me, but they would scarcely know how to start trying to locate me. I knew from what had happened to others since 1959 that days, perhaps weeks, would pass before I could be freed. Yet I now knew I had no alternative but to sit still and await whatever might befall me. If that wretched man came back with a soldier I could expect the worst. . . . He came back alone and walked slowly back to his desk, and my fast-beating heart slowed down. But only for a minute. The door opened again and in came a young Cuban soldier. He too walked past me, giving me just one quick glance, and he joined the ticket man. The two talked together in low voices. Back came the soldier. This was the moment I was dreading. Nearer and nearer he walked—and straight past me! I felt better, but I was still not out of all danger. Perhaps he would be coming back with an officer. But no, he did not. As the minutes passed and nothing happened I perceived that I had survived still another peril of that remarkable day, and I guessed the reason why. The soldier obviously had not believed that I could be anything but a Czech or a Russian, because every foreigner, any European who looked like me, just had to be one or the other. He had decided against the risk of making a fool of himself. Perhaps my briefcase, conferring a suggestion of officialdom upon me, had saved me. Whatever it was, I have ever afterwards thanked my stars that, possibly for the first and only time in my life, I was mistaken that November day for a Soviet or East European communist. I do know that there was no more relieved man in Havana that evening than the one who at last pushed against the swing door of the Libre Hotel and, after passing the customary light talk with a couple of the clerks and the elevator man in his braided, cutaway toreador-type uniform, slumped upon his bed on the fifteenth floor and felt the cool night breeze wafting through the open window upon him.

8 • On the Eve
of Crisis

LIKE A MOTH to the candle, I went again to Havana for the eleventh time in September, 1962. This was just one month before President Kennedy and Premier Khrushchev were forced at last to face the realities and the deep dangers of their duel over Cuba, and the visit was one of the most disquieting and physically alarming of any I had made up to that time. It was the sort of a challenge that had to be met, for there was much to find out.

Contradictions, obvious exaggerations, and pure confusion so muddied the thin trickle of news coming into New York from several sources that I decided there was only one thing for me to do to maintain my own first-hand understanding of what had been and was going on—this was to go to Havana and seek out the truth, or as nearly as I could get to it, for myself. This was the challenge I wanted to meet.

Castro and Khrushchev each had something to hide and between them were doing everything they could to make sure that professional inquirers, journalists and diplomats alike, would be prevented from discovering anything approaching the full, ugly truth of what the Russians were doing while the Cubans were perforce looking on helplessly. Castro now had to cover the humiliating fact that because of his own incapacity and inconstancy he had lost his revolution to the communists; and they in their turn were lagging so disastrously in their effort to harness Cuba to a communist machine that the Soviet Union had had to take over from them to save the country from total collapse. As for Khrushchev, he was at the same time taking the most dangerous and daring gamble of his career. He was building sites for offensive rockets and thereby turning Cuba into a base from which not only the United States but a big portion of Latin America could be attacked. He was hoping to pull off this monstrous gambit undetected. Until it matured all prying eyes must obviously be kept at a distance. It was small wonder that from the moment I arrived I found myself forbidden by the Ministry of Foreign Relations to go outside the city limits of Havana, was watched and shadowed by agents on foot and in cars from the moment I left my hotel bedroom every day until I got back to it, and in the end left Havana in circumstances more appropriate to a spy film than a supposedly ordered country.

To begin with I must say that I am sure nobody had the remotest suspicion even as late as September 12 of the enormity of the gamble Khrushchev was taking. It was known that he was sending men, material, and arms that together would make Cuba invulnerable to anything less than a massive assault, but if any person had said at this time that offensive rockets were already on their way to Havana and other ports in ships from the Soviet Union he would have been laughed at as mad.

The sequence of events that were destined to lead to the grand climax in October had begun, so far as I was able to learn from painstaking inquiries in non-Cuban and non-Soviet quarters, with the arrival during the early summer of about a thousand Russian and Czech specialists who were to undertake the salvage of the tottering Cuban economy. It was deduced that Khrushchev had decided after much deliberation that Castro was still worth propping up; that Khrushchev also had much bigger long-range plans for the revolution was, of course, not suspected.

The specialists were engineers and experts in irrigation, water conservation, soil improvement, and the maintenance of Russian and Czech equipment such as trucks, cars, tractors and mining machinery. There were also economists, bureaucrats, and others who began to work with and through the Cubans in the great rescue operation. This was simply to turn Cuba again into a working unit after the havoc caused by the severance of all trading and other connections with the United States, the mismanagement by the regime, and the defection of almost the whole of the country's qualified professional force.

These men had settled in cosily enough by September, even though the results of their efforts to date were apparent only in the fact that decay had been barely halted. They were quartered in the former luxury hotels, all now looking very much the worse for wear and neglect, and I wondered, as I watched them moving in and out of the hotels and going in carloads to their places of work, whether their masklike faces hid emotions of any kind and, probably more to the point, how on earth they were managing to make contact with the Cubans. They were quiet and prim. They seemed to have no Spanish at all. I heard only one item suggesting that they had any kind of life outside their work and the daily routine of existence. It was said that two of them had had to be sent home for getting drunk in one of the few bars open in the city. But, all in all, the silent demeanor of these zealots added to the new eeriness of Havana—once the gayest, noisiest, and perhaps the wickedest of all capitals. They seemed unable or forbidden to do anything to soften the hard fact that they were totally out of place here in Latin America. For centuries the two countries to which Cubans and Russians belonged had lived in worlds apart, and they now had nothing in common except a directive from Khrushchev. In the eyes of Khrushchev during the summer of 1962, however, Cuba was just a piece on a chessboard, to be used for all it was worth as long as it survived. And he had to work in a hurry to set it up adequately covered from attack, because he could not count on his American opponent, so handily placed across the Strait of Florida, to hesitate forever in trying to take it. To sum up, he did it all in three phases. First he stopped the rot in the Cuban economy by sending enough materials of many kinds to keep the wheels turning and enough of his experts to see that the best use was made of what he supplied. Second, he sent shiploads of arms and other military equipment, plus companies of noncombat troops and artisans, to turn Cuba as swiftly as possible into a fortress that would be invulnerable to anything but a massive assault of the sort that could only be made or sustained by the United States. Third, as the rest of the world was to learn to its intense alarm before the winter came, he quietly smuggled into Cuba a number of offensive air-to-ground missiles that could paralyze Washington, New York, and many another hive in the United States, as well as industrial and strategic centers over a big circle of Latin American and Canadian territory.

He carried out the first phase of his great scheme smoothly and without interference. The United States looked on uneasily as the salvaging of Castro's revolution was made, but there was little short of military interference it could do to stop it. The alarm bells began to ring when Khrushchev turned to the second phase. A handful of British and other correspondents went into Havana from Miami—the reciprocal arrangement by which Cubans and Britons could enter each other's country without visas was still valid—and came away with their reports that Russian troops were being stationed on Cuban soil. Inevitably the inference was drawn that they were fighting troops, and speculation about their purpose in the island electrified the western world.

The bare facts of the Russian intrusion were not difficult to establish from the Cuban and foreign sources that had been so trustworthy since 1959. But the hazards of pursuing one's journalistic vocation were now even greater in Havana than they had been some months earlier in Varadero. I was advised to be always on the watch for the Cuban agent on my trail, and I was recommended to be most careful about straying far from the main thoroughfares or being too inquisitive by act or word as I roamed the city.

I learned that the total number of Russians imported into Cuba since July had reached about thirty-five hundred in September, and it was believed to be still increasing as Russian ships quietly came into the harbor by night, stealing past the celebrated monument of the Morro Castle and making for a dockland area some miles beyond that point, where it was most certainly unsafe for the foreigner to venture.

The first arrivals had been, of course, the technicians, who were estimated to number rather more than a thousand. It was the second batch of men that had caused all the commotion. They had come into Havana during July and August in four Soviet passenger liners, and after they had disembarked they had been whisked out of the city to transit camps in the lush countryside not far away and probably also to places further afield. One big detachment had been settled into a former reform school three miles outside El Cano, a village ten miles

from the capital. Some inquiring foreigners had managed
earlier to drive down a road close to the reformatory and had
watched the men moving around their encampment, some of
them obviously suffering from a most painful sunburn after
injudicious exposure to the roasting Caribbean sun. To go out
now to El Cano was to ask for arrest and a none-too-gentle
expulsion from the island.

Cuban and Russian intelligence and security services had
reacted predictably to the hullabaloo provoked by the first
reports in the United States about these "troops." They were
chasing away anybody outside the diplomatic services who
went within miles of El Cano and they were taking the license
numbers of the cars of diplomats who ventured near. But I
did not need to leave Havana to see the men. I could see them
being moved across Havana, standing up in Russian and Czech
light trucks as these were driven, often under Cuban police
escort, through the streets. Sometimes they seemed to be on
organized outings of some kind, for they had their cameras
slung across their shoulders and were singing and laughing and
otherwise showing themselves to be in holiday mood, but still
not going so far as to wave at the pretty Cuban girls or even
take much notice of anybody looking curiously at the truck-
loads of human cargo.

These men were "disguised" by civilian garb of white summer
shirts and light trousers. They were all in their early twenties
and were muscular and husky. I placed them as farmers' sons,
laborers, and petty craftsmen. They did not have the stamp of
the fighting soldier—the straight back, the tough look of the
trained man, and even the discipline. Yet they were just the
age and type to be fulfilling their military service, and the
more I saw of them the more strongly I felt that this was just
what they were, conscripts drafted for special duty in digging
and constructing gun emplacements, rocket sites, installing
electrical equipment and signal services, and doing the hundred
and one tasks that the military machine demands. Where else

but from his conscripted legions could Khrushchev have found such men? I think they came from his motor corps, his pioneer regiments, and his other special units—but not from among his infantrymen or tankmen.

They would be of great value in many ways, of course, as long as they were kept in Cuba, even after their construction tasks were ended. If an invasion came, or in the highly remote event of some domestic trouble, they would man the rear positions and keep the supply lines open, liberating Cubans for the fighting. And the fact had to be met that some of them might get hurt. Russian blood would be shed. The danger to the peace of the world could be serious, even though I was as sure as any of the diplomats that those men were not combat troops. Sobering indeed were the implications of their presence in this troubled and troublesome island.

It was taking a lot of shipping to support this extensive Russian effort, and the transport of nonmilitary or only semi-military cargoes from the chilly bounds of the Baltic to the humidor of Havana was being carried out by the ships of many nations, including some of America's allies within NATO. This fact was not being ignored in Washington, and some of these trading nations, particularly Britain, were being given one of those senatorial dressing downs that periodically take the Anglo-American relationship out of the humdrum.

I went to special trouble to find out the British involvement, and it was disturbingly light for those seeking ammunition to aim at old Albion. One British ship was reaching Havana every six weeks on the average. After all, nobody was at war yet with anybody else, and Britain and the other nations involved were wholly within their rights in engaging in trade in non-strategic materials with the Soviet Union. In any case, the British aspect of the ships concerned was not very pronounced, apart from their flag. None belonged to any of the big British shipping lines, and the crews were lascars under the command of a British captain and perhaps three British officers.

The other nations whose vessels were coming to Cuba on behalf of the Russians included Italy, Greece, West Germany, and Liberia. The Russians were attracting the shipping they needed by offering long charters at rates higher than the ruling average. The bait was especially enticing to owners who had many vessels tied up because of the depressed state of world shipping.

With as much nonchalance as I could summon, I walked one day close enough to a part of the waterfront where I could see some of these ships. There were two Greeks, the *Atlantic Gladiator* and the *Protostatis*, and one West German out of Hamburg, the *Carola Reith*. I met one of the men from the German merchantman in a small bar on Via Jesus Maria and we chatted over a beer. "Yes, it's all a bit confusing when you come to think about it," he conceded, with a grin. "Here we come from Russia with a load of airplane parts and such like. When that's all been taken off we shall be going to Texas— Corpus Christi, I think—to pick up a return cargo for somewhere in Western Europe. Then, off we go again to a Soviet port for another cargo for Cuba. . . . The Russians are all right, you know, and so are the Americans and the Cubans. Here's to no more war, anyway."

I was appalled at the deterioration in the spirit of the Cubans during the months I had been away. Most of them were listless, apathetic, and suspicious—as far removed from the Cubans of old as it is possible to imagine. Severe rationing of food and the necessities of life had come on top of the imposition of the barren communist system and had just taken from them whatever spirit had been left after Castro's betrayal of his own revolution. The scramble for food for themselves and their families, and the effort needed to grab a little extra (the Cuban has always enjoyed looking after his stomach), was so preoccupying that they seemed unmoved by the constant propaganda flung at them about the massive help being given to them by the Soviet Union and about the plans of the United States for another invasion of their homeland.

Their diet was miserable and enervating enough to explain much. Adults could have no fresh milk. The main foods available were a ludicrous half-pound of fish per person per fortnight—and this in an island with well over a thousand miles of coastline—two ounces of butter per month, and one chicken per month. It was almost impossible for the visitor to get a square meal in Havana. The menu usually comprised two or three concoctions, and one had to get to a table early at lunchtime or in the evening to seize one of these. Just one or two establishments seemed to be more equal than others. One of these was La Roca, in Vedado, and I soon found out why; it was where several members of the Cuban government were eating. Another restaurant in Vedado, which at one time had made a speciality of first-class Chinese food, now presented a menu of four items of which only one was generally in the least tempting. One day when I went there it was an offering of roast lamb. That sounded fine and I ordered it. What I got was exactly what the menu promised—a plateful of slices of lamb without potatoes or other vegetables, sauces, or anything else, and it cost $4.00 at the parity rate of exchange that once again had been imposed on me when I landed at the airport.

I must say that this device of enforced exchange of dollars for pesos on arrival had been effective in stamping out almost completely any trafficking in currency by foreigners. It was still technically possible for the speculator to obtain six Cuban pesos for one dollar, if he cared to take the enormous risk. There was always a likelihood that any Cuban with whom a would-be trafficker sought to deal was an agent of the regime, and the penalties for currency offenses were imprisonment in a Cuban jail in conditions of misery and squalor or summary expulsion. The game simply was not worthwhile, and not even such hazardous speculation could alter the facts of life very greatly as far as food was concerned. Not even a millionaire could do much about the monotonous breakfast served every morning in the coffee shop of the Hotel Libre. It consisted of coffee without milk, toast without butter, a glass of fruit juice, and guava jelly.

But somebody inside the regime with a sharp estimate of Cuban psychology had arranged for the Soviet Union to supply enough oil to make civilian gasoline rationing unnecessary. So driving your car, if you still had one, and if you were reasonably sure that it would not break down and need an unobtainable spare part, was one recreation left to offset so much else that was missing now. Cubans love motoring, preferably as fast and as showy as possible. In their present chastened state, however, they had little taste left for showing off; I was told that for a while they had been using their cars to drive into the countryside to buy food from peasants and farmers who were only too willing to sell it at somewhat higher prices than the unrewarding ones offered by the National Institute of Agrarian Reform or the other organs of the wobbly economic machine. This unofficial trading had stopped suddenly when the government announced that death would be the penalty to be paid by anybody found engaging in it.

With conditions so bad, and in the absence of any glimmer of hope for any improvement for as far ahead as any Cuban could see, it was no surprise to find, as the mood of the capital impressed itself upon one, that most people now had no interest whatever in the revolution. They were far too preoccupied with the dreary business of getting enough to eat from day to day. The most common estimate I was given was that active support for the revolution among the population had dwindled to less than one quarter of what it had been in the honeymoon days of 1959, and it was still seeping away.

The professional observers in the foreign embassies who were the most reliable assessors had some unusual but effective yardsticks for estimating the strength of revolutionary fervor at

any period. Of course they all compared notes and opinions
whenever they met at the receptions and cocktail parties that
represented about the only compensations for working in the
drab Havana of the day, but they also always noted such facts
as the number of television sets they heard working whenever,
say, Fidel Castro was speaking, and how many Cubans were
showing at his meetings in the open air and what their reactions were to what he had to say. They also became expert
in reading between the lines of telltale promotional or propaganda paragraphs in the newspapers or exhortations on the
radio and television. One ambassador used to tell all on his
staff to note every significant fact, however seemingly trivial,
wherever they chanced to be when Fidel Castro was speaking
or (rarely!) making a public appearance without speaking;
next morning all the reports were considered so that a compari-
son could be made with similar reports of the previous time.
One way and another a surprisingly accurate reading of the
barometer of popular opinion could be produced. There was
rarely much difference in the estimates of the embassies, and
they all reflected the current slide.

Support for the regime was now limited to three sections
of the community. Some of the peasants in the agricultural
provinces such as Pinar del Río and Oriente were said to be
still faithful, in spite of the hardships they were feeling as a
result of the bunglings of inexperienced young administrators
attached to the National Institute of Agrarian Reform. (I had
to take this information at second hand because I was confined
to Havana.) Youthful idealists serving in the militia or enrolled
in one or more of the cultural and artistic institutions created
by Dr. Armando Hart, the Minister of Education, and his vigorous wife also still were under the influence of the Castro
magnetism and would concede nothing against him.

The third segment of revolutionary support was provided
by those many thousands who in one way or another were getting something out of the new order. They would go on sup-

porting it as long as it supplied a living or privileges, but I
felt, as I dealt with those bureaucrats and others in the tedious
task of keeping myself within the law while I was in Cuba,
that here was a re-creation of the person one met in Berlin
after the war. If Castro went, like Hitler, these would be the
people who would say, "Oh, no, I was never *Fidelista*. I didn't
know anything about the shootings and, of course, I had nothing to do with the Russians. I just did my job."

Yet, even though three out of four people in Havana were,
at heart, soured with the revolution, I saw no chance at that
time of any popular uprising against Castro even in the most
extreme circumstances. The State Department or the hundreds
of thousands of exiles longing and plotting for the liberation
of their country would have been foolish indeed to have counted
on support from within in any attack upon Castro. An invasion would have had to be on the verge of success before the
imprisoned population would or could do anything to help it.
The only people with arms were the militia and the regular
army. I reasoned that the army, which still had much of the
toughness and tight discipline inculcated in the days of the
campaign in the Sierra Maestra, would not rise against Castro
and would see to it that the much more lightly armed militia
would do always what it was told. The rest of the populace
was so dejected and so overborne by the prohibitive surveillance of G2, the Committees for the Defense of the Revolution,
and other spies and informers as to be incapable of making the
slightest effective gesture of protest or defiance now or plotting any plan of action if circumstances changed.

We have been told that when the invasion on the Bay of Pigs
was being planned, both the Central Intelligence Agency and the
exiled leaders based in Florida and elsewhere were counting
upon a popular uprising from within once the invaders had
installed themselves in strength upon the mainland. I find that
hard to believe. All who like myself were visiting Cuba with
any regularity, and certainly the journalists and diplomats

living there, would have been unanimous in saying, had they
been asked, that such a thing was utterly out of all reckoning.
It was so in the fall of 1962 and so it will be, I believe, for a
long time to come unless there is a completely unexpected and
highly unlikely change in the way of life on the island.

Fidel Castro was doing very little to make his presence
known in the island. My friends told me that he was in one of
his quiet periods and was not even believed to be in Havana.
They also said he was doing nothing to dispel the impression,
which was general within the foreign colony, that he had had to
recognize the harsh truth that the man (Khrushchev) who was
paying the piper was also calling the tune. Castro did not make
a single speech or other pronouncement in the two weeks I was
in Havana, an item of circumstantial evidence in favor of the
theory about his minor role, for it had been found since 1959
that if Fidel Castro was not talking he was also not doing
anything else of much consequence.

His substitute in the limited social world of Havana at this
moment was Che Guevara, who had just come back from another visit to Moscow. Guevara turned up one evening at a
reception given by the Brazilians in celebration of their Day
of Independence. The party had been held on the lovely grounds
of the country branch of the Zarragozana Restaurant, which
in the pre-Castro period had been one of the choicest restaurants in the Caribbean. There was a notable rise in the tempo
of conversation as Guevara ambled into the gardens through
a path zealously cleared for him by Raul Roa, the Cuban
Foreign Minister, who was also making sure that the government photographers did not miss recording the vice-regal entrance.

I had not seen Major Guevara in the flesh for over two
years and I was shocked at the deterioration in his appearance.
He had put on at least twenty pounds, and most of the youthful elegance had gone. He was also none too well-tended physically. His beard was untrimmed and his dark hair unbrushed;

and, worse still, he was wearing dirty and creased fatigues, which fitted him ill. I thought he was looking far more like a reincarnation of the late *homme fatal* of the Czarist court, Rasputin, than a dashing young revolutionary who had just come back from a powwow at the Kremlin with Nikita Khrushchev. But he seemed not altogether to have lost his celebrated sex appeal, for the diplomats' ladies swarmed around him as he settled into the party. To be sure, they were the wives of the ambassadors and secretaries from countries associated, like Cuba, with the left-hand side of the world, and it could be that they were making diplomatic as well as sexual responses to the rather frayed, bearded Caribbean potentate.

I talked with him for a few minutes on my own after the fuss had subsided. H. S. Marchant, soon to be knighted by his Queen for magnificent service in Havana as the British Ambassador in the most tedious but also most significant phase of the Castro period, reintroduced me to Major Guevara. But I fear it was a profitless interview. Guevara knew precisely who I was and why I was in Havana. Obviously, this was a moment when he must give nothing whatever away. He achieved this by using one of his favorite and most effective tactics. He simply gave a minimal answer to any question or approach and let the conversation die into an embarrassing and, if necessary, permanent silence unless I reopened it. I had to give him best in the end and was very relieved when still another of his feminine admirers sought him out. When I told the doleful tale later to Marchant and some others who knew Guevara well, they just laughed. They had all had experience of the artful major and his stonewalling. I must say, however, that he was apparently a little more free with one or two people that evening. He gave them some free propaganda for Khrushchev and the Soviet Union.

He had found Khrushchev in splendid health in Moscow and believed he would be "there" for a long time to come. Guevara also claimed that an agreement he and Khrushchev had just

made for a steel mill to be built by the Russians in Cuba was
another proof that the Soviet Union was now the strongest
nation in the world. It must be, he argued, if it could so defy
the United States just off Florida and in what had hitherto
been claimed to be the American sphere of influence. This was
a characteristic piece of Guevara logic.

I scarcely needed his button-mouthed reticence to make it
hard to find out what was going on. It was partly by intent
and partly by pure Cuban inefficiency that the Ministry of
Foreign Relations caused one to waste more time in complying
with nonsensical regulations than in doing one's work, and it
was most certainly by sinister intent that G2 kept watch round
the clock upon the harassed visitor. I spent almost a whole day
getting an ordinary identity card from Raul Lazo, the young
Cuban in charge of such matters, after one preliminary visit
that was abortive because nobody had disclosed that he worked
the improbable hours of 7:30 A.M. to 3 P.M., with an hour or
more off for lunch. I had to spend more wearying hours in
going to the Department of Immigration, miles away in downtown Havana, to get an exit permit several days before I was
due to go. And the only result of such effort was, so far as I
could see, to make it easier for the intelligence services to keep
their eye upon me. One particular car haunted me. It was an
old white and green Chevrolet, carrying a crew of three. It
was particularly unmistakable at night because it had only
one headlight. Its driver would always keep it handily placed
two cars behind the taxi or other vehicle I happened to be
using. More than once its occupants had to wait, sitting in the
car with its lights out in a side street or even in somebody's
garden, while I had dinner or attended a party at a house or
club. I found that to be so relentlessly observed and shadowed
induced some curious feelings. I did not feel afraid once it became clear that I was not going to be arrested automatically
at the end of a shadowed visit but only if I strayed out of
bounds or behaved suspiciously in any way. Instead, I felt

steadily more unsettled and unsure of myself, not able to talk
to people—even those I knew well—easily. There was always a
third presence.

I suppose this psychological undermining is one of the
purposes of sleuthing. I was glad that I had resolved before I
left New York that I would not write and cable any despatches from Havana. It was obvious that in the strained
circumstances they would be censored and probably "lost"; and
I was in no state of mental coolness to be able to write with
the objectivity I had tried always to achieve in dealing with
the Cuban revolution, in spite of the willful harassments
pursued by its minions. I jotted everything down into a small
brown notebook that fitted easily into my jacket pocket.

All the time I was in Havana during this visit I had the
uneasy feeling that something unusual and probably unpleasant
was going to happen before it was over. But when on the eve
of my leaving for Kingston, Jamaica, I was still unscathed, I
began to think my fears had been the result of sheer nervousness. Two colleagues were missing, to be sure, but they had
been too venturesome. John Bland, the Reuters correspondent
in Havana, had gone for a Sunday ride in a car used by two
Cubans who were the only links with Havana still enjoyed by
the New York *Times,* now that the newspaper's correspondent, Ruby Hart Phillips, had had to go at last. Neither Bland
nor the Cubans had come back from that ride outside the city.
(How thankful I was that I had turned down an invitation to
join them in the excursion!) Another Englishman, John
Barnes, visiting Cuba on behalf of *Newsweek* magazine, had not
been heard from or seen after leaving Havana on a supposedly
authorized trip to Oriente Province, and it turned out later
that he, Bland, and the two Cubans had all been arrested and
were to be held for many days before the British Embassy
could get them out of confinement.

But I was congratulating myself too soon. I rose at
5:30 A.M. and, with a companion, Robert Betts, of San Diego,

California, made ready to get to the airport at 6 A.M., even
though the plane for Kingston would not be leaving until after
midday. The first suspicious occurrence came after I had paid
my bill at the Havana Libre, bade good-by to some of my old
friends behind the counters there, and began to look for a taxi.
The bell captain came up, and I pointed to a taxi waiting
outside the hotel door and said we should take that one. "No, no,
Señor Tel-low," the man answered. "Not that one. I'll get
you one." He seemed to be in some embarrassment but I thought
little of it. He was away several minutes and when he came
back I noted that he had summoned our taxi not from among
those parked by the hotel but from around a corner. We got
into it and started off. Automatically I looked through the
rear window—and, sure enough, the green and white Chevrolet
was on our tail. It had followed me out the previous evening
when I had gone to the home of Michael Brown, of the
British Embassy, and it had followed me back. It must have
stayed outside the hotel all night. Here it was again, shadowing
me to the last minute, and the agents inside it had clearly made
sure that their task that morning would be easy by choosing
our taxicab and telling the driver to keep them in sight all
the way to the airport, without any monkey business. I was
half-amused to see how the poor man kept glancing continually
into his driving mirror, making sure that the Chevrolet was
always close behind. He even stopped prematurely at a traffic
light because he calculated that if he went on the Chevrolet
would be held back by a red light.

I did not need to be psychic to perceive that the taxi driver
was obeying his orders with some distaste. He glanced back at
me once with a pathetic look in his eye. I gave him one of the
few packets of American cigarettes I had left, and further
tried to tell him that we bore him no ill will by saying, "All
right, friend. We understand." I was trying, probably left-
handedly, to say a lot of things. I was trying to signal that
we understood that he had been brought into this affair of

cowboys and indians unwittingly and unwillingly, and that
Castros and Russians might come and go but the *Yanqui* and
the *Britano* would be back again some day. . . . It was all
emotional and I think much of it sprang from the pure funk
within me. I was scared now that I might not get aboard the
K. L. M. plane for Jamaica that day and that I would probably
be joining the others in some Cuban dungeon before night fell.

We reached the airport without incident. The taxi driver
shook my hand with warm friendliness, and perhaps some relief,
after we had got out of his car and handed over our luggage to
an airport porter. The Chevrolet had gone. Even as we walked
along the ramshackle airport building toward the K. L. M.
counter on the right-hand side of the long hall, it became clear
that we had been handed over to other agents on foot. They
were unmistakable—youngish Cubans wearing trousers and
jackets and open-neck shirts, with a cigarette hanging from
the lips, and an unconvincing air of indifference enveloping
the whole. We checked in and saw our names ticked off in the
list of passengers for the day. This was promising enough. We
went for a cup of coffee in the mean cafeteria, and the agents
followed. One stood at one door of the cafeteria and another
at the exit, and one walked casually through as if he hadn't
a care in the world. I was now finding it hard to keep my
temper, but I was checked by the warning stolidity of Betts.
His father had been an inspector at Scotland Yard and some
of the lore had been absorbed, thank goodness, by the son. I
had almost to ask his permission to carry out a task that I
had arranged in advance—to telephone the British Embassy
as soon as it looked as if we were getting through the formalities
without trouble. I walked to a telephone affixed to a wall outside the cafeteria and put in my five cents (one of Fidel Castro's
popular moves after nationalizing the telephone company still
survived), and, surely enough, one of the three agents ambled
up to within a few yards of me. I do not think he was trying to
eavesdrop, for all telephone calls to the British Embassy were

being monitored anyhow, but I think he was just making sure that I did not intend to make a last-minute break from the airport. I do not know to this day really why they were hanging on to us so closely. I should have been angry if I had not been so frightened. There was still a long way to go before we were out of this never-never land.

After two hours, one of the appallingly raucous loudspeakers that have marked Havana Airport for years summoned the hundred passengers seeking to go to Jamaica to the main processing hall, an oblong salon that had long ago acquired the grim nickname of the "Cage." Once inside, nobody could turn back unless thrown out, as happened often enough. The walls were debased by the crudest symbols and drawings likening those who would flee the revolution to worms. Although fearful about my own prospects of getting out of Havana that day, I was still fascinated and horrified at the pernickety rites and indignities confronting the Cuban who would leave the Castroite paradise. Three officials looking like the members of some grotesque Star Chamber sat in a line at one end of the Cage. As each passenger's name was called he and those with him had to go through no fewer than eleven checks and inter- rogations. It was a final humiliation on top of the months of unnerving bureaucracy, selling of possessions, and official obloquy, which had gone before. Now the thick folder of documents had to be gone through once again, the one piece of baggage that a passenger was allowed to take had to be ransacked, and trinkets such as earrings and watches and even children's toys had to be checked. The process took hours. It was watched apprehensively by passengers' relatives and friends who, locked out of the Cage, kept their worried faces pressed against the glass as they waited to see whether a passenger would at last be accepted for passage out of the country or despatched out of the room and told to start again because of some trifling irregularity.

That day, the only intending passengers who had trouble

were, of course, Betts and myself. It was inevitable after all that surveillance and harassment. I think that the Cubans had made up their minds that we were spies and were now doing their best to prove it. We had cleared the hurdles of documentation, not so rigorous for us as visitors as for departing Cuban nationals, at the hands of the Star Chamber characters, and I was actually beginning to relax, my stomach no longer taut, as I was told politely enough to join a line of other passengers passing through a guarded opening on the runway side of the Cage to walk along a pavement to benches where luggage was laid out in front of shabby and untidy—but, as it was soon to be shown, very alert young militiamen and militiawomen serving as customs officers.

I located my one suitcase lying on one of the benches and at a gesture from a soldier placed an old and opened briefcase and my portable typewriter alongside it. The soldier searched the suitcase with practiced hands, checking that I still had an electric razor, a watch, and of course the typewriter, recorded on a form inside my passport. I was thereby cleared of any suspicion of being a black-marketeer. Next he dipped into the open briefcase and pulled out a folder of papers and documents. They included cuttings from American newspapers, various letters, telegrams from my London office, and, alas, a mimeographed despatch written for the North American Newspaper Alliance by one of its correspondents in Miami and circulated to its clients by that agency. The despatch was harmless enough, for it had been published in many newspapers in the United States long before I left New York for Havana. But it discussed the plans of various groups of anti-Castro counter-revolutionaries in Florida, and it was to cause me much woe before the morning was out.

The soldier looked carefully at it and, although it was written in English, I am sure he sensed its tenor and theme. With a show of indifference, he showed it to the next agent working alongside him, a young militiawoman, and she also

professed indifference after looking briefly at it. But in fact
those two knew what they were going to do, although they
gave me no inkling at that moment. The young rebel soldier
thrust the despatch back into the folder with the rest of my
documents and papers and directed me to go further along
the passageway into the airport buildings for one of the last
rites of all—to change back into dollars my surviving pesos.
I was joined there by Betts and I was naive enough to think,
with him, that we had now got through and would be on that
airplane to Jamaica.

Even while we were changing our pesos another trap was
being laid for us. At the next wicket of the airport branch of
the National Bank of Cuba was a man who had caught my
attention earlier because he was so obviously a North American
and had been displaying rather ostentatiously a B. O. A. C.
air-travel bag that had seen much use. He looked like a tourist,
even to the box camera he was carrying slung over one
shoulder. I suddenly became aware that he was making some
fuss about his currency. "I am a visitor from Canada and I've
spent only $7.00 because I've been entertained by friends,"
he said, loudly. The young Cuban teller pointed out in poor
English that there was a regulation that visiting foreigners
must spend a minimum of $10.00 a day while in Havana. It
was a reasonable stipulation, for there had been much black-
market dealing in pesos at the rate of six to the U. S. dollar,
and I knew one or two visitors from the north who had in
fact done well in the past out of their dollars. Our so-called
Canadian tourist was now blustering about losing $33.00 for
the four days he had been in Cuba.

I was warned by a furtive, most unmistakable nudge from
my cautious companion, Betts, against following my impulse
to walk over to the Canadian and try to help by explaining
what the young Cuban was trying to say in his wretched
mixture of Spanish and English. It was as well that I heeded
Betts. The man was nothing else than an agent provocateur.

He was behaving thus simply to draw us on—to get us to talk about what we had been doing in Havana, how we had spent our money, and to tell him about some of the people we had seen. In short to get us to say anything that might give him and the regime some useful information or operate to our discredit or damage. Fortunately, he had overplayed his part and aroused the police instinct in Betts. The nudge in the ribs put me well on my guard.

It became obvious that Betts was right about the man very soon after we had gone back into the Cage to continue the long wait for the plane. I noticed that the Canadian was the only person among the waiting hundred who could move freely in and out of the room. He even walked over to a window giving a view upon the runways and, without a word or other interference from any of the armed guards or anybody else, lifted his camera and seemed to take a photograph of the airfield. This was going a little bit too far in the police state of Cuba! I had seen many people arrested merely for taking a picture in the street. The truth broke upon me even as I was watching the man at work. He was really photographing Betts and myself. The camera was at right angles to us as he pointed it toward the airfield—where there was nothing to take, as I now confirmed—but in reality it was pointed at us because its shutter and lens were set in the side of the camera instead of at the front.

The incident aroused again my old uneasiness. We were marked men this day, without a doubt. I was digesting this unpleasant reality when the blow fell. Two rebel soldiers with their rifles unslung from their shoulders stumped into the Cage and tapped us peremptorily. I do not believe they said a word. They just edged us out of the Cage with our briefcases and our documents and, with one leading and the other following us, escorted us out. I was now more dismayed and fearful than ever. I knew very well what was happening. We were being taken to the G2 Intelligence Headquarters of the airport—I

had been there only briefly once before when some inefficient
Cuban had made a wrong entry into my passport—and I
knew that anything could happen to us. Judging by what had
been happening to other correspondents lately, I felt that our
chances of getting free again within days were pretty poor.

After we had reached the poky little cluster of rooms in
which G2 operated, we were told to sit down and an officer,
probably the man in charge, told me to empty my briefcase.
Out again came all the papers, cuttings, letters, picture post-
cards, keys, pencils, revolutionary proclamations by Fidel
Castro, everything—including that N. A. N. A. despatch. This
was what had given G2 its chance to hold us. I said nothing
and I did nothing except exchange a depressed glance with
Betts as the officer picked up the despatch and took it away.
Betts was taken away to another room. I was left with a
young militiawoman, who looked silently and without expression through my papers. She was sorting them into two piles,
presumably the suspicious and the harmless. As she did so, I
could hear that N. A. N. A. despatch being read over a telephone in Spanish translation by, of all people, a uniformed
official of the K. L. M. airline, by which we were waiting to
travel.

The fact that nobody in the G2 unit was fluent enough
in English to be able to make the translation was illuminating.
Although my present situation was precarious enough, I could
still spare a thought for this confirmation of a decline in the
use of the English language which had struck me on my last
three trips to Havana. In the old days, when American tourists
and businessmen helped to fill the city, the use of English had
been general, and a visitor could get along well without knowing much Spanish. One now was hearing the language rarely
indeed, so rarely that the sound of it being used was enough
to draw one's instant attention to the source. Most of those
Cubans who had had dealings with Americans and had consequently spoken good English were gone. The Cubans still in

Havana now had small need either to keep up their English or to learn it. There was hardly anybody, except the occasional visitor such as myself, on whom to practice.

As the translation by the Dutchman of the N. A. N. A. despatch over the telephone to G2 Headquarters in the city progressed, the militiawoman went on sorting and resorting my papers and other oddments. She remained silent and expressionless even when I was not able to contain myself any longer and told her that one Western Union telegram that she kept on picking up and putting down again was merely a routine service message from London to my office in New York. It had been sent three weeks earlier, as I showed her by pointing to the date, and I said to her that it had no significance to anybody outside my newspaper. She merely listened and ignored me.

I sat back on my chair defeated and deflated, and I saw that Betts, who had been brought back into the room, was giving me a pained look. He told me much later that outbursts such as I had made were precisely what the Cubans were hoping to provoke. It was all part of intelligence technique, he said, to goad a victim into giving something away or otherwise betraying himself. He was probably right.

At last the labored translation over the telephone in the next room was over. I became aware that a low conversation in Spanish was going on between the K. L. M. official and the Cuban officer in charge. I could not catch what was being said, but events showed soon enough its purport. The Dutchman came into the room of detention followed by the Cuban officer, and addressed himself with great formality to me, in English. "I am sorry to have to tell you, Mr. Tetlow . . ." My spirits fell, almost audibly as it seemed to me. I felt sure he was going to tell me that I was to be detained and heaven alone knew when I should get out now. As he went on I could scarcely credit my good fortune. ". . . that none of these papers can be allowed to leave Cuba." I had the wits, fortunately, to hide my elation. I even put on a show of protest. I pleaded with great earnestness to be allowed to keep just one or two of the papers that the militiawoman had laid into what I had mentally labeled the harmless pile. I wanted them to think that they had got hold of something worthwhile from me, whereas, in fact, I did not care a hoot about any of the papers and cuttings now. I had read them all through once and believed that, if necessary, I could recall anything of importance from them. No, my real and essential possession was the small brown note-book in the right-hand pocket of the jacket I was wearing. It carried telephone numbers in Havana, names, all the items of information I had gathered and would want to use when at last I reached the sane outside world. It even contained a tabu-lation of the facts and figures about Soviet penetration of Cuba, which I had gathered from my own observations and from the British and many other embassies and sources I had found. This was something I really did need to keep, for I could not possibly have memorized all the information in that book.

The Cuban took the bait. The show of protest, the apparent dismay, made him feel that they were all doing the right thing in grabbing my papers. The man shook his head sternly, and exclaimed, "No . . . nothing . . . not one!" I gave a shrug of defeat. The gesture was the more convincing because the actor within me had been released by the indescribable relief I was feeling that, at last, it looked as if I should be able to get away that day after all and tell my story to the world. I picked up my violated briefcase resignedly—it was carrying only my passport and other travel documents now—and got up. As I did so, the Cuban gave me one of the biggest sur-prises of the day. He put out his hand, and as I accepted it and shook it he murmured a courteous good-by. I do not re-call him using any expression of regret at having put me to such inconvenience or for having had to steal my property, but at least the unfailing politeness of the Cuban had again been made manifest. Somehow, illogically, it made me feel that perhaps the country did have a future after all. It also made me wonder momentarily whether any of the Cuban executioners who had lately been so busy had gone to the length of shaking hands with their victims before having them shot. It seemed doubtful; but at least I had certainly seen photographs of officers lighting the last cigarettes of victims before these wretched men faced the firing squads. I had even been told that in 1959 Raul Castro had so lit a doomed man's cigarette.

I began walking back toward the Cage escorted by the K. L. M. officer. He suddenly began talking to me in a murmur from one side of his mouth while he still looked straight ahead. "British Embassy been on phone. . . . Worried about you and Betts. . . . I'll phone them now and say it looks as if you're going to get away." I nodded.

Betts and I took our seats once more among the waiting passengers in the Cage. They looked at us curiously, silently, perhaps wondering anxiously if we had caused all the delay and whether the plane would go that day after all. The pseudo-Canadian tourist pretended to be engrossed in a study of his travel papers and documents. But it did seem at last as if our bizarre and disquieting ordeal was over. "I think it is," I said to Betts. "I'm sure they'll be calling us all to the plane soon. How long have we been here?" It was five hours.

Again I was comforting myself too soon. Even as the names of passengers were being called to go through the exit door of the Cage to the waiting plane, a militiaman thrust his way through the queue and again tapped Betts and myself and motioned to us to follow him. Real despair surged through me now. Were we to be taken at this last moment? What could they possibly want of us now? Once again we were marched along the passageway, under the grilling midday sun, to the same old headquarters of G2. The faithful Dutchman was still with us, and he supplied the one glimmer of hope. "They say it will be for only a few minutes," he said. "We are going to hold the plane for you."

Betts was taken off first into a small room while I was left in a kind of waiting room. An agent, a Negro, lounged in a chair opposite me. I saw that his eyes were not leaving me for a moment. They followed every slight move I made. Now I was thinking of that notebook in my jacket pocket. If I tried to hide it or threw it away he would pounce on me, I was certain. If I let it rest in my pocket it would assuredly be discovered during the coming search, for I had guessed that this ritual was the reason for our new detention. They must have decided upon it as an aftermath unless, as anybody who knows Cubans will agree is wholly possible, they had just forgotten about it earlier.

There was simply nothing I could do about that notebook. As the Negro watched, his cold gaze fixed upon me, I considered that the chances were very high that the notebook would be taken from me and that I should not be leaving Cuba for quite a time, after all. What could I possibly do to lighten my predicament? They *might* let me get in touch with the British Embassy. It was worth trying. There was a telephone on the table alongside the Negro. I leaned forward and asked him, "*Teléfono?*" He did not even open his mouth to reply. He merely shook his head.

Betts now came back, looking somewhat ruffled, and I was hustled in his stead into the small, square search room. Another of these none-too-clean militiamen gestured to me to take off my coat. Seediness seemed to be one of the common characteristics of these servants of the Cuban Intelligence; another was economy of speech. The man took hold of my jacket and emptied the pockets. He put everything, including that damning notebook, on a table. He held up the coat to the light and probed every corner of every pocket, every seam, and all the lining. He found nothing, of course. He now turned his attention to me. He searched me, running his hands lightly but probingly down my sides, across my chest, and down to my shoes. As he did so, I sensed that he was in a hurry. Well, so far they had

discovered nothing incriminating about me, and the plane for
Kingston with the hundred people aboard was waiting. He did
not even make me take off my shoes, as I had heard from other
Britons and Americans was the usual thing. Now he turned to
my wallet. He pulled everything out of it and here again he
searched every corner, fold, and crease before stuffing back
into it my money, my cards, and the rest, most untidily. He
had left the notebook to the end, and as he dealt with it an
unbelievable thing happened. He picked it up and carelessly
flipped back its pages—and he was holding it the wrong way
round for my notes to show! I had filled about two-thirds of
one side of it, and his perfunctory flipping had exposed the
unused sheets. He gave it back to me, along with my loose
change, pens, wallet. My hands were trembling with the relief
I was feeling, and I fumbled as I put everything again into the
pockets. I was still blessing my good fortune when I suddenly
noticed that the agent had his hand outstretched toward me.
That routine again! I had nothing against him at this stage,
and I shook hands heartily with him.

Now we were marched away again from that unpleasant complex of buildings occupied by G2. The faithful officer of
K. L. M. was once more our escort, and this time he took us
straight to the waiting plane. It was my turn now to give him
a message through the corner of my mouth. "Please tell Embassy we were searched but nothing more found or taken. . . .
Call them only when we are in the air, please, not before. . . .
Thanks and good-by."

The officer nodded, smiled, and shook hands with Betts and
me as we mounted the steps of the jet. Two seats had been
kept for us, in the front of the aircraft. The pseudo-Canadian
tourist was sitting four rows behind us. So he was following
us to Jamaica. I just did not care. I told Betts I felt like
walking over and punching him in the nose. Instead, I sank
back in my seat, wiped the sweat off my forehead, let my
muscles relax, and stretched out my hand to take the most

welcome gin and tonic it had ever been my good fortune to be offered. The plane was airborne and Cuba, the hot little island, was vanishing from view under its envelope of humidity. I hoped I should never see it again until it had shed its revolution and its communists—all those Russians, Czechs, Poles, and other incongruous interlopers. But I knew the end was not yet. I should be there again, I was sure. I laid my portable typewriter across my knees when the gin and tonic had gone and began to write my story. I wanted to get it all down while the facts were hot in my mind. I did not know it, but only three weeks were to pass before the great confrontation between Kennedy and Khrushchev.

What, in fact, were the impressions and opinions I was bringing out of Cuba at this uneasy phase? As I basked briefly in the restorative tranquility of Jamaica, I was conscious that two strong convictions were occupying my mind. One was that Khrushchev had embarked in Cuba on one of the most venturesome, dangerous, challenges of his career during the cold war. The other was that, sooner or later, the United States would have to meet this challenge and beat it off if it were not to lose, perhaps forever, any claim to control over the areas of Central and South America that it considered to be within its charge and an essential element of its scheme of defense as a major nation. I did not think that at this time the United States needed to go to the limit by mounting an invasion of Cuba and throwing out Fidel Castro and the Russians and the rest of the unwelcome lot with him. I did not think that if it did so it would plunge the world into war, but I did think that the United States had to be cleverer than that. It seemed to me that it might profitably take the course of giving all possible help and encouragement to the hordes of Cubans waiting in Florida and elsewhere in territories around Cuba for the day when they could deal with Castro themselves. It might also promote the creation throughout the hemisphere of a well-armed and trained anticommunist brigade. The U. S. could use all economic and diplomatic measures short of war to make it increasingly difficult and perhaps finally impossible for Khrushchev to keep his hold upon Cuba.

I felt there was even a great chance for Kennedy to be able by the use of courage and cunning to turn Khrushchev's spectacular but fundamentally unsound gamble to good account by giving him and international communism a severe and long overdue setback. It seemed to me that if all the cards held by East and West in this particular hand in the grim game of international diplomacy were to be played, Khrushchev must lose, for he would not be able to sustain his effort in Cuba from the Soviet Union with his antagonist, the United States, on Cuba's doorstep. Once faced with an ultimatum that he must withdraw from Cuba, he would do so without going to the fatal limit of starting nuclear war. He might seek redress in Berlin, Vietnam, or somewhere else, but he would not go to war over Cuba. I repeated my belief that the Soviet Union will never go to war unless and until it feels sure of winning. In 1962 that was still, "Not yet."

When I got back to New York I was surprised by the intensity and bitterness of the debate over Cuba. I had been too close to the center of the storm to realize how strong it was. This was a midterm election year, and the Republicans were jabbing hard at Kennedy, prodding him to do something not very clearly specified. Loud were the cries for a blockade of Cuba to squeeze the Russians out, noisy was the outcry that the Monroe Doctrine was being defied. There were even a few shouts of, "Send in the Marines!" Less vehement but equally convinced were those Americans who surprised me by putting forward an argument that the United States had no right to interfere in the domestic situation of Cuba, no right to object to the help that the Soviet Union was giving her; no right indeed to do anything. President Kennedy was taking a holding position. The Soviet moves concerning Cuba, coupled with the regimentation of the island's forces and resources, did not at that time present a threat to the security of the United States, he said. The moment any effort was made via Havana in any form or direction to spread Russian or Cuban communist influence outside that country, the United States, he promised, would intervene.

This sounded all very well. But as I listened to the debate, argued the circumstances with Americans and others, watched the television programs and took part myself in some of them, I found myself concluding more and more firmly that the United States would have to do something very soon, no matter what the hazards, to preserve her position in Latin America. I despised the contention that, since the United States had a ring of bases around the Soviet Union, it should not now object to the establishment of just one close to her own territory. One does not win wars, cold as well as hot, by that kind of thinking. If you have an advantage you guard it and improve it. You certainly give nothing away.

The voices raised, fearfully, against the United States doing anything at all about developments within Cuba were loudest of all in the United Kingdom and Western Europe. Very soon after I had got back into New York I read a leading editorial in the *Economist* arguing that the United States was getting excited about something that was only an irritant and should not do anything to remove it so long as it did not become a military threat. I simply could not understand such reasoning. I wrote a long letter to the *Economist* and my respect for that influential periodical was increased when the letter was printed, although its contents ran completely counter to what the editor believed. I wrote as follows:

This sounds ominously like the kind of defensive thinking which has caused our own [British] recent history to be marked by so many dangerous and nearly fatal episodes in which, as the saying goes, we have lost all battles except the last one—and won that one only at awful cost and at least twice with decisive help from our friends. It sounds indeed in the present instance like asking a man to stand by quietly to allow his enemy to take an attacking stance and prime his gun and only do something about him when he pulls the trigger. Not many Americans accept this kind of patient forbearance, as you admit, and I must say I have sympathy with them.

I suggested that as part of her reply to Khrushchev the United States should offer to Cuba the terms of a new relationship that would wipe out memories of exploitation in the past and give real attraction to a Cuban-American future. I went on:

Too much nervousness is being shown in and out of the United States, in my opinion, about the effects upon Latin American feelings of any American action about Cuba. Fairly regular acquaintance with events in Central and South America over the past ten years leads me to think that the United States will be much more respected there in the long run if she disposes of Mr. Khrushchev in Cuba than if she lets him go on defying and goading her there. The Latin, like the American, always admires a winner. One final word.

I ask Britons who support the recommendation of passive containment of Communism within Cuba if they would take the same calm and detached line if circumstances were to make it possible for Mr. Khrushchev to set up a handy base for himself in Eire?

The letter was published on October 9, 1962. In a matter of days, Khrushchev's gamble in Cuba was to be exposed as far more deadly than anybody had dreamed. President Kennedy grasped the nettle, and was not stung. Still another new phase in the history of the Cuban revolution was to unfold.

9 ♦ *Viability*

ONE OF the telltale facets of the thrilling or, to most, the nerve-racking encounter between President Kennedy and Premier Khrushchev about the placing of Russian-made offensive rockets in Cuba was the temporary but total eclipse of Fidel Castro. He was like an actor who had been rehearsing and building himself up for a leading part in a drama and had then found on *the* night that the two other principal players had written out his part completely and had sent him off into the wings. He suddenly became a person of no account —an appalling blow to a man of his self-exaltation. He might have had some late inkling or premonition that another of the periodic international crises that have marked the course of

his revolution was brewing, for, as we have noted, he was unusually quiet while I was in Havana only a few weeks before
the biggest one of all erupted. But I am sure he had not the
slightest idea that he was going to be so brusquely and inexo-
rably elbowed aside. He did in fact make one or two pronouncements, but they sounded like mere bleatings, or even noises-
off, and were given scant attention indeed by a world that
was watching breathlessly the main show.

Castro was meeting the same fate as so many figures in
world history who have been the nominal cause of or reason
for clashes between great powers and have then found to their
dismay and humiliation that they did not really matter any
more because the issue between the principals was about something much more fundamental. From the standpoint of any
student of the Cuban revolution, this particular crisis served
to transform theory into fact. It gave confirmation, if any
were needed, that Khrushchev had picked up Castro's tottering
revolution only because he intended to use Cuba coldly and
callously as an ideological and military tool and cared only
for Fidel Castro as long as he were handy and useful. At the
same time it indicated glaringly how Castro had abdicated to
an alien master the control of both his revolution and his
country. He had done so at least as thoroughly as any of his
predecessors had made Cuba a handmaiden of the United
States.

This, however, was obviously not what was gnawing at his
mind in the late fall of 1962. He was suffering the tortures of
the spurned, and he was suffering them far more deeply than
would almost anybody else in the world because for four years
his ideas about his own grandeur had been greater than anybody else one could readily call to mind. Hurt and dismayed,
he retreated once more to the restorative peace of the Sierra
Maestra, but not before those in Havana who were able to
observe him had noted that, as one of them put it to me, he
looked like a man broken beyond repair.

Yet it turned out, even while the crisis had not yet passed, that if Fidel Castro were down he was not out. His astonishing resilience did not fail him in this moment of extremity. After only a short silence he made an impressive effort to rationalize everything. He broadcast a speech in which he argued that since the United States and the Soviet Union were arguing about whether offensive missiles in Cuba represented a threat by one of them toward the other there had been no real reason why Cuba, meaning himself, should have been consulted during the negotiations. He conceded that there had been differences between the Soviet Union and Cuba about the withdrawal of the missiles, but he promised confidently that these would be settled. His purpose in that speech was to salve his badly bruised self-esteem and also to reassure those many Cubans who had been wondering and worrying about where he had landed them at last.

As his confidence grew, he turned to meet a fearful internal turmoil within his regime. Once more by no means the whole story has ever emerged, but enough has become known to show that Khrushchev's decision, based on the earthy realism that was always one of his strongest characteristics, to accept Kennedy's demand for the withdrawal of the rockets came closer to toppling Fidel Castro from his post as standard-bearer of the revolution than anything that had happened since 1959. It also shook the grip of Moscow-communists like Blas Roca and Carlos Rafael Rodriguez upon the domestic administration.

The most bitter attack upon Castro came from the survivors of his original 26th of July Movement. They had followed him from the beginnings in the Sierra Maestra and had tolerated, with many misgivings, the close Soviet embrace into which he had brought them. His was the responsibility for it no matter whether he had done it deliberately or had been maneuvered into it by shrewder politicians than he. The old faithfuls of the movement wanted to know what was to be done now that

Khrushchev had let them down so hard and had treated their Maximum Leader as a mere nothing in the bargain.

Another attack burst upon Castro from a section within his regime that had always had a preference for the Chinese brand of communistic dogma but had had to go along with the stronger Moscowites. This pro-Peking group now pressed him to break away from his traitorous friend Khrushchev, and the shadowy battalion of Chinese diplomats and others stationed in Havana added their pressure. They suddenly became much more visible than usual during this phase and were to be seen talking earnestly to Cuban communists and officials of the regime, obviously making the timely point that they had been right all along and that Khrushchev was not to be relied upon. One fact that I could not clear up was whether Che Guevara joined those who wanted a shift in ideological orientation. It would not have been at all surprising if he did, and an effort must have been made to cause him to do so, but one informant whom I had always had good reason to believe told me that Guevara's deep loyalty to Fidel Castro survived even this severe test.

Castro himself went into something close to physical decline from the stresses of this grueling period. His features, which are usually well padded behind the beard, went gaunt and his olive-green fatigue dress began to hang limply around him as worry stripped pounds off him. But he won the battle, survived the challenge to his leadership, and preserved the bond with Moscow. He knew that Communist China could not possibly keep Cuba viable, and he knew that without the massive help—perhaps a conscience payment—being given by Khrushchev his revolution would collapse. He also threatened again to play the one trump card that represented salvation for him and his policies. All right, he would resign and leave the island —and where would everybody be then? Everybody knew that the revolution still stood or fell with him. There was just nobody who could possibly replace him. This one inescapable

fact had saved him many times since 1959, and it saved him
again now. It looked, too, as if it were going to save him many
more times no matter how loudly men around him muttered and
no matter how the fortunes of the new Cuba withered, for even
after four years nobody looking even remotely like a rival for
local power was in sight.

This most remarkable man, indestructible as one is sometimes tempted to believe, was again well on the road toward
physical recovery when I saw him for the first time for many
weeks in the middle of January, 1963. He had taken up his old
habit of driving to the Havana Libre Hotel late at night for
a quiet glass of cognac or pink champagne in the Castro
Suite on the top floor, followed by a hefty supper in the kitchen
with the hired help flitting around him, and then an hour or so
of badinage and chatter in the lobby with the cluster of Cubans
who were sure to have gathered there once word of his presence
spread.

Castro's resumption of this ritual was a sign that he was
feeling sure of himself again. He had by no means regained
all the lost weight and physical luster that had always marked
him when he was in his top form. His cheeks were still sunken
and his complexion was waxy. His enormous black eyes looked
even bigger than ever. He was loose-muscled and relaxed, but
his movements were for him rather lethargic as he ambled
around the lobby, play-acting and gossiping with those who
were about him. His only companion, apart from a guard of two
or three lightly armed soldiers, was Comandante Rene Vallejo,
a gray-haired doctor of repute in Havana, and, although one
must assume that his political views would not endear him to
either the American Medical Association or the British Medical
Association, he was charming enough to meet. He was Castro's
most regular companion at this period and he was probably
keeping a medical eye upon him. If so, he was assuredly not
getting his patient early to bed. Several nights during the first
fortnight of January he and Castro sat up until close to dawn

talking, half-seriously and half-banteringly, with a Canadian
social worker, an ingenuous and attractive young woman who
had gone to Havana because she thought the revolution was
still an idealistic crusade and wanted to see it and her idol,
Fidel Castro, in action. She had caught Castro's attention—
he always did have a keen eye for a pretty girl—and he had
found enjoyment in her company. I must say I could understand her attractiveness for him. She was coquettish, but not
naughty; ingenuous but not foolish; a most refreshing personality for a man recovering from the ravages of an exhausting
political ordeal. He and Vallejo had taken her off, on an impulse, for a weekend by the sea at Varadero, and had treated
her like a princess.

She was not there that evening in the Libre, but there were
several dozen young Cuban women, as well as a few from elsewhere in Latin America, to supply him with an audience. He
put on a good show for a convalescent Maximum Leader. He
fooled about with his forage cap, pulling it off and slapping it
back upon his head at odd angles, as he dealt with the none-
too-substantial questions that came to him from the maidens
and the outnumbered men in the crowd of about a hundred. He
also used one effective mannerism of drawing his index finger
down the side of his nose and he put on one comic expression
after another. Quite a few of his listeners wanted a favor from
him. One wanted a scholarship in some subject or another. "All
right, you may have it if you can earn it," he told her. Another
girl made some other request. Castro listened gravely and when
she had finished he did a quick swivel turn to say to one of
the soldiers, "Get that girl's name and give it to me tomorrow."
So it went.

I reflected as I watched the scene what a surprise it would
have given many Americans if they could have been there to
see it with me. I knew, because I had left New York only a
few days earlier, that the picture people there had of the post-
crisis Castro was of a man who had been so discredited and

humiliated by the disdain with which he had been treated by
President Kennedy and Premier Khrushchev that he no longer
counted for anything; that he was probably cowering somewhere in a corner, fearing for his life because of the poor pass
to which he had brought both his revolution and his country.
How different was the truth as I was now seeing it enacted as
I stood only three yards from him on the fringe of the eager
crowd, pressing around him in the marbled lobby of the one-
time Hilton Hotel! He clearly was not caring a cent for his
personal safety, and he was thriving on the adulation of these
Cubans as a child thrives on mother's milk. I could have pulled
out a pistol and put a bullet through his head with certainty
and ease, from where I stood. To be sure, it would probably
have been the last thing I ever did, but it would have been
done. The two or three soldiers grouped close by him, or Vallejo
standing by his side, could have done nothing to hinder the
deed.

I marveled as I watched that scenes such as this had been
going on, with periodic breaks, for over four years and yet
nobody had ever tried to kill Fidel Castro in these most favorable circumstances. I had never heard since 1959 one authen-
ticated story of any attempt on his life. The fact that he had
survived for so long without a scratch was a sobering one for
those who had been saying almost from the time that he entered
Havana that he would fall to an assassin at any moment. Tonight he was giving even less thought than ever to his safety.
Not surprisingly, in view of what he had been through lately,
he seemed to be needing the comfort and reassurance of the
friendly crowd. Vallejo told me that they were already late
for another engagement, but still Castro dallied, ignoring
Vallejo's gestures and appeals. Even when at last he turned to
the exit door, he did not go to his waiting Cadillac. Instead he
swung to the left and went into the hotel bookshop, which was
still open even though it was so late in the evening. Works by
Lenin, Marx, Engels, Mao, and many others were prominent

on the shelves. Almost everything in the shop had some association with communism—treatises, pamphlets, excerpts from
speeches and the like. Castro took several at random from the
shelves and handed them to young Cubans crowding around
him. "Read this—and this," he said as he thrust the books and
the treatises into their hands. I felt he would have gone on
like this for hours, but at last Vallejo cried, "Enough!" He
gave an order to two of the soldiers, and the next thing I
saw was the ludicrous sight of Castro being shoved toward his
car by them, one grasping each of his elbows. Castro returned
to his comedian's role as they did so, assuming a look of comical
resignation and murmuring hoarse comments to those nearest
to him about the way he was being treated. He was bundled into
the back seat of the car, the others piled in around him, and
he was off into the night. It had been an entertaining as well
as illuminating episode.

If Fidel Castro could afford to be indifferent to his safety,
others in his regime could not. The very next day one of the
few western correspondents still operating in Havana got hold
of a detailed story of yet another attempt on the life of Carlos
Rafael Rodriguez, head of the National Institute of Agrarian
Reform and one of the leading Moscow-line communist intel-
lectuals in the island. About a year earlier Rodriguez had run
into an ambush while being driven back to Havana from Varadero and had been wounded. I believe his bodyguard had fought
a battle with the ambushers and one or more of these had been
killed. Now, according to the story by Alan Oxley, he had
been ambushed again and had been wounded in the leg. Once
again there had been a brief battle and, the story went, two
soldiers in the Rodriguez bodyguard had been killed. Oxley
had even the number of the hospital room in which he said
Rodriguez had been lying for some days, and he knew the
identity of the nurse who had been tending him. He also had
other details that sounded most convincing. Greatly daring, he
tried to broadcast his story over an American radio network

and he was cut off the air, presumably by the Cuban censor in Havana, before he had got half of it over. The Cuban Press Office now saw to it that not another word about the story got out of Havana. Cables were stopped, overseas telephone calls were monitored and ended if a word about it was mentioned, and I even found that local telephone calls made on press phones such as that used by the Associated Press would end abruptly if the word "Rodriguez" was mentioned. Oxley was summoned to the Ministry of External Relations and given a severe warning by Señor Piniati, the Cuban in charge of press matters, for trying to disseminate a "false" story. The fact that he had escaped with only verbal punishment was a relief to Oxley. He had been in and out of Cuban custody some twenty times since 1959 and had had some juicy experiences.

In spite of the denials and devices used by the regime to convince everybody that there was no truth in the report, I still believe that Oxley might have been right. I witnessed one interesting occurrence that tended to confirm him. Presumably as part of their program to show that Rodriguez had not been attacked, the Cubans arranged for him to attend a formal reception being given by the Foreign Ministry in the Sierra Maestra Suite of the Havana Libre in honor of Vasily Kuznetsov, a Soviet Deputy Foreign Minister, who had been on a mission to the United Nations in New York and was now visiting Havana before going back to Moscow. I attended the reception and watched Rodriguez closely as he arrived and when he left. He was sprightly enough as he walked without help from the elevator to the suite to shake hands with Roa, the Cuban Foreign Minister, Kuznetsov, and others in the receiving line. Then he walked over to one of the big circular tables in the suite. He sat down at one being used by the Russians and Cubans and their friends of the East European bloc (the Chinese with *their* friends from North Korea and elsewhere were at another table), and he did not move from his chair until it was time to go. He was now a very different Rodriguez from the one who had walked in an hour or so earlier. He could walk only slowly, limpingly, and with hesitation. Perhaps to screen him from eyes such as mine, several Cuban men and women guests, and others, hastened to form a circle around him and they held him in conversation between each step he took.

I had no doubt whatever, as I watched, that Rodriguez had had some kind of trouble or mishap. I believe Oxley had the right story. The affair fitted into the blurred and bizarre aspect of most events connected with the revolution. Even when one sought possible reasons for an attempt to kill Rodriguez, there were uncertainties and alternatives to be taken into account. One obvious reason would be, of course, a desire by some counter-revolutionary personage or organization to be rid of him because of what he had done to deliver Cuba to Moscow and because of what he might still do. Then there could be some motive of personal political revenge. But I found that there was still another more piquant possibility. Rodriguez had always been an enthusiastic and successful "ladies' man," even for a Latin, I was told, and was thought to have been concerned in a number of notable romances. He had a dashing personality and a keen brain to go with his handsome appearance, in which a neatly trimmed spade beard and laughing eyes were assets of which he made full use. So the reason for one, and possibly two murderous assaults might well have been revenge on the part of an outraged husband or an ousted suitor or—could it even have been?—a woman scorned. The blood runs hot in Cuba, as it does anywhere in Latin America, and many a Cuban will kill for love or money.

Dr. Castro had had one compensating success, of a kind, to offset the debits of his downgrading during the rumpus over the Soviet rockets. He had negotiated with James Donovan, the lawyer from New York, an arrangement whereby the thousand-odd prisoners who had fallen so easily into his clutches during the invasion on the Bay of Pigs were to be exchanged for medical supplies worth many millions of dollars—more mil-

lions by his reckoning than by anybody else's. It was a success
if ever any trafficking in human flesh can be so described. He
had made the most of it by delivering bombastic statements
that through him the new Cuba had been able to hold the United
States to ransom. He would have crowed even louder, it was
thought in Havana, if he had not been halted by President
Kennedy's statements to the counterrevolutionary leaders in
Miami that the flag that had been their symbol during the
Bay of Pigs invasion would one day go back to Cuba and
that the removal of Castro was the firm objective of the United
States.

There were many, myself included, who thought that Kennedy
might have gone too far by making so much of the defeated
Cuban invaders, with Mrs. Kennedy standing at his side during
the rather theatrical proceedings. But when I got into Havana
soon afterward, I found that there had been a tactical dividend
after all. The demonstration had carried to Castro the warning
message that the Cuban-American current account had by no
means been settled by ransom. It was a warning that he apparently heard loud and clear. It angered him, but it stopped
his gloating.

He scarcely needed to boast about the exchange he had
negotiated with Donovan for it was enough in itself to lift
his prestige among the Cubans. The shortage of medicaments
of all kinds had become dangerous, and the deep need of them
had caused Castro to negotiate for them instead of for the
tractors that had been considered in the first place. Incidentally, few people in Havana ever believed that Castro was
serious when he blurted out his first proposal for the exchange
of prisoners for tractors; he had made it characteristically as
a gibing joke and had been taken aback when he found it accepted at face value by Americans, who are permanently human-
itarian and often naive.

Travelers to Havana who used the daily plane from Miami,
as long as it was running, were constantly being reminded in

an unusual way of the shortage of drugs and medicines. Cubans who now lived in Miami but had relatives still in Havana would get up at four or five o'clock in the morning to go to the International Airport to plead with the passengers to take small packages of medicaments with them. I was several times so waylaid as I walked along the covered ramp to the departure gate, and I yielded to the tearful appeal of Cubans, invariably women, to take a package to Havana and just telephone the number written on a piece of paper around it, although I realized well enough that I was foolishly letting my heart rule my head. It was quite conceivable that a package would not contain medicine at all but incriminating contraband of some kind, and I should have been in serious difficulties indeed if ever the Cuban customs in Havana had opened a package and found some illicit commodity inside. They never did ask me to open a package of this kind, always accepting my explanation of how I had come to have it with me. I refused only once to take something from one of the women suppliants at Miami airport. It was a small bottle of hair dye addressed to Señorita Somebody or Other in Vedado, and I thought she and the consigner in Miami were trying masculine gallantry a little too far in seeking to use me in such a manner in the cause of vanity. I was also a little suspicious at this time, for I found it hard to understand why a woman would get up in the middle of the night just to send over a small bottle of hair dye.

One surprising fact that was evident in early 1963 and became more marked as the year lengthened was that the support of Castro from the civilian population was stronger than it had been the previous autumn, in spite of the letdown by Khrushchev and the tightening Russian grip on the revolution. One reason for this was that the controlled press, radio, and television in Havana had given such a suave and extremely distorted account of what had been happening during November 1963 that Cubans simply did not know the real facts. One had to realize that by this time they were almost completely cut off from the rest of the world in which they had once lived. They had been told, for example, that as part of an agreement made with Khrushchev the President of the United States had given an unqualified promise never to invade Cuba again, and they had obviously accepted this as a fact. The effect had been to erode still further any will to resist the revolution among many Cubans, who felt that it was now pointless to hope for any succor or rescue from the United States, and they might just as well make the best of their predicament under Castro and even work with the revolution in the hope of making it function better and so improve their lot.

Another reason for the slight but noticeable increase in tolerance of Castro in 1963 was that, with the settlement of the crisis in November, tension had gone out of daily life. The feverish stirring of national feeling about the danger of invasion and war had abated, thousands of members of the militia had been demobilized, and the basic necessities of life were becoming slightly more broadly available as the Soviet Union kept up its supplies by sea, and the labors of the imported technicians from the Soviet Union and other Eastern European countries brought results in the form of higher efficiency and better production. As a result of all these influences and drifts, the diplomats were estimating that Castro was enjoying the solid support of about 30 percent of the population, compared with 25 percent in the fall of 1962. They also thought that a further 40 percent of the people were forming a kind of floating vote, varying from warm to cool toward the revolution according to conditions, and that the remaining 30 percent were still hostile to Castro at heart and, although powerless in themselves, wanted to see him go.

Officials of the regime were always interested to hear about those foreign assessments of the backing enjoyed by Castro, and most of those with whom I discussed the topic professed to be satisfied that he should have 30 percent of the people still actively with him. One Foreign Office man, who at the time

had the rather barren job of improving relations between Cuba
and Western Europe, put it this way to me: "We are doing
very well if after four years we still have that proportion of
people actively behind us; and we are doing even better if, as
I think you will agree is likely, we have at the moment most
of the 'floaters' with us. It puts Dr. Castro into a much
stronger position than your Prime Minister and into one at
least as strong as President Kennedy."

As I roamed around Havana—without hindrance or open
shadowing or other surveillance this time—I could not help
feeling with growing conviction that this revolution was going
to envelop Cuba for a long time to come, unless some unexpected disaster overtook it. This permanence was, of course,
just what the Soviet Union was intending. Even if events had
shown that Cuba could not be sustained as an effective military
base, it could certainly be kept going as a communist entity
and a Caribbean ideological base, provided Moscow was prepared to foot the growing bill and the United States was not
goaded into enforcing a full blockade or going to alternative
extremes. The picture that came to mind was, as I wrote at
the time, of a shabby and somewhat careworn Castro sitting
at the wheel of a battered old car, staggering along at only
two or three miles an hour in one low gear and on wheels that
had not yet acquired tires. But the point was that the car *was*
going and there seemed a good chance that, provided Castro
could keep his hands on the wheel and the fuel kept coming in
from afar, the road might get less bumpy in the end and there
might even be enough money to buy tires.

The change in the situation in Havana since October was
astonishing—but this was Cuba, after all, and I had had many
experiences in the past four years of the volplaning and soar-
ing that the spirit of the revolution could make quite unpre-
dictably. Policies, even petty regulations, moods and attitudes
—all could change from one visit to another, even though the
interval might only be one week or two. But I did feel most

strongly in 1963 that the revolution had at last taken root, and this, of course, was a most unpalatable fact that had to be faced by anybody who still thought there was a chance that it had not done so and might yet wither if left alone.

Perhaps there *was* a chance of this happening, but I felt as I surveyed the Havana scene that it was a slim one indeed and a mighty catastrophe would be needed to make it a reality. Castro's long and relaxed visit to the Soviet Union that summer tended to prove the point that he also felt as I did and as did many others who were even closer to the domestic drama. He must have been relaxed and confident to be able to fly away to Moscow and to stay away from Havana for many weeks, for the first time since 1959. He now knew that Khrushchev was going to keep Cuba intact as part of the Soviet strategy and would go on doing so—if not to the extreme limit, very close to it. There was no hint that the United States was preparing any kind of challenge.

This was a phase of the revolution that the orthodox communist thinkers had been awaiting—a phase when the early dislocations and shakiness had passed and a process of consolidation would start. I believe that many such communists in the Cuban regime must have doubted often since 1959 that it would ever be reached by their rickety and daredevil venture. But here it was at last, thanks to three years of American bewilderment and inability to strike it down and now to the phenomenally lucky circumstance for the revolution that it was being preserved and succored by Khrushchev because it was on his conscience and could also still be used by him with advantage in the continuing struggle with the United States.

So time was working for Castro. He could safely go to Moscow and play the part of grateful protégé and (here was something that warmed his actor's heart!) enjoy the plaudits of a vast Russian audience to whom he was romantic and unique, beard and all. But nothing happened while he was in the Soviet Union to change my opinion that he was an ideological fake, a time-serving communist and not a true one, a man who had always known on which side his bread was buttered.

We sometimes forget that the Latin is usually carefree and fey, and that his temperament is one of the most mercurial of any in the world. This natural sprightliness explains why Castro has always been able to show a ready recovery from adversity, and it explains why I could find such a change in the mood of the people of Havana between September and February. Whereas earlier they had been so listless, nervy, insecure, and silent, they were now laughing occasionally and they were even industrious in a Cuban way. I watched men tinkering with ancient cars in the sunny, dusty streets and enjoying it. The women waiting in line for many hours at a time for some of the pitiful textiles coming into the island from Eastern Europe were not muttering and grumbling as they had the year before. I felt as I watched all this basic living going on that I was seeing yet another demonstration of the toughness of the human spirit—the same kind of show I had watched in beaten Germany after 1945, in Italy while the country was being used as a bloody battlefield by the same still-warlike Germany and the advancing Anglo-Americans, and in Santo Domingo many years later after the awful despotism of Trujillo had been ended.

I think Italy had provided me with the ultimate in human defiance of uncontrollable circumstances. The day before Rome fell in May, 1944, the probing patrols of General Mark Clark's army were held up by a well-placed German rearguard with a big gun and out of the smoke and dust provoked by shells being lobbed between the two forces walked a gay Italian wedding party, into the gaze of dumbfounded Americans and Britons, taking whatever cover they could find from the last stings from their retreating enemy. Now in Havana, eighteen years later, the defiance of, and resigned indifference to, the plight into which the follies of lowly persons' so-called betters had betrayed them was taking the form of expression in humor, as it might well have done in similar conditions, of course, in Brooklyn or in Cockney London.

I walked one morning all the way, perhaps two miles, from the Havana Libre to the Prado, and by the time I had turned off the Malecon into the last stretch, I was thirsty and in need of a quiet sit-down, for Havana is warm and humid in what passes there for winter. I saw that an open-front refreshment bar of the kind every visitor to Havana has seen still seemed to have something to offer. I dropped onto a high stool, and, my hopes raised by the sight of a line of bottles standing on a musty shelf behind the barman, tried my luck. "Beer?" "No, señor." "Rum?" "No, señor." I went along the line and in the end it turned out that all he had to offer was milkless coffee. Wearied, I accepted the inevitable, and as I sipped I asked the man what had become of all the beer and liquor, even the rum for which Cuba is famous. Before he could answer, a Cuban smoking a cigar as he sat on a stool a couple of yards from me broke in and announced without the flicker of a smile, "They're aging it."

The same kind of cynical banter met me in the restaurants where I forayed, like everybody else, for an occasional piece of meat or a slightly more appetizing fillet than the wretched dabs of fish caught via string and a bent pin in the murky shallows opposite the Morro Castle. One lunchtime in the Restaurant Miami, which still functioned but only as an insubstantial ghost of what it had been, I did not bother to look at the penciled menu but asked the waiter what he had to offer. "Lots of wonderful music, señor," he told me, expressionlessly.

Such interludes showed that the psychological and physical stresses of the last four years had not smothered the Cuban sense of humor once and for all. Now that the tensions of 1962 had passed and there seemed no more point in worrying about the morrow, it was blooming again. Its reappearance fitted into the picture one now had of the revolution taking on the

shaky outlines of a viable organism or machine. It was foolish
for any onlookers, especially Americans, to delude themselves
with thoughts and hopes to the contrary.

The diet was still thin, expensive, and unattractive, but nobody starves in Cuba, for this is one of the most fertile and
comfortable islands in the world. It is warm all the year
round, and that solves many problems. There is never any
worry about getting and paying for fuel for the furnace or
the fire, no anxiety about frozen pipes, not even much of a
care about clothes, unless one is on the hunt for a husband or
seeking to cut a dash about town as a dandy. Even in civic
Havana I have never seen any results of undernourishment or
privation. The diet there in the later days of the revolution
was still dreary, but people managed. As I have mentioned, the
scale called for three-quarters of a pound of beef per person,
one chicken per person per month, half a pound of fish per
person per fortnight, and no milk for anybody over seven
years of age. Yet there was plenty of money around for Cubans
to dine out where they could, for everybody was now earning
more, if less valuable, pesos, and the American blockade was
drastically reducing the fields in which it could be spent.
What was available was expensive. I remember paying $3.00
at Willie's Club, a mediocre place at the best of times, for a
meal of bean soup, tough white rolls of bread, a small glass
of red wine, and a salami sandwich made up of heaven knows
what. The Zarragozana Restaurant, which had always been
one of Havana's choicest and to which one now turned in hope,
was showing signs of stress in the form of a skeletonized menu
and sickening wall paintings of Fidel Castro scaling the heights
in the Sierra Maestra and the late and almost canonized Camilo
Cienfuegos gathering the little children unto him, but it still
had faint reminders of its former elegance. I felt almost privileged to pay $6.55 for one glass of beer (served only with a
meal because the one million bottles from Czechoslovakia
brought in for the New Year by the Soviet freighter *Baltika*

were dwindling), a bowl of vegetable soup, lettuce, some chicken and rice, coffee without milk, and no butter, pepper, salt, or other commodities to garnish the meal.

There was evidence everywhere of the great leveling, to a drab plateau, that the revolution had achieved. Earnest little parties of girls and youths, guests of the government at the Havana Libre, talked politics endlessly and possibly out of duty, under the palms alongside the artificial fountains that used to beguile the American tourist. The proletariat had made a wreck of the famous Red Salon of the Capri Hotel, a sad fate for a gilded showplace of a room even if, as was said, it had been the product of American gangster money. They had turned it into a kind of cafeteria, in which on Saturday nights, when the revolution meant little to Cubans, they danced to a marvelous band, though with scarcely room to move, and answered the call of the music with Latin passion. Marriage was still an approved and encouraged institution; couples from the distant fields, as well as those living in the city, could get a government permit that would let them spend their honeymoon at one or another of the former fabulously expensive hotels at the cut rate of $6.00 per day and night. I often saw pairs registering, with appropriate blushes, after they had arrived at a hotel with their luggage from the bus or train from Oriente Province, Pinar del Río, Las Villas, or other distant habitat.

Like everybody else, they had to take the propaganda and the puerile ballyhoo of the posters and the newspapers as part of the revolutionary bargain. This was the Year of Organization, and as anybody who knows Cuba will agree, it was long overdue. The effort to put the national house into some kind of order at last—and I must say I saw little visible evidence of it in Havana—was being buttressed by just the kind of vacuous slogan and appeal that one has come to associate with communism everywhere. There was one poster proclaiming "Cuba is not alone," showing a shadowy Soviet soldier standing behind the militiaman; another depicting two young-

sters on a peak in the Sierra Maestra and saying to a saint-
like Castro, "Commander-in-Chief—give your orders." I also
saw another saying, "Cuba is not the Congo," but, for some
reason that I never fathomed, this had proved a highly unpopular placard, and almost everywhere in the city it had been
slashed and partly torn down by objecting Cubans. Still another poster showed the communist dove of peace carrying via
its beak the five conditions laid down by Fidel Castro as terms
for negotiation with the United States: no economic blockade,
no subversion, no infringement of Cuban sea and air space,
yielding of the base at Guantanamo, and an end of "piratical
attacks." One city garage at which former maidservants were
driving cars to supplement the dying bus service had a placard
all its own. The notice on the gate said that the workers there
had agreed to: 1, give better service; 2, lift their political and
cultural level; 3, be more revolutionary every day.

One might snigger at some of the puerilities, but they were
part of an appeal appropriate enough to an uncomplicated
people who had been led by Castro into an impressive administrative and economic muddle and were now being rescued
slowly and expensively, watched by many hostile neighbors,
by the tough and self-serving Soviet Union. Every day
that the Russian, Czech, Polish, and other specialists and
teachers stayed in Cuba sped the process of rescue, even though
difficulties of language and clashing temperaments got in the
way. I found also that a third force was taking part in the
salvage work. It was composed of several hundred individuals
from many parts of the world who had felt a stirring of inspiration from Castro and his revolution and had gone as
volunteers to help build the new Cuba. They had come from all
over Latin America, from Western Europe, the Far East,
Canada, and even the United States and Britain. The most
interesting one I met was a Scotsman who was a specialist in
refrigeration engineering and similar work. I bumped into him
one evening while he was waiting to chat with a party of left-

wing British Members of Parliament who were being given a
sightseeing trip to Cuba by the Castro administration.

The sandy-haired youngish man told me his name was Alex
Scott, but I was not surprised to hear later that this was
probably not his real name, for most of these communistically
inclined disciples fron noncommunist countries tried naturally
to hide their identity; they might one day want to go back
home. "I came over here more than a year ago because I had
read a lot about this revolution and I felt that Dr. Castro was
on the right track in taking his country away from the control of the United States," he said. "I wanted to size it up
for myself. I found it was all I had expected and I decided
to stay on and work for it. After all, I could offer it some
special knowledge."

For a while Scott did routine engineering work. Then the
Cubans offered him one of the biggest and most important posts
they had. They asked him to take charge of all the engineering
work that would have to be done in the building of a massive
new fishing port in Havana, which, as Castro had announced
some months earlier, would be built by the Russians. Scott
told me that the first batch of materials for the new port had
just reached Havana from the Soviet Union, along with the
advance guard of Russians and other technicians who would be
cooperating with him on the job. Five ocean-going refrig-
erated fishing boats of the latest type had been ordered from
Japanese shipyards by Cuba.

As Scott gabbled all this information to me I wondered
about him and his credibility. I could have spared myself. Two
days after I had talked with him his appointment to the post
he had outlined to me was announced officially by the regime,
and so were many of the details he had given me. "I've signed
a contract for five years," he said. "But I shall stay longer if
things go as well as they are at present. These Cubans are
working magnificently for me." There was now no doubt in
my mind that Scott was a genuine, if misguided, idealist. "They

offered me a wonderful salary when we were talking about my
appointment," he recounted. "I told them I did not want to
make a fortune out of them. I just wanted to help, I said. So
I asked them to let me take much less."

Not all the volunteers were of the usefulness or caliber of
Scott. Some were shifty-looking persons who, one suspected,
had come to Havana with the idea of making an easy living
out of the revolution. Others were political idealists with nothing but enthusiasm to offer. One couple who had just arrived
were Austrians who had fled Vienna from the scourge of Hitler
and had now come from Peru to escape what they considered
to be almost as oppressive a dictatorship, to help Fidel Castro
on his way. The wife spoke several languages, but she was a
boring busybody and, having no other skills except linguistic
ones, simply could not be found useful employment by the
revolution. She just got in the way. Another couple, whom I
found much more pathetic, were Canadians. The husband was
a wealthy builder from Toronto who had come, with his wife,
to try to lure back home a lost son. The boy had been given
everything that doting parents could lavish upon him, and as
the father said, he had "gotten some advanced views from his
college chums." He had decided against joining his father's
business and had come instead to Havana to look at the revolution at the closest possible range.

The parents had made the complicated and irritating journey from Toronto to Havana, via Mexico, to try to talk him
into going back with them. I met them when they had failed
and were preparing to go back home without him. "He just
feels he has to stay and work for Castro and I think I understand it," said the father, gamely. "We aren't going to try
any more. We shall miss him. . . ."

It seemed to me as I listened, and watched the mother quietly
weeping, that a revolution—and a revolutionary-like Castro—
that could do this sort of thing must not be airily brushed
aside as a bad joke. I felt that this was an important element

in the message I had to take back to the United States and to
Europe. This revolution was showing after four years that it
was not merely the toy of a wayward madman but still a symbol, faulty and distorted to be sure, of the human craving for
self-determination. This was certainly how it looked to many
of the young idealists now laboring for it in Havana who had
not yet discerned the pitiful treason of Fidel Castro in yielding his revolution and his country to a system that nine out of
ten Cubans abhorred. "This is pure socialism, dad, don't you
see?" the young Canadian had said, naively, to his father.
"It isn't communism, which is bureaucratic dictatorship. I
must stay with it and help it."

I have since wondered many times, how long it took for the
boy's eyes to be opened. He was by no means the first to confuse socialism with communism, and he would be by no means
the first to let himself be hoodwinked into believing that socialism could live with communism. It is because they wish to preserve these delusions that the Russians use the word socialism
to cover their creed and practices when, as we all should clearly
understand, they mean communism.

Cuba was now cut off from the rest of the hemisphere except
for an erratic air service between Havana and Mexico City.
This was maintained by only three British-made Britannias,
which between them somehow managed to provide two round-
trips a week. A plane would leave Havana, with every seat
taken, usually after hours of delay, and would get back some
time late the same night or, more often, in the early hours of
the following morning. This precarious link was the only
means whereby embassies of many countries could keep in
physical touch with their capitals via couriers and diplomatic
bags. It was also the only means whereby a handful of Cubans
at a time could leave the country or get back into it.

The Mexicans naturally kept tight control over the traffic,
especially after they found that Cuban agents were being sent
in from Havana and that propaganda literature and other em-

barrassing commodities were being transported into Mexico
City for distribution around Latin America. There used to be
some pretty bonfires at the airport as the Mexicans detected
the literature and disposed of it thus in spite of the noisy protests of the Cubans bringing it in. Passengers not protected by
diplomatic privileges had tedious and harassing experiences
as they arrived from Havana. Their passports were taken away
from them, and they were not allowed to leave the airport if
they were in transit. They were kept for hours in one big
waiting room and were usually only allowed to go to the airport restaurant, or even make a telephone call to their embassies, after making a lot of noise. Quite often arriving passengers whom the Mexicans found suspicious were simply put back
on the Britannia and sent back to Havana.

Cuba was for all practical purposes a prison, and this was
another reason for the growing docility of the Cubans. If you
had no chance of getting away you might as well make the best
of what was offered around you. This was what more and
more Cubans were doing. Determined spirits were still trying
to escape by boat and some were succeeding, although one considerable deterrent was a watch being kept by day and night
offshore by four patrol boats that the Russians had towed to
Havana across the Atlantic. These craft, plus five motor torpedo boats manned by the Cuban Army, formed a kind of floating Berlin Wall against escaping fugitives from the regime as
well as a defensive screen against incursions and raids from
the counterrevolutionaries in Florida.

The regime also had agents planted among the boatmen
and fishermen along the coast who would make a bargain to
take a load of fugitives to Florida and elsewhere, gather
their handsome fees in advance, and then take their unfortunate
passengers straight into the night patrols. Many dramas and
tragedies of this and other kinds happened off Cuba without
a word of them reaching the newspapers or the radio stations
of the world. It has seemed always to me that Cuba is a place

where even minor happenings can often be slightly more tense and unusual than if they happened almost anywhere else. The country has a tendency toward the theatrical, and Fidel Castro's histrionic quality is in keeping with the national characteristic. People coming out of Havana in the latter days of the revolution often have a bizarre story of some kind or another to tell. Even the staidest of diplomats seem to become drawn sometimes into the unexpected and outsized event.

One Sunday afternoon in the summer of 1963 the then British Ambassador, Sir H. S. Marchant, was enjoying his favorite antidote to the stresses of official life in Cuba—underwater fishing—with two or three members of his staff in the bay on the coast between Havana and Varadero. He suddenly became aware that a young militiaman had somehow got into difficulties in the water and was being swept out to sea by the strong undertow. He and Joseph Pethybridge, the British Consul, put out with the Ambassador's homemade raft. The man was well over a hundred yards from shore and was in poor state indeed by the time they reached him. They slung him upon the raft and hauled him to the beach. As they lay gasping to get back their breath—neither man was in the early flush of youth—they heard some Cubans who had watched the rescue telling others who had raced late to the spot, "Yes, they've saved one of our men. They're Russians."

10 ◆ *Guantanamo Interlude*

BACK AGAIN in New York in March, 1963, I pondered the Cuban conundrum afresh. Was there a possible solution for the United States anywhere to be found? As an Englishman, transplanted to be sure but still European in viewpoint and by affinity, I was not so passionately concerned in the struggle for the heart and body of Cuba as an American. But I felt that this probably gave me an advantage in following the problem and measuring its developments. I also felt that circumstances had placed me in a remarkable, possibly unique, position as a privileged, unofficial observer of the affair since 1959. Although I had felt from the beginning that Fidel Castro had earned the right to bring emancipation to Cuba, I had been appalled to see how during the last five years his revolution had been used as a vehicle for the transportation into the Caribbean of an extreme political philosophy abhorrent both to the United States and most of the people within the hemisphere that she dominated; and I had been dismayed by the American inability to stop it all from happening.

Perhaps there *was* something I could do, before it was too late, to exploit to the ultimate benefit of both Cuba and the United States the facts I had obtained and the firm impressions I had gained in my unusual situation as a man in the middle. Perhaps it was my obligation to do all I could on behalf of the United States, in particular, because I had profited greatly from it as my adopted home since 1950. After thinking deeply about these considerations, I decided that there was in fact something I could do, even at the risk of being considered presumptuous, self-inflated, interfering. I was prompted to act because I had come back from Cuba this time with a keen feeling that, since the confrontation between President Kennedy and Premier Khrushchev had seriously weakened the political position of Fidel Castro at home, and probably even caused some of the people running a communistic revolution to have temporary second thoughts about where they were going, this might be an opportune moment for the United States to make a new diplomatic initiative. I decided to go straight to the top by writing a letter to the White House.

After outlining my credentials and using my old friend, Pierre Salinger, the then Press Secretary, as a reference, I wrote for submission to the President:

I have found that the greatest worry among Americans to whom I have talked about Cuba—and that means practically everybody I meet—is what can possibly be done about Castro. There are various obvious possibilities, but I have been considering in the last two or three days an idea I have not seen discussed anywhere. It is that some distinguished and respected American communicate in whatever form might be considered most useful—by a speech or a radio or TV broadcast—to Dr. Castro and his Cubans an indication that the U. S. is at all times prepared to seek a new *modus vivendi* with them. It might even be possible to make a hard and practical offer of a new type of relationship for the future between Cuba and the U. S. and perhaps to outline it in great detail. Mr. Dean Acheson who has recently been making pronouncements of some incisiveness [!] about my own country and France might be the person to make such an announcement.

My reasons for offering this suggestion are as follow:

1. It is my firm opinion that Dr. Castro is not, and never has been, a conforming and convinced Communist but has been taken over by his own Communists and, through them, the Russians, and to preserve his position as the nominal leader of the revolution has been forced to proclaim a political belief to which he does not subscribe.

2. I do not believe that all the propaganda which has been used upon Cubans in the last four years has yet turned them irrevocably against the United States.

3. I believe there is still time to drive a wedge between Dr. Castro and the Russians and that he and his people might well react to a carefully framed announcement of the kind I have in mind.

4. I think that in undertaking his revolution Dr. Castro was impelled by a missionary-like zeal to liberate his country, as he saw it, from economic and other bondage from the United States. I think he then was what he said he was—a crusading patriot—and I think he still is in spite of all that has happened. He is also, of course, an ill-balanced egotist and an opportunist.

5. Although he has so ingloriously reduced his country in all material senses he has undoubtedly opened the minds of Cubans to the possibilities of a new and better future, and I do not believe that Cubans will ever settle down, permanently, to anything like a return to the old relationship.

You might agree that the United States will be acting with great vision and political acumen if she recognises this fact now and at the same time turns the recognition to her possible advantage.

I trust, Mr. President, you will understand the motives prompting this letter. I write in all sincerity and with a wish to contribute something of possible value to a country which has given me a great deal in the past 12 years.

So ran the letter. I mailed it on March 18, 1963, and I had a reply on April 4. It came from McGeorge Bundy, the President's special assistant, and it told me that President Kennedy had read the letter and had been interested in my comments and suggestions "and asked me to let you know of his appreciation for letting him have the benefit of your views." One could scarcely expect more than that. I was gratified to feel that at the very least I had been able to put my deeply felt views to the President, the man to whom they might conceivably be of some use.

We shall never know, because of the criminal lunacy of Lee Harvey Oswald, whether President Kennedy would eventually have negotiated some form of coexistence with Fidel Castro or otherwise have extricated the United States from its dilemma about Cuba. There *is* evidence, however, that he recognized that the United States owed Cuba some recompense—perhaps it could be more accurately described as atonement—for past errors and sins, and that he wished Fidel Castro to know this. Learning that a French journalist, Jean Daniel, was passing through Washington on his way to Cuba with a good prospect of seeing Fidel Castro there, the President gave Daniel an interview at the White House on October 24. This was twenty-nine days before he was assassinated. According to a detailed account of the interview written in the issue of the *New Republic* dated December 14, 1963, the President said to Daniel:

I believe that there is no country in the world, including all the African regions, including any and all the countries under colonial domination, where economic colonization, humiliation and exploitation were worse than in Cuba, in part owing to my country's policies during the Batista regime. I believe that we created, built and manufactured the Castro movement out of broad cloth and without realizing it. I believe that the accumulation of these mistakes has

I never saw such zeal as these men showed. Whenever they were escorting him anywhere, even only a matter of a few yards, they were all round him with their fingers on the triggers of their automatic rifles and their eyes darting in all directions. They would have mown down instantly anybody who had tried to molest their leader; yet I never saw them get in the way when Castro wanted to talk to the simple Cubans who mobbed him constantly. Their performance as devoted watchdogs was truly phenomenal.

Castro often went to bed around dawn, after taking a satisfying breakfast in the coffee shop of the Hilton, and he got up as and when the impulse took him. Ambassador Fordham at last gave up trying to see him until he had settled down, if he ever would. But early one morning, some hours after the ambassador had gone to bed, he was awakened by a call telling him that Castro was on his way to his residence. Fordham dressed hastily and managed to be at the door as Castro came up in a car. "Come on, let's take a ride and do some talking," Castro said. The ambassador joined him and the two were driven around Havana for most of what was left of the night, talking things over. It was one way of conducting foreign affairs, to be sure.

About the same period Castro held his first mass press conference in the Havana Hilton. The Sugar Bar, an elegant room at the top of the hotel giving a bewitching view of Havana, was cleared for the momentous event. Television cameras, microphones, and miles of wire were put into position, and Castro was surprisingly not more than one hour late in appearing. He answered questions easily and with good humor, even the hostile ones put to him by some of the American correspondents who were already becoming suspicious of him as a man who was not going to be as pliable and friendly an ally of the United States as most of his predecessors had been. But he did not always answer truthfully that day, notably in saying blandly that he knew nothing about the Peoples' Socialist Party (the communist party) in Cuba. It was a silly thing to say, for it took in jeopardized all of Latin America. The great aim of the Alliance for Progress is to reverse this unfortunate policy. This is one of the most, if not the most, important problems in American foreign policy. I can assure you that I have understood the Cubans. I approved the proclamation which Fidel Castro made in the Sierra Maestra, when he justifiably called for justice and especially yearned to rid Cuba of corruption. I will go even further; to some extent it is as though Batista was the incarnation of a number of sins on the part of the United States. Now we shall have to pay for those sins. In the matter of the Batista regime, I am in agreement with the first Cuban revolutionaries.

This was strong stuff indeed. It must have sounded like music in the ears of Fidel Castro when in an all-night session on November 19–20 Jean Daniel relayed it to him. Daniel later related that this was one of the parts of his interview with President Kennedy that Castro asked him to repeat three times. The Castro reaction was a typical one. He spoke volubly, roving all over the field of politics and often giving an impression rather than saying anything directly. But there were two sentences he spoke that could be interpreted as giving President Kennedy an answer. One was, "I ask nothing; neither dollars, nor assistance, nor diplomats, nor bankers, nor military men—nothing but peace and to be accepted as we are." The other was, "So far as we are concerned, everything can be restored to normalcy on the basis of mutual respect of sovereignty."

Finally, Fidel Castro said to Jean Daniel, "Since you are going to see Kennedy again, be an emissary of peace, despite everything. I want to make myself clear: I don't want anything, I don't expect anything, and as a revolutionary the present situation does not displease me. But as a man and a statesman it is my duty to indicate what the bases for understanding could be."

In other words, it seemed to me when I read Daniel's remarkable account, Fidel Castro was making an indirect acceptance of an equally indirect preliminary invitation to the

waltz. Alas, there was not to be any waltz. Two days after
Fidel Castro spoke thus President Kennedy was murdered in
Dallas. His successor did not pursue the dialogue and, indeed,
for some years afterward did not seem to have anything like
the preoccupation with Fidel Castro and Cuba that President
Kennedy had had.

Daniel's second talk with President Kennedy never took place,
of course, and the world might never have heard much about
the episode if it had. There was an understanding that the
first interview had been "off the record" and that nothing
would be published until after the second. The White House
was displeased that Daniel should have reported the episode so
fully. On December 11, Pierre Salinger was asked about the
long account appearing in the *New Republic* and he commented
curtly that the Kennedy-Daniel interview had been "off the
record" and should have remained that way. Daniel's reply to
that was that he considered that the assassination of the
President had made that commitment void. We need not concern ourselves here with that point of ethics. Let us just rejoice that we have the advantage of knowing that the President of the United States in 1963 was prepared to concede
the original validity of the Castro revolution and to acknowledge that the United States had some guilty responsibility toward Cuba. I had the satisfaction, sterile though it now had to
be, of knowing that I had addressed my letter to a realist.

Fidel Castro was aglow when he came back to Havana in
mid-1963 from a visit to Moscow that had lasted five weeks. A
report soon spread in the foreign colony that while there he
had had some form of corrective surgery at the hands of a Russian surgeon. This was, of course, quite possible, for the best
Cuban surgeons had long ago fled from him and his revolution
and he could scarcely go to the United States for medical
help in all the circumstances prevailing at the time. There
were two theories about the nature of the ailment that the

reported surgery had been meant to correct. One was that it was tuberculosis or some other respiratory condition; the other that it was hemorrhoids.

There had been some evidence at intervals in the previous four years to support either theory. He had had one or two illnesses in that period suggesting a weakness of the chest or lungs. I remembered also that when he was taken ill in 1961 and had to retire from the public scene for several weeks I had a report in Havana that the doctors were suspecting that he might be suffering from cancer of the rectum. This deadly diagnosis must have proved unfounded, for years later he was still going about his tangled business with no sign of any such fatal physical disability. Perhaps the report was an exaggeration of the truth that he was afflicted with piles.

But there was a more solid reason to account for his mood of exhilaration when he got back from Moscow. As one diplomat put it obliquely to me, he was in the same state as a man who had found that luck rather than judgment had led him into the embrace of an inspiring soulmate. It seemed clear enough that all he had seen and heard in Moscow had deeply impressed him. It had fortunately confirmed all that he had been saying not from conviction but from necessity about the ally toward whom the Cuban communists had been piloting him. The Soviet Union had survived his physical inspection. When he took to the microphones in Havana, once again, after the visit, he was silken-voiced and he was still awed, just as a lucky suitor in a *mariage de convenance* should be. He told Cubans that the Soviet Union was so well protected morally as well as militarily that she could repel any assault from anybody who tried to do her harm in any way whatever. Even if the imperialists made a surprise attack this would inevitably fail. She had a superiority in rockets and other armaments that must ensure her survival and ultimate victory. Everybody in the country had work to do and everybody had social security. It was all very wonderful. Even to the subway. Whereas the one in New

York was noisy and filthy the Moscow subway was smooth, clean, and delightful to ride on. And so on. . . .

The fact that Castro had been able to go out of Cuba and stay away for five weeks showed not only that he and the revolution were secure again after the devastating upheaval of the confrontation. It showed also that relations between Cuba and the Soviet Union were no longer unsettled. I found in fact by the end of the year that the Soviet position in Cuba had become stabilized in a form that was to last for a long time.

Cubans were still in charge of all arms of the administration, but Russians were in positions of supervision in all sections connected with the disposition of material and commodities supplied from the Soviet Union and, of course, in the maintenance of all those parts of the military machine using equipment from Russia and other countries of the communist bloc. Cubans were told in their newspapers during the year that one-third of the Soviet fleet of merchantmen based in the Baltic had been put on the Cuba run and four ships of ten thousand tons each were being built in Finland to join the trek to and from Havana. One Russian or communist-bloc ship per day was putting into Havana on an average. There were rosy reports that in time ships and planes would be available to take Cubans on cruises and excursions to the Soviet Union and Eastern Europe. It was all very good for morale.

In the meantime, Fidel Castro was in the position of branch manager for Khrushchev. He seemed not to be disturbed by the thought that this was an ignominious status indeed for a man who only four years earlier had had the opportunity to become his country's George Washington, its Winston Churchill, or even, ultimately, its national saint. Now the chance had gone forever, and he was just the agent of another man and another power. There was an element of unintentional irony in the award to him of the honor of Hero of the Soviet Union, the medal for which he wore so proudly when he got back from

Moscow. It kept jingling against the microphones as he made his first fulsome speech after his return.

There were in 1963, as there had been the year before, considerable discrepancies in the estimates of the number of Russian troops on the island. I was not surprised, for the size and disposition of troop units is a matter kept always close to the military breast, and it is one subject to an unusual dose of deliberate lies and distortions as well as mystery. One point I can make appropriately at this juncture is that since the first hints of the presence of Soviet troops in Cuba became known early in 1962, the estimates given to me by military attachés and other observers in Cuba itself have always been much lower than figures quoted by senators in Washington, Cuban exile spokesmen in Miami, and others outside Cuba. For instance, when early in 1963 some Americans in Washington were claiming that there were at least twenty thousand Russian combat soldiers in Cuba, I was being assured in Havana by one West European informant whose authority I respected that the total number of Russians in uniform in the island had never been higher than about eight thousand. That was in the fall of 1962, and the figure had been reduced by about a thousand after Khrushchev had agreed to withdraw his rockets.

I should now make a few observations on the topic of *combat* troops in Cuba. I never saw one such Russian soldier for myself, and in 1963 everybody with whom I discussed military matters in Cuba told me firmly that there were no trained combat troops from the Soviet Union on the island. My memory is quite clear about this, and it is confirmed by notes I took at the time. Yet, four days after I returned to New York from one trip that year, I was astonished to hear President Kennedy say at one of his televised press conferences in Washington that the Soviet Union had about six thousand *combat* troops in Cuba.

I cannot explain this contradiction. I can only record it.

I do know that, in and around the city of Havana, I never saw any Russian who looked like a combat soldier: the ones I saw all seemed obviously to belong to specialized service units of one kind and another. But as I have recorded, I was not allowed by the Cubans to go out of the area of Havana, and it is highly likely that the combat troops to whom Kennedy was referring were stationed well out of sight of anybody in the capital. I have also no doubt that American intelligence in Cuba was and is still functioning efficiently in spite of the revolution, for it is improbable indeed that all the links forged in an association between the two countries that has lasted for sixty-five years have been cut because of the coming upon the Cuban scene of Fidel Castro. Indeed, he has mentioned many times in his speeches and conversations that he knows very well indeed that agents of the United States have been active within Cuba all the time since his regime took power. Of course they have. The United States and Cuba have been closely associated ever since they fought the Spanish-American War in 1898 as allies, and Cuba's accession of independence in 1902 did not greatly change the terms of the relationship.

I am quite sure that, in spite of what has been done by Castro and Khrushchev and his successors in the Kremlin, America still has many firm and active friends within Cuba who let her know via intermediaries and possibly some peculiar means of communication what is going on within the island. The United States cannot be expected to be forever disclosing all she knows about events there. So, when President Kennedy said almost in passing that the Soviet Union had about six thousand combat troops in Cuba I accepted his statement, even though it scooped me, in journalistic parlance.

It was certainly known in Havana in the spring of 1963 that some of the Russian military specialists—I will still call them such, for that is how they were always described to me and how I saw them for myself—had been withdrawn from Cuba after the unprecedented assertion of American determination

by Kennedy in the previous November. Some one thousand of
them had gone in two big Soviet transport ships, perhaps
with some joy in their hearts at the end of a sojourn in the
unnatural surroundings of semitropical Spanish America.
These were almost certainly the specialists who had been sent
to Cuba to install and maintain the medium-range and inter-
mediate-range ballistic missiles, and the bombers, which had
provoked the American challenge, or counterchallenge.

It was felt within Havana that all the offensive rockets had
also been shipped back home by Khrushchev in accordance
with the assurance he had given President Kennedy. But for
many months there was doubt outside Cuba, particularly among
Americans, as I was to find, about whether Khrushchev had
in fact fulfilled his promise. I met nobody in Havana in a position of any responsibility inside and outside the regime who
would concede that this doubt was valid. Nobody seemed to
believe, as so many Americans suspected, that the Russians
still had rockets hidden in underground caves or in caverns
in the hills and mountains of central and eastern Cuba.

The reasons advanced to explain why Khrushchev would
have carried out his pledge to take away all the offensive weapons seemed to me to be convincing. It was argued that, for
one thing, it had been proved in November that he could never
hope or expect to be able to use them without provoking the
very thing the Soviet Union wanted to avoid—war with the
United States. For another thing, he could not expect to be
able to keep rockets hidden in Cuba without the United States
locating them and learning all about them either by direct
surveillance from the air or by the more secret but perhaps
more certain agency of human beings on the ground, including
those agents whom I have already mentioned. Discovery of
deception by concealment would obviously put the Soviet Union
in a worse tactical position in the tussle for Cuba than did
the original gamble in putting the rockets there in the first

place. I believe the realistic Russians would be as quick as anybody in perceiving this.

The Russians sent the rockets to Cuba in the first instance with the idea of testing the resolution of the United States in the face of such a threat. One simply cannot accept at face value Castro's explanation that the rockets were installed because the Cubans and the Russians had evidence that the United States was going to attack Cuba again. I had seen the Russians pursue this same kind of testing tactic in Berlin in 1948 when, step by step until the process was complete, without determined resistance by the Western powers, they managed to impose the blockade of Berlin—and they determinedly kept it going until the Allied airlift eventually nullified it against all their expectations. Now, fifteen years later, the same thing was happening again. Once the Russians realized that their tactic was not going to work in Cuba—once their effrontery was laid bare and resolutely encountered, they moved back and abandoned the line of attack. I felt sure they would not try it again until they had some reason to suppose that it could succeed, and the confrontation of 1962 had provided some substantial evidence that there would be no use in "trying it on" again for a long time to come.

The postconfrontation drama died hard. Fidel Castro seemed either unwilling or unable to let Cuba settle down and try to advance toward the communist millennium that was now the goal he had set for it. Stimulated by his visit to Moscow and comforted by the assurance that the Soviet Union was apparently prepared to sustain him and his revolution until further notice, he rashly went once again too far by delivering another challenge to the United States about her naval base at Guantanamo. He had not yet learned the lesson, which the Soviet Union and others had been absorbing by stages since the blockade of Berlin in 1948, that the abounding resources—and the

resourcefulness—of the United States are not to be lightly
regarded in any diplomatic or military jousting. He calculated mistakenly that, at best, he might be able to force the
Americans out of Guantanamo and, at the very least, score a
political victory over them by cutting off the water that he
supplied to them on a commercial basis by pipeline from the
Yateras River four miles outside the perimeter of the base.
He was provoked into this costly error after the U. S. Coast
Guard had arrested a party of Cubans fishing illegally in somewhat suspicious circumstances in American waters off Florida.
Fidel Castro demanded their release and, after the American
authorities had turned him down, he eventually threatened that
he would cut off Guantanamo's water supply until the Cubans
were released.

Once again I had the astonishing good fortune to be in
the right place at precisely the right moment, thereby perpetuating the uncanny sequence that had begun on New Year's
Eve in 1958. I have no doubt whatever that a lot of people
in Washington believed that I had been "tipped off," as the
saying goes, by Fidel Castro or somebody speaking for him,
and I must say the circumstances made everything look that
way. But two official personages who knew that the timing
was entirely my own were Pierre Salinger and Arthur Sylvester, the Assistant Secretary of Defense for Public Affairs. I
had seen both of them in their offices two weeks earlier and told
them I wanted to visit the base, and Sylvester had in fact arranged the trip. On February 5, 1964, the day before I flew
to Guantanamo in an enormous transport plane of the U. S.
Marine Corps from Cherry Point, North Carolina, I had had a
long chat with Sylvester, talking about assignments we had
covered together, including presidential election campaigns, in
his days as a journalist and laughing over the fact that Pierre
Salinger had once worked for me as a correspondent in San
Francisco. (Salinger tells with much relish a story of how I
commissioned him on the telephone from New York to cover a

frog-jumping contest in California, asking him to make sure that he gave us a particularly detailed account of the performance of one frog that had been sent all the way from Australia to compete.)

I left Cherry Point in a thick rainstorm at dawn on February 6. I was the only civilian among about forty-five other passengers and Marine crewmen, and I was greatly flattered when the U. S. Marine Corps honored me by calling out my name first when boarding-time came, ahead of a Navy captain and several other notabilities; I presumed that as a taxpayer (and I wish to stress here that although I am not an American I pay my full whack of them) I was really a paying passenger, the only one in fact, and as such was entitled to pride of place and choice of seat.

This was not such a concession as it sounds, for the Hercules transport had a stripped-down fuselage and only a mesh of webbing for seats. I marveled at the mass of equipment it was taking down to Guantanamo and Roosevelt Roads in Puerto Rico on this once-a-week run. The belly of the plane was filled with jeeps, tires, computers, and bundles of many other materials all securely strapped down and stowed away with precision. The passengers, including the civilian taxpayer, got just enough space to be comfortable and enough elbow room when the time came to eat the box lunch comprising the inevitable chicken, apple, five cigarettes, chocolate, and hard-boiled eggs with which all veterans of the wars and military travel are familiar. As it turned out, I did not spend much time in my webbed seat, for as soon as we became airborne and had left the stormy mainland behind, the captain of the Hercules invited me forward. The piloting area was so roomy that it reminded me of the bridge of a warship. There was ample space to stroll around, and there was even a small galley on the portside where hot coffee was constantly available.

What a wonderful sense of power as one sat in the copilot's seat while the plane reared southward! Ahead and below

stretched the island-studded, sunlit Atlantic. Then, as a dark
smudge to starboard, loomed the northern coast of Cuba. "We
fly far enough away to keep out of any trouble but close
enough to be able to see if there is anything interesting going
on over there," said the navigator as he peered out to the west-
ward with a pair of extremely powerful binoculars to his eyes.
"They'll be watching us as usual anyhow." I was standing behind the copilot's seat when we landed at Guantanamo. It all
happened remarkably quickly, like a maneuver which had been
plotted minutely. One moment we were flying in the sunshine
over the browned grasslands and the palms of eastern Cuba;
the next we were diving down steeply over warships at anchor
off the serrated bay shore, and then we were speeding down the
massive runway of McCalla Airfield.

A reception committee of two awaited me as I stepped down
from the Hercules, blinking like an owl as I accustomed myself to the glittering sunlight. It comprised Lieutenant Commander B. D. Varner, Public Information Officer at the base,
and his assistant, Chief Koze. They had come in a smart-look-
ing cutter to take me across the water to the Bachelor Officers'
Quarters, where I was to rest and be fuelled. As we sped
through the slightly choppy water with sparklets of spray
spending themselves against our grateful faces, Commander
Varner handed me a thick package in an envelope. It contained
every possible fact I should need to know about Guantanamo
and an invitation to dine that evening with Rear Admiral and
Mrs. John D. Bulkeley at the Admiral's Quarters (RSVP
8-5441; Coat and Tie). It was a friendly and hospitable gesture, and I appreciated it. But Commander Varner slowly un-
veiled an even more appetizing journalistic welcome. "There
are two alternatives for you to choose from," he said. "You
can stay forty-eight hours during which we can give you the
works—show you everything, tell you everything. If you do
that you can catch your plane back on its return trip from
Puerto Rico. If you would like to stay longer you will have to

stay eight days to await the next round trip by air. It's up to you. . . ." Commander Varner was silent for a moment. Then, as the boat ripped on through the water, he delivered the day's big news, the item that was going to put the name of Guantanamo on the world's front pages for days to come. "Oh, by the way, we have a report that Castro has turned off our water, as he has been threatening to do," he said quietly, eyeing me shrewdly to observe how I would take his news. I took it with a chuckle. "In that case, I'll be taking the eight-day package, thank you," I told him. "I imagined you might," observed Commander Varner. "You're on to something that looks rather like a scoop."

They took me on a motorcar ride around part of the base before they stowed me away in the Bachelor Officers' Quarters. I marveled at its completeness. There was everything in Guantanamo that the American way of life demanded—from church to dry cleaner and from hospital (where an average of twenty babies per month were born) to roller-skating rink and photographic darkroom. A self-contained community of some sixty-two hundred Americans was neatly and comfortably ensconced in a little enclave of the United States here by the sunlit Caribbean—a replica of any one of a thousand small towns in the eastern, middle-western, or south-western states in the homeland far to the north; an efficiently run unit comprising some forty-five square miles of land and water but sealed off from a hostile foreign country, on whose territory it sat, by a forbidding wire fence line stretching for twenty-four miles without a break around its flanks and rear.

"We'll give you a helicopter trip round the perimeter tomorrow," Commander Varner promised, as he left me to the ministrations of the staff of Filipinos who welcomed me to the B. O. Q. "But before that you'll meet the admiral tonight. You'll like him."

And that I did. We got on famously from the moment we met, perhaps partly because he told me very promptly that his family had its origins in the same county of England as my own (it is Cheshire) and that many of his forefathers had served in the British Navy. But this apart, I enjoyed seeing him in command here at this acute phase because he seemed to me to be just the kind of man, a fighting admiral with a flair and a liking for the impetuously histrionic, to take on Fidel Castro in this skirmish in the war between the United States and Cuba. His record as a sailor in war had been a dazzling one. He had specialized in motor torpedo boats in the Philippines and in European waters, and he had gathered an imposing row of decorations—including the Congressional Medal of Honor—for daredevil deeds, citations that spoke of "fearless determination" and "dynamic forcefulness and daring in offensive action" and the like; and once when he went back to the United States from the Philippines in the spring of 1942 he had already become such a national hero that he was given a ceremonial parade in New York. He was the sort of man whom nothing but obliteration could stop, and with this quality of doggedness went the priceless one of leadership. He had exhibited this inspiringly in one episode in March, 1942, in which he commanded a motor torpedo boat that took General MacArthur, Mrs. MacArthur, and their son through 560 miles of Japanese-controlled waters on the first dangerous leg of a journey to Australia, so that MacArthur could rebuild American and Allied forces for the ultimate recapture of the Philippines. Once again, nothing could stop Bulkeley. He delivered MacArthur exactly on time on Mindanao Island, despite setbacks and breakdowns and enemy interference, so that a bomber could pick up the general and take him on to Australia.

Now, twenty-two years later and at the mature age of fifty-two, he was electric in his excitement at the challenge delivered to him and Guantanamo by Fidel Castro and at the prospect of certain action of one kind or another. His eyes were almost throwing off sparks and his tanned face (a trifle fleshy now but remarkably unlined) glowed as he welcomed me

and his other guests into the spacious colonial-type small mansion that served as the quarters of the man in charge of the
base. We were a considerable company—four Navy captains
and their wives, Lieutenant Commander Varner and his wife,
Admiral and Mrs. Bulkeley, and myself. The admiral lost no
time in telling me his account of what had gone on that day
at the pumping station where the water from the Yateras
River came into the base through massive pipes. As we sat
sipping cocktails in the cool of the evening on the big patio
of the mansion, he drew his chair close to mine and, fishing a
piece of paper from his pocket, he recited all the times—the
very instants—at which the water pressure first faltered, how
it drooped, and when it finally vanished altogether. "I went
down there myself and noted it all down—wanted it exactly
right for the record," he said. "Now I'm waiting to see what
Washington wants me to do tactically. One thing I do know.
We can beat this move; we just aren't worried about that. My
mission here is to maintain the *status quo* of the base and,
believe me, this I shall do. . . ."

He told me the illuminating story of the Cuban functionary
who for some years had been in charge of the water-control
station up the river and had always been on good terms with
the Americans at the base, upon whom he made a daily call as
part of his duties. His master's act in cutting off the water
was just a little too much for him to take. When he made his
formal call at the pumping station just inside the perimeter
of Guantanamo he announced that he wasn't going back. He
asked for and was given asylum. He wanted to be among
friends, it seemed, if there was going to be any shooting.

The admiral's dinner party that evening was a lively and
enjoyable affair. Two of the guests were Captain Raymond
E. Peet, commanding the nuclear destroyer U. S. S. *Bainbridge,*
and Captain G. E. Miller, commanding the aircraft carrier
U. S. S. *Franklin D. Roosevelt.* These two ships were in Guantanamo for maneuvers. Their captains did not quarrel with

Admiral Bulkeley's confident declarations that the base would
not wither from thirst. Nobody, in fact, seemed to be in the
slightest degree concerned.

Mrs. Bulkeley was seated next to me. Like me, she is British, and it did not take long for us to find topics of mutual
interest. Halfway through the meal, I happened to notice that
on the wall opposite me was a reproduction of one of those
paintings depicting the death of Admiral Nelson on the deck
of H. M. S. *Victory* at Trafalgar. As I gazed at it I was moved
to say to Mrs. Bulkeley, "I wonder what Nelson really said
as he lay there dying against that mast. Did he say 'Kiss me,
Hardy,' or was it 'Kismet, Hardy,' meaning 'It is fate, Hardy.'
I hardly believe, Mrs. Bulkeley, that . . ."

I did not get time to finish the sentence. Admiral Bulkeley,
sitting at the other end of the table, had heard what I was
saying, and, as quick as lightning, had perceived that I had
given him a perfect cue. "I'll tell you what Nelson said," he
boomed out at me. "He said, 'Send for Midshipman Bulkeley,'
and I'll prove it." He got up from his seat and picked up a
book lying handily close. I cannot swear to it, but I *believe*
it was opened at the appropriate page. The admiral brought
it round to me and there, surely enough, was a paragraph re-
counting that the dying Nelson had in fact told one of the
men tending him as he lay there fatally wounded to send Midshipman Bulkeley, his favorite middy, to him. "That was my
ancestor, Richard Bulkeley," said the admiral. Hastening
around the table to the painting, he placed his finger upon one
of the figures standing near Nelson. "And there he is," he announced, triumphantly.

That evening and during the next morning I learned the
basic facts of the situation in which Fidel Castro and Guantanamo now found themselves. Firstly, Castro was not breaking any treaty or international agreement by turning off the
supply of Cuban water to the base. It had been delivered under
a purely commercial arrangement whereby the United States

paid Cuba $14,000 a month for it, and this useful contribution of precious U. S. dollars he would now lose. He had been regularly cashing the checks paid to him for the water—but he had not been cashing the other annual checks of $3,500 made out to him as rental for the territory on which the base was established, and it was presumed that he had been not taking this cash because he wanted to buttress his claim that he did not recognize the treaty under which the United States had acquired the base in 1903 and a new treaty in 1934 that guaranteed Cuba's ultimate sovereignty over Guantanamo but gave the United States complete jurisdiction and control over the base as long as she continued to hold it.

Fidel Castro now stood to lose not only his income of $14,000 a month. He had also placed in jeopardy a much bigger revenue of over $5 million per year that he obtained from the three thousand or so Cubans working on the base for the Americans, because if the unpleasantness over the water continued these Cubans would almost certainly lose their jobs. Their average rate of pay was about sixty cents per hour, very high by domestic Cuban standards, and when they took their wages with them into Cuban territory through the frontier at the northeast gate they were required to hand over nine out of every ten for exchange into pesos which, though still pegged artificially at parity with U. S. dollars, were worthless outside Cuba. It looked as if Fidel Castro was going to find his latest tactic an expensive one.

Indeed, as I weighed one fact against another I could not see how he could possibly expect to gain anything at all by depriving the base of its water. One had only to spend a few minutes with Admiral Bulkeley or anybody else in authority to be sure that there was not the slightest chance of the base being abandoned. Nor, judging by the reports coming in from Washington and Florida over the radio, was there any chance whatever of the United States saving his face by releasing the Cuban fishermen still in custody. I thought he would have been wise to have found some reason or excuse for calling off the one-sided Battle of the Taps before it got really started.

Guantanamo had over fifteen million gallons of water stored in reserve in anchored floating reservoirs in the bay and in clusters of enormous tanks within the perimeter of the base. This reserve was always maintained against the possibility of any natural failure in the water supply from the Yateras River or, ever since Fidel and Raul Castro had started agitating for the evacuation of Guantanamo by the American Navy, against just such a contingency as had now come up. Even at unrestricted use of about two million gallons per day there would be enough water for over a week. Under restrictions imposed as soon as the Cuban supply was cut off there would be enough, it was calculated, for well over twice that period— and less than twenty-four hours after the emergency began, Admiral Bulkeley was able to tell everybody via the base television station that barges from both Florida and Jamaica were already on their way to Guantanamo with supplies that would be coming in at the rate of 1.3 million gallons per day when the relay system got really working.

Within forty-eight hours the base was already using less than one million gallons a day, and Admiral Bulkeley told me gleefully that he was certain he could get the figure down much lower as time went on. "We've got fine cooperation and discipline here, as you'll see," he said. Actually, everybody on the base was permanently conscious of the need to save water because there were some restrictions on its use even when Water Condition Charlie, as it was called, was in force. Charlie was the least restrictive of three conditions regulating water usage that were proclaimed from day to day over radio and television, in the *Gitmo Gazette* (the daily newspaper), at base movie houses, and over public address systems in the residential areas. Even when Charlie ruled, a man could only water his lawn between two hours on Tuesday, Thursday, and Saturday, clean his car only if he used a self-closing nozzle or a bucket, and if he lived aboard ship his daily ration of water was twenty-five gallons.

When Condition Bravo took over—"when existing or anticipated circumstances indicate that the Base water supply may be reduced"—nobody could either water his lawn at all or clean his car, and even in the public parks and gardens only freshly planted areas could be sprinkled, and not without the permission of the commanding officer of the Public Works Center. But it was when Condition Alfa was decreed, as now— "when a serious casualty occurs in the water supply system that will require a shutdown for an extensive period"—that every drop was measured. Water valves in many parts of the base were shut off altogether; valves elsewhere were opened by Masters-at-Arms for an hour at a time thrice daily; all swimming pools were drained; men stood by day and night at the Base Fire Department to open valves there only when there was a fire; and I found as I went about the base that expedients not mentioned in the official instructions were being used. Paper cups were being issued in restaurants and canteens to save the use of washing-up water. Sailors were wearing dungarees instead of whites. Drums of salt water were being issued wherever possible for the flushing of toilets.

Morale was high, dangerously so in the case of some spirited young officers with whom I chatted and played pool in the B. O. Q., who told me as they thumped the billiard balls that there was nothing they would like better than to lead raiding parties up the Yateras River to turn on the water again and make sure it stayed turned on. I was sure that, of course, none of these young men would take it upon himself to do something rash, but it did seem that their fiery mood would ensure that if called upon to deal with any provocation, however slight, from Cubans outside the base fence they would obey orders to the full, to say the least. I had the impression that the frustration which had been building up within such young Americans because of the unchecked progress of the

hostile revolution since 1959 would now explode most readily
if given a chance. Therein lay one of the serious aspects of
the present tension.

Social life, always highly organized and intense on this base,
now became more important than ever to keep everybody occupied. I found that Admiral Bulkeley was especially sensitive
to any suggestions, however vague, that dependents might be
evacuated because of the lack of water, and such diversions as
mass bingo parties, sports of all kinds and a lavish Mardi
Gras party (complete with a well-supported fancy dress com-
petition) were just the thing to keep people's minds off topics
like possible impending separations. Admiral Bulkeley showed
himself determined to scotch all rumors of evacuation. He
sought me out to tell me, with repeated apologies, that he had
felt bound to delete from one of the reports I tried to cable
out of the base a paragraph stating that dependents might
eventually have to be sent home. It was only an incidental
point in the story as far as I was concerned, and I told him
I would make no fuss or protest about the deletion. It would
have made little difference had I done so, for I was wholly in
the Navy's hands as far as communications were involved. They
could despatch—or not despatch, as I was to find—whatever
suited them, because all my cables to New York had to go
through the Navy signal organization and I had no means of
knowing what happened to anything once I had handed it in.

The resolute admiral also went directly via television to the
families on the base to emphasize that nobody was going to be
sent home. "There's no parallel between now and the situation
in October, 1962, when those Cuban missiles were threatening
American security," he said. "We stay here."

On February 8, two days after the water had been cut off,
seven Navy specialists were flown into Guantanamo from Washington to make a survey and decide where a plant for desalting
sea water could be built so that the base could be made permanently secure from any interference with its water supply

by the Cubans. I ran across some of them on the afternoon of Sunday, February 9, while they were examining the lie of the land in the neighborhood of Kittery Beach, on the south-eastern tip of the base perimeter. Kittery was reserved for the use of families, and I had gone there this Sunday afternoon to observe for myself a weekly farce in which the Cuban soldiers keeping guard on their side of the seven-foot fence marking the limit of the base were the chief players. On a Sunday afternoon the beach was always well filled, and pleasantly so, by the wives and pretty daughters living on Guantanamo, and it was the regular thing for a half-dozen Cuban soldiers to post themselves on a slight slope overlooking Kittery and spend an hour or two idly "girl-watching" through field glasses. But this afternoon they were doing more than that. They were there in twice their usual force and they were using long-focus cameras as well as the customary binoculars. They had spotted the Navy specialists, easily discernible because they were wearing civilian clothes or uniforms not usually seen on the base, and they were making a photographic record of what the visitors were doing, presumably for intelligence purposes. For once the pretty girls were being neglected. Even I came in for some of the picture-taking, for I also was wearing more or less formal civilian clothes, certainly more formal than either the pretty women or their escorts.

That evening there came another message from the admiral, a rather mysterious one. If I would be outside the main door of the B. O. Q. at 6 A.M. next morning, a jeep would come to pick me up and take me on a sortie that might be interesting; something might happen that should be recorded, and I was just the chap to do it. In the meantime, I should not say a word to anybody. Nor did I, although I enjoyed a comradely evening with a dozen of the residents of the B. O. Q., first at the bar after it had opened at 5 P.M., then at supper, and eventually at an open-air cinema of a sort in the garden, where we sipped coffee and liqueurs and watched what was surely the

first experimental sound movie ever made. It was a hilarious
production rather like *The Great Train Robbery*, and we all
had a great time jeering at its out-dated naiveties, hissing the
villain with the handle-bar moustaches and the glinting silver-
plated pistol as he crawled over the coals and dodged tunnel
after tunnel and bullet after bullet until the hero got him at
last, and we most ungallantly gibed at the girls in the long
skirts as they turned up their white faces (appealingly as the
producer hoped) toward their saviors who had rescued them
moments before the train carrying the dead villain plunged to
awful destruction in the river bed. I was to find that several of
my fellow bachelor officers had been alerted, like myself, to possible happenings early the following morning and, again like
myself, were not saying a word to anybody about it in advance, as they had been ordered. I reflected that there was not
much really wrong with a service that could command such
decorous obedience.

Promptly at 6 A.M. the promised jeep called for me at the
B. O. Q. and my escort then explained what was afoot. Word
had reached the base during the weekend that Raul Castro
had been touring Oriente Province and had made some inflammatory speeches about the crisis over the water. These had
provoked mass meetings and demonstrations in the town of
Guantanamo outside the base, and there had been signs that
the local revolutionary activists and communists might be
organizing some form of anti-American display—such as a
propaganda march to the perimeter of the base, stone-throw-
ing, taunting of the guards, or something similarly provocative—when Cubans employed at the base presented themselves
this Monday morning after a weekend off. Admiral Bulkeley
had made his plans to meet any such development and we were
now driving to the gate to see what would happen.

This celebrated gate was, as I had noted from a helicopter
earlier, as complete a frontier post as I had seen any-

where in the world. On the Cuban side was a row of low but substantial buildings flanking a central arch on which was painted in big letters *"República de Cuba: Territorio Libre de América,"* the familiar slogan of the revolution. Guards armed with machine pistols and some carrying the inevitable binoculars were stationed close to the arch. Anybody wishing to cross into the American base had to walk along an open-air passage traced by high wire and submit to examination of documents and a search before being allowed by the guards to pass into a neutral zone leading to the American guard post. Here again the formalities were strictly followed. Americans and Cubans kept constant watch on each other, as they did at many other observation points along the fence separating the base from Cuba proper, but for the most part there was no contact between them. Occasionally the need would arise for a formal exchange of words and sometimes, I had been told, the Cubans would stage some crude display of revolutionary senti-ment; once when a dog had tried, in all innocence, to dart through their checkpoint toward the Americans they had cal-lously shot it and then hanged up its body in full view with a notice calling it a *"gusano"* (the term used to describe de-spised fugitives from the revolution). Usually they ignored such rituals as the raising and lowering of the American flag at dawn and dusk, but I found that on this particular morning they had all stood rigidly at the salute during the flag raising, and the Americans were wondering whether this did not in some way confirm that something out of the ordinary was brewing.

If so, Admiral Bulkeley was prepared for it. He had set up modest field headquarters on a slope behind one of the buildings a little way back from the American checkpoint, and he was sitting there sipping coffee with two or three of his officers when I presented myself. The first thing I noticed was that he was wearing a blue baseball cap. He grinned at my look of surprise and explained, "Didn't want to advertise my presence

here this morning to those boys over there and this should
fool them."

Nor was the gallant admiral advertising the forces he had
gathered at the spot to deal with any disturbance that might
occur. He had fire engines with hoses at the ready parked behind hillocks just off the road leading to the frontier post,
and he had Marines and others, plus armored vehicles, similarly hidden from view. He had also arranged that this morning the buses used to go to the checkpoint to pick up the
Cuban workers as they emerged in ones and twos should be
driven by American sailors instead of the usual Cubans, so
that in an emergency the vehicles could be deployed promptly
and efficiently without complications of language or other
handicaps.

We waited with growing interest as the number of workers
coming through the checkpoint grew from a trickle to a flow.
Nothing whatever unusual happened, although we waited patiently until the last worker of all had emerged. Then the
admiral, reluctantly, called off the alarm and drove back to
take on the more humdrum routine of the day, exchanging his
baseball cap for his braided naval one on the way to his office.
I do not know to this day whether the Cubans had planned
something for that morning. But I shared a general opinion
on the base that they had and had called everything off because of the precautions taken. There was no doubt that they
had spies inside the base and these would certainly have advised them that Admiral Bulkeley had resolved to tolerate no
nonsense. They had probably weighed the circumstances and
decided that there would be more to be lost than gained by
promoting an hour or so of trouble at the gate, especially as
Castro's maneuvering with the water taps was already going
awry as a challenge to the Americans. Reports and photographs of Cuban troops and civilians being sprayed with hoses
might evoke more comments of "serve them right" than of
sympathy when published in countries where Fidel Castro's

hasty reprisal had harmed the prestige not only of himself
but of the new Cuba.

It now became time for me to try to get out of the base at
Guantanamo so that I could tell my story of what had been
happening there while all the diplomatic duelling had been
going on between Washington and Havana. Although the Navy
was later to reproach me for complaining of censorship, it
was ludicrous for either of us to pretend otherwise. One report
I handed in for cabling on Friday, February 7, was simply
stopped in entirety. Other stories were handed back to me for
complete rewriting and shortening into terms suitable to the
Navy. The limit in futility was reached during the weekend of
February 8–9, when I was not allowed to report the fact that
a team of experts had reached the base to prepare the way
for the establishment of a water desalinating plant, even though
this same fact had already been reported to the whole world
from Washington. I am afraid I just gave up after that.
I realized that—for some reason that I could not then fathom
but that amused and flattered me when I learned of it later—
the Navy and the Pentagon had to make as little as possible
of my fortuitous presence on the base at this particular moment. This was the cause of the censorship and the cutting
down of my messages to the bone; why an arrangement was
made, but apparently collapsed, that everything I wrote should
be circulated to all the American news agencies; why my messages often took the incredible time of over twenty hours to
reach New York.

As I have indicated, I knew nothing of the background while
I was in Guantanamo, but some journalistic sense prompted me
to make no fuss about the verbal strangulation, hard though
it was to endure. For one thing, I suppose, I realized that I
simply had no cards to play. Once I had handed in a message
to Lieutenant Commander Varner I had no further control over
it; and, as for myself, if I became obstreperous they could just

ship me out. So I contented myself with doing and writing more or less as they decreed for the time being, knowing that I should have a chance later of writing a balanced summation of what had gone on there.

On Monday, February 9, I intimated that, if there *happened* to be any kind of plane flying out of the base to, say, Jamaica I should like to go with it. Conveniently for all concerned, it turned out that one was going the next day. So off I went to Kingston in a small naval scouting plane, seated back-to-back with the pilot and with a holiday-making naval officer as the occupant of the only other seat. As we flew the short south-westerly hop, I tapped away on my typewriter. As soon as I reached Kingston I raced off to the office of cable and wireless and sent off a long despatch of some eight hundred words to London—the first full and untrammeled message the world had had from Guantanamo since the Cuban water stopped flowing into the naval base. Then I made my way back to the United States in comfortable easy stages via Grand Cayman Island and, after a hop high over Cuba, Nassau in the Bahamas, and Miami.

Here I received my first inkling of the fuss that my presence in Guantanamo had caused. The immigration officer who was checking me in asked me according to routine where I had been while out of the United States. I told him and he immediately broke out into a laugh. "So you're the Britisher we've all been reading about," he said, glancing down at my battered British passport. "It's in the papers here today." Now I found out at last why I had become an embarrassment to the Pentagon as a whole and Arthur Sylvester, my old comrade, in particular once my presence in Guantanamo had become known. Naturally there had been a clamor from American correspondents to be flown down to the naval base after the water had been cut off. They were told curtly that it had been decided that it was "not in the national interest" to have reporters in the base while the situation between the United

States and Cuba was once again so tense. Back came the
Washington reporters to Arthur Sylvester. If that was the
case, what was this Britisher, "named Tetlow," doing there?
Poor Arthur! He had to explain, convincingly, that my visit
had been arranged two weeks before the crisis started and it
was pure coincidence that I should be there. I hope he was believed. The outcome as far as I was concerned was pleasant
enough to compensate for the stifling time I had had in Guantanamo. The Associated Press, showing the acumen that one
has come to expect from it, arranged to acquire the material
I had compiled while at the base. This was circulated all over
the United States and elsewhere, and for a day or two one
could scarcely pick up a newspaper without reading some of
this exclusive journalistic product.

What in fact did I feel about this extraordinary episode in
which I had become so closely involved? First and foremost, I
never wavered for a moment from my early conclusion that
the only sure loser was going to be the unfortunate Fidel
Castro. I was also inclined to agree with the theory that was
aired by quite a number of Navy people at the base that he
had been prompted to try and cause American evacuation of
Guantanamo by Khrushchev while the two were together in
Moscow so recently. The Russians might well have had their
eye on the base for use by themselves. Although it had been
made obsolete in some respects by the coming of the military
era of long-range rockets and missiles, it would still be a useful tool in their hands in their cold war with the United States
for a long time to come. Russian warships based on Cuba
would exert far more than their practical military influence
upon Latin and South America, and the knowledge that they
were there would scarcely make Americans sleep more easily in
their beds in time of crisis. The prize must have looked very
glittering when viewed on a map in the Kremlin, but the chance
of getting it now by American default or local defeat was so
small as to be almost negligible. The defensive-offensive reac-

tions of the United States to Fidel Castro's sudden thrust were
prompt and efficient. They had three chief elements:

1. Not to yield one iota beyond the bounds of legality and justice
in the case of the thirty-six Cuban fishermen caught operating in
four boats in American waters off the coast of Florida.

2. To strike back at Fidel Castro via his pocketbook by permanently depriving him not only of the revenue from supplying water
from the Yateras River but also of much greater returns. This could
be done by gradually reducing the number of Cubans working on the
base. As we have noted, he had been acquiring from them some
$5 million per year by forcing them to change most of their U. S.
dollar earnings into pesos.

3. To make Guantanamo invulnerable to any further Cuban interference by installing a desalinating plant that should supply the
place with all the water it needed. Once this were done the base
would be permanently in a much stronger defensive position than it
had been before Fidel Castro turned off the taps.

The objectives had either been achieved or were in process
of being achieved by the time I got back to New York. Plans
for the desalinating plant were being put into operation, Cuban
workers were already being dismissed, and there was talk of
arranging for them to be replaced by men and women from
Jamaica who could supply all the labor needs of the base,
and Washington had announced that American dependents
would be gradually "phased out" so that the least possible
quantity of water would be needed. It did not automatically
follow that all this planning would be carried out rigidly,
for military and quasi-military tactics have to be flexible
always, but as a policy created to meet an emergency it was
admirable.

For this reason, I felt sorry that the Navy had not found
it possible for the story of Guantanamo to be told fully and
without delay while it was happening during the week I was
there. There was nothing to hide but a tale of triumph. The
United States was winning—no, it was almost being presented

with—a tactical victory in its local tussle with Fidel Castro and in the more significant struggle of the cold war with world communism. Such victories were scarce enough. To let one such as this go mostly unexploited was unfortunate. If it were "not in the national interest" to allow a lot of reporters in Guantanamo, then either I should have been given every possibility to tell the story for everybody, for surely my presence on the base at this time was a piece of luck for the Pentagon, or one American correspondent should have been flown in to complement me. This type of "pool" coverage had been used often and with great success in the war with Germany and Japan, and it could have been reintroduced effectively in this near-warlike episode at Guantanamo.

11 ✦ *Regal*
Revolutionary

THE DEFEAT at Guantanamo had been absorbed and put aside as something not worth discussing by the time I made yet another trip to Havana in June, 1964, about four months after it had all happened. I put out suggestions through diplomatic friends and some officials serving the revolutionary regime that if Castro felt so inclined I should be most pleased to give him my eyewitness story of some of the events at the base while I had been there in February during the water crisis. I must add that I had no intention whatever of betraying any American military secrets—not that I was aware of having learned any—but I should have been most interested to hear how he would have rationalized the episode. Would he have conceded that it *had* been a mistake to cut off the water, and that he had met a consequent defeat? I scarcely think so. I was offered no chance of finding out, for my approaches came to naught and I assumed that he just did not want to talk about Guantanamo, especially to a western journalist.

I did, however, spend a long session in his company in a salon of the British Embassy residence in Vedado on the evening of June 5, 1964, and into the early hours of the next day. It had been forecast with as much confidence as may be used in the case of Fidel Castro that he would be attending a party at the residence to be given by the Ambassador (Adam Watson) and his wife to celebrate the Queen's official birthday. He not only attended but arrived, with astonishing promptness for him, within a few minutes of the time on the invitation and stayed on until almost 3 A.M., to make absolutely the most of the occasion both socially and diplomatically. He stalked, loose-limbed and with long strides, into the elegantly appointed house with a beret crumpled up in one hand. He was wearing a new uniform, dark olive in color and made of what I took to be a really fine sateen. His thick dark hair was well groomed and glossy, his beard had been somewhat trimmed, and his face had a well-washed look—giving him the air, I amused myself by thinking, of a schoolboy with shining evening face. But there was nothing of the schoolboy about the pistol resting in the black holster suspended from the webbing belt between the tunic and the well-creased trousers.

His urbane host ushered him through the groups of other guests. He shook hands with some, smiled or waved at others, and bowed now and then to a lady. From the moment he arrived the party just ceased to be a party. This unique man, simply by being there, turned it into a shapeless thing. It was now as if the people had come to the residence not to exchange social pleasantries and perhaps transact a little diplomatic business over a cocktail but to wait on him and obey his will. Watson escorted him into a reception room that had been

cleared in advance. There he sat himself easily into an arm-
chair and, after only a slight delay for incidentals such as
accepting a drink, prepared for business. Subordinates directed
by Roa, the Foreign Minister, were stationed as guards and
couriers close to the double doors of the salon. And then King
Castro started to hold court and conduct his audiences. I
marveled at his regal dominance. First this ambassador, then
that one, was discreetly summoned into the salon by the Roa
couriers and allowed through the double doors by the Roa
guards. This was the new diplomacy in action—the latter-day
revolutionary using the ambassadorial amenities of an ancient
kingdom and monarchy to conduct his fledgeling country's
affairs.

But for all the Castro regality there was one circumstance
that showed that he was perhaps not a king after all but a
subking. The only important ambassador who could not be summoned into the Presence was Aleksandr Alekseyev, of the Soviet
Union. He could not be summoned because he was already
there. He had seated himself at the outset on the chair immediately to the left of Fidel Castro and, so far as I was able
to note, he never left it all evening. I mentioned this permanent
proximity to one of the other ambassadors and he told me that
since Castro had come back from his visit to Moscow it had
become the regular thing. The deduction being drawn was that
the ambassador had had orders to keep a close check on Castro,
an impulsive man prone to the occasional blurt and one who
had shown himself often in the past to be capable of deciding
upon a new and contrary political tactic on the spur of a
moment. Watching the devoted attention being given to him
that evening by Alekseyev, one could scarcely avoid drawing the
conclusion that Khrushchev just did not trust Fidel Castro to
keep strictly to the party line. I regarded it also as another
small item of evidence to support the judgment I had made
since 1959 that Fidel Castro had never been and was not now
a convinced and reliable communist.

The diplomatic representatives attending this reception which had so dramatically changed its aspect watched the events of the evening with deep attention—noting such points as how long one ambassador spent by the side of the Maximum Leader and how abruptly another was dismissed after the merest contact. They milled around and quizzed each other smoothly but thoroughly, trying to detect the directions into which the volatile mind of Castro was darting. I joined the game as an amateur and was rewarded before very long with the information that only the representatives of the Vatican, Spain, and Switzerland had "done business" (as the phrase went in the foreign services). It was something to know this, one friendly ambassador assured me. He believed that Fidel Castro was courting the Vatican because he now wanted to become respectable and to be accepted as one who did not intend active enmity toward the Church; Spain because there had been hints in the newspapers and some substantial gossip in the embassies in Havana that the Spaniards had been trying, either on their own initiative or at the instigation of an interested party (perhaps the United States), to see if there was still any possibility of an accommodation between Cuba and the United States; and Switzerland—well, that was easily understood, for Switzerland was the protecting power of the United States in the absence of normal diplomatic relations between the two countries, and there were always matters that one or the other wanted to air.

At last, I imagine it was somewhere around 9:30 P.M., the serious work of the evening by Castro was finished. It was time to have something to eat and to acknowledge the reason for the occasion. He was served with a handsomely filled plate of supper, but before he started tucking into it he did a most gracious thing. He asked for his glass to be filled—I believe he was drinking Cointreau that night—and, rising to his feet and bowing to the British Ambassador, he proposed the health of the Queen. "*La Reina!*" he said, giving a beaming smile to all around him in the salon.

When supper was over and most of the guests were preparing to leave he was ready for the final ritual of all. He asked Watson to bring in the foreign correspondents to see him. At most this could mean a session lasting until dawn, and at the very least it meant four hours. A handful of us—two British correspondents and two American, followed by some Cuban and other reporters—were ushered into the Presence in the same fashion as the diplomats had been. I had the distinction of being presented first to Fidel Castro by the Ambassador, and I noted as soon as he grasped my hand that after six years he had learned the knack, used by so many Presidents, Prime Ministers, and other public figures, of pulling with some decision at the hand being shaken so that the person to whom it belonged was propelled to the right. It is a most useful device to prevent a would-be dawdler from holding up the line of presentation.

But, once again, the overpowering sensation I always experienced whenever I met him enveloped me. I am going to take this opportunity to describe it, emphasizing the messianic aspect of Fidel Castro when encountered face to face, even though I might be accused of fulsome partisanship toward this unique man when I do so. The truth is that Fidel Castro *does* have the aura of a Messiah. I will go so far as to say that if I were an artist wishing to do a painting of the Saviour, he is the man I should want as my model. The cartoonists have created such a grotesque image of him, and photographs convey such a veiled and partial suggestion of the soft and appealing radiance that emanates from his face, that I have found that people who have never met him just do not realize the quality of his physical presence. (Ask any intelligent and mature woman who has met him for her assessment of his physical attraction as a man and, judging by what such women have told me, she will confess that he casts a most powerful

spell, perhaps more powerful than any other man she has met.)
I think that most of his appeal radiates from his eyes, but it
is supported by the finely drawn outline of his oval Spanish
face. This evening the impact of his gaze was as strong as
ever. His large dark eyes seemed to be transmitting a message
of hurt wonderment at the manner in which the world was
treating him, as if he would say, "I want to help everybody . . .
carry everybody's burdens . . . but nobody seems to understand. . . ." I confess that even I, cynical veteran though I
am after forty years of experience with the complexities and
contradictions of human nature, found it almost impossible
that evening to believe that this could really be the man who
had done some of the things I knew him to have done since 1959.
I could readily understand some of the naiveties and the impulsive errors in his record, for they were just the faults
that one could expect from a man giving out this air of sim-
plicity and anxious earnestness. But what of the ruthless
thrusting aside of anybody who got in his way, the vindictive
bloodletting, the callous imprisonment and other degradations
accorded to men who had been his comrades in the long guerilla
war in the Sierra Maestra? Here in the flesh, sitting within
four or five feet of me for one hour after another in the
middle of the night, he was as docile, humorous, and appealing
as any man—say a senior college student—discoursing on his
favorite topics. He answered, sometimes at inordinate length,
question after question about his revolution, agrarian reform,
foreign relations, his attitude toward the United States, his
demands for the full sovereignty of Cuba. He had still not
learned, of course, how to keep still, but even in this he was
more controlled than I had seen him in the past. Mostly, he
vented his inward restlessness by fiddling about with the brass
handles on the drawer of a small table in front of him. He
scarcely seemed to be aware of Alekseyev still sitting quietly
by his side; perhaps he had become so used to the Russian
presence that he now accepted it as a part of his public life.

There were one or two points of topical interest in the rambling answers he gave to the questions put to him. The most
significant to me were those answers and observations, made
with such apparent clarity and sincerity, that helped one to
perceive or deduce the current trend of revolutionary foreign
policy. The Maximum Leader conceded that some "interested
persons" had been trying recently to serve as mediators between Cuba and the United States, but he added with em-
phasis that Cuba had turned down overtures made by these
unnamed persons because at the time it was being harassed
by American "threats and pressures." He did not elaborate,
but one presumed that he was referring to the blockade being
maintained by the United States and the efforts being made
from Washington to stop other countries, including Great
Britain, from nullifying it by trading with Cuba.

I followed up by asking him to give his estimate of the state
of relations between Cuba and Great Britain and Western
Europe. He liked this one. "Our relations with Great Britain
are magnificent," he said, with surprising enthusiasm. "I hope
and expect that trade between us will go on and grow greater.
We are splendid customers for Britain and Western Europe,
you know. You make just the things we want now—machinery,
motors, equipment, and so on."

There was one other segment of the interview that caught
my attention. He said plaintively that he still could not understand why he was finding it impossible to get on with the
United States when he was doing so well with most of the rest
of the world. All right then, somebody quizzed him, what were
his terms for an understanding with the United States? He
enumerated them, ticking them off with one finger against
another: an end to all harassments and interferences, total
independence for Cuba, and an acceptance without any quibbles
or qualifications of himself and his revolution. No change here,
I reflected, in the Castro stance. It would *still* have to be the
United States that must make the first move, and there was

precious little chance of this coming in 1964—an election year, an election that Fidel Castro now forecast would be easily won by President Johnson.

The interview was still meandering on when I had to leave at 2 A.M. to make ready for a telephone call from London. In the following two days I pondered what Castro had said to us and I gathered the reports of some of the things he had said to the ambassadors before that. I read the controlled newspapers of Havana for their versions of what had happened at the British party, talked with the few Cuban friends and official acquaintances I met, exchanged information and impressions with the handful of American, French, and other journalists still based there, and checked the lot with diplomatic friends and contacts whom I had come to trust. Slowly, a credible picture of what was going on began to form, although a few blurred lines had to be filled in with assumption. It seemed certain that Fidel Castro was now trying to free himself from almost total dependence economically upon the Soviet Union and her satellites, who between them all had seen to it for so long that he did not collapse on account of the American blockade of Cuba. He was even trying to find out if Algeria could supply him with oil. And he had really meant it when he told me that he hoped and expected that trade with Great Britain and Western Europe would flourish.

The first decisive breach in the American blockade of Cuba had been made a few weeks earlier by Leyland Motors, the British engineering concern, which had agreed to sell Cuba a total of 950 buses, worth about $25 million, to ease the chronic shortage of civilian transport in the island. While I was still in Havana in June, 1964, the Cubans took up their option on the second consignment of buses under the original contract. This considerable deal had predictable consequences. It aroused resentment in the State Department and other organs of the United States administration, and it drew some bitter comments in the American press, sections of which were furious

that, once again, it was the British, who were supposedly
America's best allies, who were defying and frustrating American policy toward Cuba. The British answer, given to me in
Havana, was that the United Kingdom was not yet a tamed
satellite of the United States and had to trade or die; that
nobody was yet at war with anybody else, and the American
blockade was proving ineffective in causing a Cuban collapse;
and that if the British did not supply the buses somebody else
would, probably somebody within the communist bloc.

The British followed up the sale of the buses with other
promising commercial ventures in Cuba. I learned about one of
these by chance as I was following my invariable habit of enjoying a final rum and squeezed lime juice on ice in the
Antilles Bar of the Hotel Libre before going to bed. It was
the evening before I was due to catch a morning plane to
Mexico City on my tortuous way back to New York. I was
sipping my drink in the company of Morris Rosenberg, one
of the few visiting American journalists to be seen in Havana
that year, when I spied two unmistakable Britons at one of
the marble-topped tables a few yards away.

How is it that Britons *are* so unmistakable when encountered in foreign parts? One or another attribute gives them
away—the fresh complexion, the Saxon look, the excellent cut
of the clothes, or the huffing and puffing in temperatures only
slightly above man's mean of sixty-eight degrees Fahrenheit.
On this occasion, it happened to be a combination of all these
factors. I knew I was taking no risk at all of their turning
out to be Germans, Russians, or even Hottentots, when I walked
over to their tables and introduced myself. They were a Mr.
Scott and a Mr. Rydehalgh, representatives of the well-known
firm of Sir William Halcrow and Partners, consulting engineers, and their mission in Havana added notably to the picture I had been getting of a confident Fidel Castro spreading
his economic wings and planning for the future of the new
Cuba that he hoped to create in his new status as manager of

a revolution if no longer its inspiration. The Halcrow concern had agreed to draw up plans for the modernization of six of Cuba's biggest ports—including Havana, Mariel, and Santiago —to handle the ten million tons of sugar per season that Castro was saying would be harvested from the plantations by 1970. Scott and Rydehalgh had inspected all the six chosen ports and were now going back to England with their diagram and their recommendations. They told me that within four months the first British engineers would be coming to Havana to start the impressive task that Castro had set them.

It so happened that this was the second piece of evidence I had gathered that day of the Cuban aim to improve relations with Western Europe. I had been told on about the best available authority in Havana that emissaries of Fidel Castro had invited the British Foreign Office to serve as a go-between with the Anglo-Dutch owners of the expropriated Shell refinery in Havana to find out whether a figure for the amount of compensation for the expropriation could be agreed upon. The Cuban regime had always given the impression since 1959—in the vaguest terms, to be sure—that it considered the acquisition of the Shell refinery to be not quite so absolute as the seizure of property belonging to American oil companies, and I had heard that Castro now considered the moment politically opportune for a settlement with Shell. (Alas, the budding negotiations of which I had learned that day had not come to fruition long afterward. I ascertained in New York that one reason why they withered was that Shell told the Cubans that it was not disposed to deal separately about its own refinery but would negotiate only when and if the American-owned refineries were included in negotiations.)

There were others besides the British, of course, who were probing the commercial possibilities of the new Cuba at this period. Spurred by the disclosure of the fat contract obtained by Leyland for the buses, the French had sent salesmen to find out if the Cubans wanted railroad locomotives, and the

Italians were offering textiles, and so on. The one-time tourist hotels were well filled with commercial ambassadors from countries of the Western world that were exploring the gaps in the American blockade, now a blunted instrument indeed. They were succeeding, too. Chartered ships carrying the merchandise of Britain, France, Canada, Spain, and Italy, as well as Japan and other countries on either side of the iron curtain, were gliding into the port of Havana by day and night, close by the American observer ship that one could see cruising constantly just outside the limit of Cuban territorial waters, reporting the traffic to Washington. Specialities such as ball bearings and a brand of light concrete produced in Denmark were among the cargoes coming in. Sugar and tobacco were the cargoes being taken out. Much of the trading was being done on barter terms, but in cases where the balance was against the Cubans they were being given almost unlimited credit by their eager suppliers, presumably on the grounds that Fidel Castro had become a good risk as a more or less permanent fixture.

Although the salesmen were obviously doing good business, many of them complained that it was an infuriating and exhausting ordeal to negotiate with the bureaucrats of the regime. There seemed always to be one man higher up the ladder to whom to refer responsibility. Che Guevara, who was still right at the top rung at that time, was forever telling his subordinates to take more initiative; with his usual bluntness, whenever he had something to say he criticized them openly in speeches that were widely disseminated by the newspapers and the radio and television. These criticisms were monitored in Miami and were seized as evidence that the Cuban economic and administrative machine was still floundering and possibly deteriorating. It struck me in Havana, as I noted the unmistakable fact that the regime was slowly improving its performance, that a safer interpretation might have been to assume that the admonitions by Guevara were having some effect. The Cubans were just finding it hard to learn, understandably

so since their tradition had never been one of brisk efficiency
in their daily lives. So, noncommercial visitors such as myself
found themselves still enmeshed in a bureaucracy that demanded
the completion of long and pointless questionnaires about themselves, the inevitable photographs at the rate of two and three
at a time, and tiresome journeys to the immigration offices,
the Cubana Airlines office, and the Department of Foreign
Affairs, far away from everywhere else. All these performances
had to be started days ahead of time to obtain exit permits,
plane reservations, and the like.

One might have thought that the Russians would put a
brake on the enlargement of Cuban contact with western nations, but in point of fact they seemed to be doing nothing
whatever to stop it. Although the Russian ambassador was
clearly under orders to keep a close eye on Fidel Castro, he
was not instructed, it seemed, to interfere with this process
of broadening the economic base of the revolution. Indeed,
some of the diplomats to whom I spoke thought that the Soviet
Union, confident that the country was now firmly under communist control, was seeking to lighten the financial burden that
the maintenance of Cuba had placed on her—a rough estimate
was that Cuba was costing her well over $300 million per
year—and was encouraging Fidel Castro in his new policy
while watching him to make sure that he did not go too far.
It was also suggested to me that the Soviet Union had realis-
tically deduced from what happened after it had taken the
gamble of placing offensive rockets in Cuba that the moment
had not yet come when it could pursue with advantage any
plans for the communization of Central and South America
by stages, for the American reactions during the crisis over
the missiles had been sharp and unwaveringly determined. Accordingly, ran the theory, Russia had placed her plans for
that area on ice and for a time would rest content with the
capture of Cuba; Russia would exploit the possibilities of co-
existing with the United States while both sized up the extent

of the menace presented by Communist China. This was hypothesis, of course, but it fitted the facts so far as these could be determined in Havana.

I had no doubt now, in mid-1964, that communism as a philosophy had gained a grip upon Cuba that would take some loosening. For one thing, those Cubans who were determined never to tolerate permanently either Fidel Castro or communism had gone at last, for the flow of fugitives had abated. It was now comparatively easy to obtain a seat on the supposedly daily plane leaving for Mexico City, provided one started early enough about booking it. The inference to be drawn here was that the remaining population, as a whole, was willing to live with communism and might eventually come to accept and embrace it. I had an eye-opener one evening when I went into a downtown district to watch the commencement ceremonies at the School of Revolutionary Instruction. Several thousand young Cubans dressed in the simple blue uniform of the militia had been brought by the truckload to fill the hall and they were gay, fervent, and demonstrative as they listened to one speaker after another addressing them from a dais that was occupied all the width of the hall by their teachers and party leaders. The chief speaker of the evening was Blas Roca, the top communist in Cuba, and he had a flattering hearing. Every point he made against the Yankees and in favor of the revolution brought applause and foot-stamping and several times he had to stop while the enthusiastic students chanted their battle cry of "Fee—del, Fee—del!"

Blas Roca himself made an interesting study for me. It struck me as I watched him that physically he was a Cuban version of Joseph Stalin, and the likeness was heightened by the plain white tunic he was wearing and the Stalinlike moustache he sported. Blas Roca had spent several years of exile from Cuba in Moscow in the days of Stalin. There was no doubt that he had become a political son of Stalin during that period, and as I watched him declaiming, in a rolling oratorical style acquired in the days before microphones became the fashion, I thought that he had gone to a lot of trouble to make himself look like a physical son as well.

He had even dutifully followed Stalin's example in giving himself an impressive assumed name. Stalin's real name was Joseph Vissarionovich Dzhugashvili—liquid-sounding but nothing like so effective, of course, as Stalin. I do not know the original name of his Cuban "son," but I have no doubt whatever that he became Blas Roca because he wished, like Stalin, to give himself an aura of implacable communistic determination and dynamism.

Apart from the kind of propaganda and indoctrination practiced at places like the School of Revolutionary Instruction, the regime was now in a position to make the revolution more palatable in other practical ways to the population in general. Food was more plentiful, and a clear effort was being made to make as much of it as possible available in the state-run restaurants. Prices had risen a lot in the past year and even a modest meal cost not much less than $8.00. But there was no lack of customers. I was impressed as I saw ordinary Cuban families paying anything between $35.00 and $50.00 for a meal together. The explanation for this phenomenon was not hard to find. There was a lot of loose money around in Havana in the form of internationally valueless pesos, and in the controlled and still strained economy of Cuba there were not many luxuries on which to spend it. A man could not buy himself a new car or a new house, and even rents were supposed not to exceed 10 percent of his income. So the regime was achieving two objects at the same time in tempting Cubans into the restaurants, all now run by the National Institute of Agrarian Reform through one of its subsidiary organisms. It was helping to keep Cubans satisfied with their new life under communism by appealing to their stomachs, and at the same time it was channeling back a lot of the loose money into its own keeping, for redistribution as and when needed.

One flew back, this time, into the rational world outside Cuba feeling that the weird experiment of imposing communism upon, of all places in the world, Havana, looked to be succeeding temporarily at last. But Havana had just not been made for this sort of regimentation and control of both the body and the mind. It had been built up over decades to cater to the pursuit of leisure and pleasure. The grandiose hotels were not intended for use by the proletariat as discussion halls for heavy political theorizing. The Tropicana and the other re-splendent night clubs and tourist haunts had not been meant for the presentation of ballets and "spectaculars" with deaden-ing communistic moral but for voluptuous and carefree and daredevil display. The very air of Havana was caressing, uniquely so. One would have said that it was just impossible to transform the very nature of this haven into something hard and drab. Yet, unmistakably, it was being done. And the im-pact of it all was even more stunning than if the same trick had been pulled upon New York, London or—damned be the thought!—Paris.

While in Havana I had been in almost daily touch with a young Canadian social worker who, as I have already described, had taken the fancy of Fidel Castro and Vallejo and had been briefly treated by them earlier as a young princess. She was still trying to make herself useful to the revolution, but the stars that had once been shining in her eyes were now eclipsed by clouds of doubt. We had many discussions over coffee and drab sandwiches in the Havana Libre, and again and again she showed that she was in the toils of indecision about whether to pursue her original idealistic course of taking out Cuban citizenship and devoting her life to serving the revolution or whether simply to give it all up and go home.

Her friend, Fidel Castro, was naturally mentioned continu-ously in our conversations. We never referred to him by his real name, for one never knew who might be listening in Havana.

We used the device of referring to him always as "Mr. Castle," so that any Cuban chancing to overhear our talk, in English, should not guess that we were discussing the illustrious Maximum Leader. She was not now in contact with him and Vallejo was also proving a little elusive. It seemed quite clear to me that they felt that my young friend had served her purpose. She had helped to tide "Mr. Castle" through a difficult period with her bright and pure personality, and that was that. Fatherlike, I told her I thought she should now go home and look afresh at Cuba from there, particularly after she had confided that a dark-skinned Cuban whose character she had not yet fathomed was pursuing her.

She countered most gallantly by defending her hero, "Mr. Castle." To her he was still the noble crusader fighting great odds and, for all his neglect of her as a friend, she still could not rid herself of the feeling that his revolution claimed her. When I last saw her before catching the plane to Mexico City she was bemused by indecision. But two months later I had a letter from her, written in Canada, telling me she had gone home in a Cuban cargo ship. The voyage had been eventful. She said that a U. S. military plane had buzzed the ship in international waters and a U. S. Navy destroyer had zipped across its bows at a range of a mere twenty-five yards "in spite of having the entire sea at its disposal." Even in harbor in Canada the freighter had been assailed. A group of Cuban counterrevolutionaries had tried to blow it up.

But the girl was now back at university, taking a course in Town Planning. I imagined her studying seriously in Montreal, cherishing only the memories of the dazzling, dreamlike experience which the workings of chance and good fortune had produced for her. But I was underestimating the allure of revolutionary Cuba. She could not get "Mr. Castle" or his revolution out of her system. Late in 1965 I had yet another letter from her. In it she said she had been again to Havana to make still another effort to decide her future. Now she was back in

Canada—but she was going back to Cuba. She thought that
the revolution had survived its most serious internal and external crises. She had found "Mr. Castle" to be as loved,
revered, and popular with the Cubans as ever he had been. So,
I mused, the magic had not vanished after that brief fairy tale
in Havana over a year earlier. Would she ever be able to put
"Mr. Castle" and all that he stood for, to her, out of her life?
I doubted that very much.

12 ✦ Clouded Skies

I HAD come away from Havana that June feeling no doubt
that Fidel Castro, for all his airy talk about not cooperating
with "certain persons," really did wish to find out if there
was any common ground upon which he and President Johnson
could build a bridge, however shaky and rudimentary, between
the governments of the two nations. He confirmed this to the
full early in July in his own bizarre style, in the form of a
serial-like interview with my friend Richard Eder, who, as the
resident correspondent in Havana of the New York *Times* at
this period, had been with me at the long session at the British
Embassy residence. The message that Fidel Castro wanted to
convey was perfectly clear, and the only difficulty about it was

that it was so one-sided. True to the tradition of twentieth-century dictatorship, he wanted a bargain in which the other side would yield the vital concessions he needed while he would only *appear* to be giving something away by performing actions that law, justice and plain decency demanded anyhow. What he really wanted was that the United States start buying his sugar again, thereby providing him with the money to build up his communist state, and that it forfeit any right to interfere with him in any way whatever while he was so doing.

It was, of course, a very saucy proposition considering all that had happened since 1959, and he sought to sweeten it in the hope of putting it over. He would stop giving material support to other Latin American revolutionaries if the United States would stop supporting counterrevolution against him. He would tacitly concede American rights to the base at Guantanamo by withdrawing his guards from a line about fifty yards from the perimeter to another one several hundred yards away. He promised, rather more vaguely, that one result of the resumption of relations would be the release of about 90 percent of the "something under fifteen thousand" political prisoners he still held; and even more vaguely he said that a later result would be discussions about indemnifying American companies whose properties had been seized in Cuba, although this would have to depend on a resumption of trade because Cuba would not be able to afford compensation until some time after this had begun.

He was making a bid, of course, to tempt the United States into accepting him as a permanency. He wanted it to stop trying to isolate him politically and economically, thrusting him as an ever more expensive luxury upon the Soviet Union, and to stop trying to bring the day nearer when his own people might grow tired of him and the privations that his revolution was still inflicting upon them. There was scant chance of the bid succeeding in the form in which it was framed, but even so I was taken aback by the speed with which it was rejected by the State Department. I had seen how Western European and other nations had been developing their trade with him and so frustrating the American blockade of Cuba, besides tending to make him permanently less dependent upon the United States, and I had detected some signs of material consolidation by his revolutionary regime within the island. There might have been some advantage in keeping him dangling. But Washington evidently had no doubt that time was on its side, despite temporary appearances to the contrary, and I must say that the trend of developments during the next twelve months seemed to confirm this. There came a series of unexpected shifts in the economic and political conditions governing this seesaw struggle between the United States and her cheeky tormentor to the south. They confirmed, once more, that it was a drama whose outcome simply could not yet be foreseen.

The change was only too apparent when I next visited Havana in July, 1965. Fidel Castro was not now the jaunty and confident adventurer of 1964, offering one-sided bargains, but a worried man who was showing both by deed and demeanor that he had some serious problems on his hands. He had had several unexpected setbacks which had hit him all the harder because they had come just at a time when his future was at last beginning to look a little rosier. The worst of them was economic. The hazards of the world sugar market had given him a bruising tumble.

In the previous autumn and winter he had turned with zest to the task of making the "Fifth Sugar Harvest of the People" one that would take him impressively further toward achieving the goal of a production of ten million tons by 1970. Some of the new cutting machines that he had obtained from the Soviet Union were put to work and, although it soon became clear that they would have to be strengthened and adapted if they were to function to full advantage on the very rough ground of the Cuban sugar fields, they certainly speeded up cane-cutting. Prompted by propaganda and probably stimulated to some ex-

tent by the modest but noticeable improvement in living conditions in 1964, thousands of volunteers surged into the fields
and helped to gather the harvest. Fidel Castro led the way.
He went to Oriente to cut sugar himself—with photographers
there to show him doing it and reporters waiting to record
how he cut faster and more furiously than anybody else.

The harvest was a revolutionary triumph. According to the
most reliable estimates I could get, it amounted to about 6.2
million tons, a notable improvement indeed on the 3.7 million
tons gathered the previous year. When the harvest was in, Cuban affairs looked more promising than at any time since 1959.
About one half of the harvest was to go to the Soviet Union
and other countries of the communist bloc at a price of six
cents a pound to pay, in part, for all the sustenance and aid
that Cuba was getting from her ideological partners and patrons. Most of the rest was available for purchase on the
world market by anybody else who wanted it—and that, importantly, did not include the United States.

But now came a big blow. The world found itself over supplied with sugar and sugar beet, and the bottom fell out of
the market. The price dropped until it held shakily at something under two cents a pound. Even if Fidel Castro could
have found customers for much of his sugar, the returns would
have been disastrously meager.

I do not know whether the collapse in the sugar market
was altogether a natural phenomenon of supply and demand.
I, for one, do not pretend to comprehend the complexities of
the world's sugar trade, but I must record that I found people
in Havana in July, 1965, who said they believed the United
States had provoked the collapse solely with the aim of squeez-
ing Fidel Castro in a classical economic grip by manipulating
the market. I think it probably did. The fact was that this
summer Cuban reserves of foreign currency had dwindled to
almost nothing. Its trade with Western Europe had dried up
because countries sensed that Fidel Castro was not now by

any means the good risk he had seemed to them a year ago,
and those splendid ventures such as the building of a grand
new fishing port in Havana and the modernization of other
ports round the island had had to languish. I reflected that
perhaps the United States *had* known what it was doing when
it had turned down Fidel Castro's bid for resumed trade a
year earlier.

Some other events had served to depress and disquiet him.
His friend and fellow-dictator Ahmed Ben Bella had been de-
posed overnight in Algiers in the spring. There had been a
bond of more than ordinary strength between these two. They
were in roughly the same position, each trying to hold together
a small country in a new phase of emancipation after decades
of control by a much stronger foreign power. Ben Bella had
visited Cuba and Che Guevara had attended a seminar in Algiers opened by Ben Bella on February 22, only weeks before
his unexpected fall. Some months earlier Fidel Castro had
caused negotiations to be opened between Cuba and Algeria
for the development of trade between them. Now Ben Bella had
gone, and his disappearance was a reminder of the truth,
proven time and again throughout history, that no man's hold
on power is so strong as to be unshakable. No wonder that
Fidel Castro, still fighting an uphill battle to hold a revolution
intact against odds that sometimes (as now) seemed to grow
instead of diminishing, was shaken when the news reached
him from Algiers. Some of his associates within the Cuban regime said that it had hit him harder than even news of the
assassination of President Kennedy.

Then there had been deductions to be drawn from the way
things had gone in Santo Domingo, so close at hand in the
Caribbean, and were going in distant Vietnam. In both these
lands the United States had reacted positively to developments.
In Santo Domingo it had intervened decisively, if clumsily and
perhaps unjustifiably, and in Vietnam it was showing beyond
all doubt its willingness to go a very long way indeed in sac-

rifice and cost to pursue a policy that it had set for itself.

Observers in Havana did not think that the rights or wrongs of American intervention in Santo Domingo were worrying Fidel Castro, for all the clamor that his newspapers and his television stations made about and against it; they felt that he saw very clearly that one reason why the Americans had landed there was to point a particular moral to him and a general one to any other would-be dictators in Latin America —the moral that, once bitten in Cuba, the United States did not intend to be bitten again anywhere else. They also argued that both in the Dominican Republic and in Vietnam there was another sobering lesson that Fidel Castro had not been slow to learn. American action of a quite determined and even extreme kind had *not* drawn any counteraction of much more substance than words from either Communist China or the Soviet Union. Suppose it had been he who had been attacked by the United States? Would his professed protectors have come in to save him? Or would they have done as they had in the instances now before him? He was reminded of the tense and perilous days of the great confrontation between Kennedy and Khrushchev, and the time when Khrushchev, after trumpeting that the Soviet Union would come to Cuba's aid if ever she were assailed, had hastily amended the statement very shortly after making it by saying that it was a symbolical one and was not to be taken absolutely literally. There was no certainty even now, after almost seven years in which his revolution had not only survived but in some respects had prospered, that some unlucky twist of circumstances would not bring the Marines into Havana. What then?

There had been an unsettling rift close to home, too. At the beginning of the year Che Guevara had set out on one of his periodic trips to keep in political touch, and perhaps to do some business, with friendly socialist (i.e., communist) nations far away from Cuba. He had gone in his capacity as Minister of Industries, on a tour lasting three months, to nine Asian

and African nations, including Communist China. Rather surprisingly, he had made some forthright speeches criticizing the
communist countries—including, of course, the Soviet Union
and his own—which were either contemplating or were actually
doing trade with the industrial nations of the West; and the
accompanying refrain of some of these speeches was that communist nations should not weaken as they strode toward the
goal of Utopia by giving sops in the form of material comforts
to their peoples.

One speech in particular, made in Algiers in the last week
of February, irritated Fidel Castro for two reasons. It showed
a Guevara who, most unusually, was expressing open disagreement with the current policy of his chief—and he was doing
so without any kind of contact or consultation with Havana.
One typical passage in the speech made in Algiers that caused
notable offense ran:

How can it signify "mutual benefit" to sell at world prices basic
materials which cause unlimited sweat and suffering to the backward
nations, and to buy at world prices the machines produced in the big
automated factories of today? If we establish this kind of relationship between the two groups of nations we must concede that the
Socialist countries are certainly accomplices in imperial exploitation.
It is possible to argue that the amount of interchange with the under-
developed countries constitutes an insignificant part of the foreign
trade of those countries. This big truth does not eliminate, however,
the immoral nature of the exchange. The Socialist countries have the
moral duty to liquidate their tacit complicity with the exploiting
countries of the west.

After he had come back to Havana on March 14, 1965,
Guevara simply disappeared from view, and he was still con-
spicuously absent when I was in Cuba toward the end of July.
Rumors of all brands swept through the capital and were
eventually aired in newspapers all over the world, with special
prominence in the anticommunist ones, which naturally just
loved such a mystery. The juiciest rumors I heard were (a) he

had shaved off his beard and was directing the rebels in Santo Domingo in their operations against the Americans; (b) similarly unshaven, he had gone to Washington as a defector and was helping the C. I. A. to prepare the doom of Fidel Castro; and (c) he had been despatched by his chief to Algiers to lead a movement for the return to power of Ben Bella.

There were several items of evidence that indicated beyond reasonable doubt that the missing Guevara was neither dead nor a defector. His photograph was still being prominently displayed in propaganda posters and at revolutionary meetings in Havana. His wife and daughter attended a massive rally addressed by Fidel Castro at Santa Clara on July 26, and were photographed in gay conversation with Celia Sánchez, Castro's faithful assistant and watchdog. During his speech Castro referred to Guevara, once only to be sure, but in complimentary terms as a "warrior of the revolution." Castro also demonstrated by his other public reactions to interest in the mystery of the missing third man of the revolution that Guevara had not been "liquidated," as the phrase of doom goes, or was yet irrevocably out of favor. Once, when reporters asked him what had happened to Guevara, he answered with unimpressive sarcasm, "If the West wants something to do, let it find out where he is"; and when questioned again later, as the absence of his former faithful friend became more widely commented upon, he answered, "You may be sure that wherever he is he is working for the revolution."

It seemed unbelievable to me that in a gossipy country like Cuba, where a secret used to be a rarity indeed, that one of the foremost figures of the revolution could be absent for months without *somebody* blabbing, but I found when I got there that this was indeed so. From the moment I landed at Havana airport from Mexico City on the evening of July 23, I tried every source I could tap for an answer to the intriguing question: Where is Che? In the end I obtained from the only diplomatic personage—a British one—who seemed to have information of merit an explanation that at the time appeared to be credible. It was that Guevara had been "put out to pasture" by Fidel Castro because, possibly for the first time in an almost brotherly association which had started when Castro was planning his assault upon Cuba in the middle 1950's, they had had a temporarily irreconcilable difference of opinion about the policy that ought to be followed. Fidel Castro had already been irritated by the independent line taken by Guevara during his tour, but, the story went, he had found Guevara unrepentant when the pair talked about this after the traveler returned. Guevara insisted that the fiber of the revolution would be permanently weakened if the recent policy of providing Cubans with more food and more consumer goods were followed. The revolution could not afford these inducements at the present time and their effect would be not to stimulate Cubans to work harder than ever for communism but to make them ultimately more slothful and unenthusiastic about continued sacrifices.

Castro's answer was said to be that the very opposite was true—that the revolution simply had to afford the incentives because if, after seven years of drabness and privation, Cubans were not given some compensation he could not feel sure about keeping their support, and this he needed now as badly as ever he did because of the serious economic pressures facing him; already he had detected an unwelcome increase in the number of people living off the revolution as unproductive bureaucrats, and production in some sugar and other factories was falling off alarmingly because, he felt, people were just getting tired of seeing little reward for the sacrifices they had made and were still making.

There was another aspect of the sudden division between the two men that, according to my diplomatic friend, seemed to have increased it. Guevara, who hitherto had always been regarded as a strong pro-Chinese supporter in the ideological rift within the camp of world communism, was said now to have come back from this latest visit to Communist China deeply disappointed with the economic state of the country and pessimistic about prospects for the future there—so much so indeed that he now urged Fidel Castro to take Cuba without reservations into the Soviet communist fold on the theory that the Soviet Union represented, for all her present limitations and deviations from the true path to communistic fulfillment, the hope for the future. Fidel Castro was reported to have made the only obvious response to this somewhat impetuous suggestion—that as a fledgeling new state Cuba had no alternative but to maintain friendship with both her big allies and, as a matter of opportunistic politics, to play one off the other whenever a chance was offered.

It was clear, my informant said, that two men holding such contrary views could not possibly go on working with each other until one or the other was proved right; but the bond between them was far too strong to be snapped violently and forever. At the end of a long discussion, it was agreed that it would be useless for Guevara to continue as Minister for Industries, and Castro resolved the matter by sending Guevara with his family into the Cuban countryside to cool off and, perhaps, come back into service when either or both of them felt that they could resume the partnership—a rather idyllic one, it always appeared to me—that had been so unexpectedly broken.

The story was later accepted as being substantially true, although Castro did his best to try and foist a substitute one upon the world. The only important particular in which it erred was in assuming that the political quarrel between the two men was repairable. It was in fact complete.

Castro was at his most tantalizing and his most cunning when he lifted the veil on the mystery of Guevara. He did so by inches and to the accompaniment of startling off-stage music composed for the purpose of distracting attention from the cutting blow of Guevara's departure. He started the process by telling an audience celebrating the fifth anniversary of the foundation of the Committees for the Defense of the Revolution that in a few days he would read to the public a document which would explain the absence of Guevara for so many months. "Read it now," clamored his hearers. "No, not now," answered Castro. "I haven't got the document with me." But he duly read it out five days later at a meeting of Cuba's only political party, the United Party of the Socialist Revolution. It turned out to be a remarkable letter which, said Castro, had been written by Guevara and handed to Castro on April 1, six months and two days earlier. It ran, in full:

Havana
Year of Agriculture

Fidel:

At this moment I recall many things, of when I met you in the home of María Antonia, of when you proposed that I come, of all the tension in the preparations. One day they came to ask who should be informed in case of death, and the real possibility of the fact was a blow to all of us. Later we learned that it was true, that in a revolution one triumphs or dies if it is a real one. Many comrades fell along the road to victory. Today everything has a less dramatic tone because we are more mature, but the event repeats itself.

I feel that I have done my duty, which tied me to the Cuban Revolution in its territory, and I take leave of you, of the comrades, of your country, which is already mine. I formally resign from my posts in the leadership of the party, from my ministerial post, from my rank of major, from my condition as a Cuban. Nothing legal binds me to Cuba, only ties of another kind, which cannot be broken like appointments.

Reviewing my past life, I believe I have worked with sufficient honesty and dedication to consolidate the revolutionary triumph. My only shortcoming of some gravity is not having confided in you more from the first moments in the Sierra Maestra and not having realized with sufficient celerity your qualities as a leader and a revolutionary. I have lived magnificent days and I felt at your side the pride of belonging to our country during the luminous days of the Caribbean crisis. Few times has a statesman shone more brilliantly

than on those days. I am also proud of having followed you without hesitation, identified with your way of thinking, seeing, and of
estimating dangers and principles.

Other lands of the world demand the aid of my modest efforts.
I can do what is denied you by your responsibility as head of Cuba,
and the time has come for us to separate. Let it be known that I
do so with a mixture of happiness and pain. Here I leave the purest
of my hopes as a builder and the dearest of my dear ones, and I
leave the people who accepted me as a son. That wounds a part
of my spirit.

In the new fields of battles, I will carry the faith you instilled in
me, the revolutionary spirit of my country, the sensation of complying with the most sacred of duties: to struggle against imperialism
wherever it may be. This heals and more than cures any laceration.
I say once again that I free Cuba from any responsibility save what
stems from her example: that if the final hour comes to me under
other skies, my last thought will be of this country, particularly of
you.

I thank you for your teachings and your example and I will try
to be loyal to you to the last consequences of my acts. I have always
been identified with the foreign policy of our Revolution and I still
am. Wherever I am, I will feel the responsibility of being a Cuban
Revolutionary and I will act as such. I do not leave my children
or my wife anything material, and I am not ashamed. I am glad it
is thus. I do not require anything for them, for the State will give
them enough with which to live and be educated.

I would have many things to tell you and our people, but I feel
they are unnecessary. Words cannot express what I would like to
say, and it is not worthwhile to fill pages. To victory always, fatherland or death, I embrace you with all revolutionary fervor,   Che

Castro's official version is, then, that Guevara, having finished his tour of duty in Cuba, had left for "other lands" where
he can continue the "struggle against imperialism." But can
the truth be so simple?

When this text was studied by the world outside Cuba there
were many who said immediately that it was a forgery. Some
believed that it was a doctored suicide note. Others felt that

Guevara, a man known for his stubbornness and individuality, could not possibly have written such fulsome sentences as appeared in it. My own opinion was that it was probably genuine, even though the story it told was not true but was an agreed version to cover the unpalatable facts of the fundamental differences about revolutionary policy which had arisen between Castro and Guevara. The note seemed to me to bear the stamp of Guevara authorship. I had always been struck by the distinctive and quite graceful literary style of Guevara and, as the reader will already have noted, I had been impressed since 1959 by the affection and obvious admiration which Guevara felt for Castro. I thought it quite likely that as a final gesture to the man to whom he had always been so loyal he would cooperate in an agreed formula to explain his departure. I also noted that a week or two after disclosing the letter Castro spoke with apparent, if unusual, sincerity about his lost friend. Describing their last meeting to a small company of journalists on October 31, 1965, he stated: "We said farewell. It was tough . . . a moment of great emotion, because of the time we had been together and the great love we had for each other." In the same informal interview Castro said that, of course, he knew where Guevara had gone but he would not say where this was. He added, pointedly: "And he is in the best of health."

Thus was one of the greatest mysteries of the Cuban revolution disclosed—and glossed over. Unlike Shakespeare's Julius Caesar, Fidel Castro did not bare his anguish at the unkindest cut of all. Not for him a cry of "Et tu, Che." No, instead, he went to spectacular trouble to ensure that friend and enemy alike was given something other than his grievous loss of Guevara to think about. In the same speech on September 29 in which he promised to read the document written by Guevara he made the electrifying announcement that Cubans with relatives in the United States could leave the island and join these relatives if they wished; and he followed up by challenging the United States to accept this proposition and make the necessary arrangements to carry it out. In the event, after considerable maneuverings, the exodus was made. For a while, the little coastal village of Camarioca, a few miles from Varadero, had its name in the headlines and on the news bulletins as the setting for the departure of Cubans going to the great land to the north. This was the place where six years earlier I had snorkeled among the coral and the tropical fish off its delectable little coves; watched the villagers play baseball in its rough fields; and, not quite hardy enough to participate myself, seen them going off to the cockfights every Wednesday evening. . . .

Of course, everybody wanted to know during this pulsating, latter-day phase of the revolution why Fidel Castro had so suddenly made his unexpected gesture. I have advanced one reason which at any rate explains its timing—to capture world attention which would otherwise have been turned with uncomfortable intensity upon the defection of Guevara. Having been so recently in Havana, I did not need much reflection to think of others, all advantageous to Castro, which would account for the move:

1. He could calculate with considerable confidence that there would be no mass departure to damage the revolution in the eyes of the world. As I knew for myself, the vast majority of those who wished, and were able, to leave Cuba had already gone. Those who would now go were people of whom he would be glad to be rid; the loss of even a considerable number of elderly, disabled and disgruntled thousands would strengthen the revolution both economically and politically.

2. Opening the gates of the island-prison, even though only partially, would do much to reduce discontent in Cuba. I had heard enough in Havana in the last year to show me that one of the most harmful factors upon Cuban morale had been a feeling of utter isolation. I had noted in July and August that the population was in bad need of just such a tonic as Castro was now delivering.

3. If the United States refused to cooperate, it would suffer diplomatically. If it did cooperate, it would be reopening contact with the revolutionary regime, and this had been an objective of

Castro for some time. And its acceptance of still more refugees from Cuba would intensify the burden it was already carrying in Florida and elsewhere.

4. There were obvious propaganda values in the move. The prestige of the revolution would benefit if, as Castro calculated, the vast majority of the population stayed with him. Pro-Castro elements all over Latin America would be given some extremely valuable ammunition.

One could advance other reasons to justify Fidel Castro's spectacular gambit. I believe the foregoing are sufficient in themselves to explain it.

With Guevara absent from his side, and his relationship with his half brother, Raul, certainly no warmer than it ever had been—and that was none too warm—Fidel Castro was now really alone at the summit of power in Cuba. The men with whom he had felt any sort of kinship had gone, one after the other, since 1959, and in this hot and bothersome summer of 1965 he seemed to have nobody at all upon whom he could draw for inspiration and the warm, comforting companionship that comes to men who have shared years of experiences, and dangers, and know sometimes without the utterance of a word what the other thinks, senses, fears, or deduces. The split with Che Guevara had brought him to the end of a long road leading to utter isolation. It had always been inevitable that he should come to this. He was unique, removed from all other men in the end by the chemistry of mind and body that gave him the mystical and mysterious quality of leadership and the power that springs therefrom. Like Churchill, he could assemble no lack of men who would subordinate and spend themselves in serving him—and I always felt that Guevara was his Anthony Eden—but eventually each and all of these men must droop and fall away because they are outshone, dried up, and burned out by the consuming brilliance of the leader who has drawn them to him.

Fidel Castro now had only two men who were just slightly

closer to him than anybody else, and he was not drawn to either of them by any deep spiritual bond forged over the years. One was Dr. Osvaldo Dorticos, his puppet President, and the other was Vallejo, his physician. Dorticos was a pallid, doctrinaire lawyer-communist, with little humor and no personality worth talking about; he was brought physically closer to Castro simply because he was the President—and Castro just had to have somebody in that position. Vallejo had rather more to give. He was alert, cultivated, and a skillful doctor, and whenever I saw the two of them in public I felt that he had a deep fondness for, and a protective instinct toward, Fidel Castro. The young Canadian social worker who, as I have related, spent a hectic week in their company, told me that Vallejo showed by almost everything he said and did that he wanted to protect Fidel Castro not only from the rigors of his lonely and increasingly desperate and demanding role at the top of the revolution but from the debilitating effects of his habit of overextending himself physically and mentally, as if he had an instinctive feeling that he might not have long to fulfill the messianic role that he imagined destiny had allotted to him; and she also said that quite often Fidel Castro would turn to Vallejo whenever some point of politics or policy came up in conversation and would check it with the calm doctor even though, she surmised, he by no means necessarily took any account of what Vallejo might say.

The diplomats now told me that Vallejo was their recognized channel to Castro. If one of them wanted to see Castro, wanted to know whether he would be attending this or that party or function, or wanted a reminder to be passed on, he would first telephone or seek out Vallejo. So there was an association of some value between the two men, but it was no substitute for the understanding he had enjoyed for so long with Guevara. And some of the diplomats thought it significant that he had never found a fellow spirit or a supporting confidant among the professional communist functionaries—such as Blas Roca and Carlos Rafael Rodriguez—who had come into his regime after the victory had been won in 1959.

One of the purposes of my visit to Havana in 1965 was to observe- whatever fun and unusual activity there might be during celebrations of the twelfth anniversary of the birth of the 26th of July Movement, from which the revolution had sprung. On July 26, 1953, a band of dedicated but rather foolhardy young men whom Fidel Castro had gathered to him in Oriente Province made a frontal attack with rifles and machine guns on a big, bare house being used as barracks by troops serving Fulgencio Batista to support his dictatorial, and by most accounts tyrannical, regime. As might have been expected—since an assault upon a barracks, of all places, is a grim proposition even when made by an experienced force heavily superior in numbers and fire power—an attack by a force of young amateur soldiers led by the twenty-eight-year-old Fidel Castro was a bloody failure. Of the 165 who took part, about sixty were either killed on the spot or were afterward tortured and slaughtered.

Among those who escaped without a scratch was Fidel Castro, as he was to escape in all subsequent adventures and escapades, including the hazardous and costly landing in the yacht *Granma* and the subsequent campaign of two years in the Sierra Maestra that brought him to power. To be sure, he was captured with almost all the rest of the survivors at Moncada and sentenced to fifteen years' imprisonment; but he was released after one year in one of the periodic political amnesties that used to mark prerevolutionary history in Cuba (there was not one during the first seven years of the Castro regime). His long record of extraordinary immunity from the risks of combat has not passed unnoticed in Cuba. Many Cubans who regard him as their country's savior have told me

fervently that they attribute it to the workings of providence
ensuring that he should be saved until his destiny is fulfilled;
the soured ones in 1965 who were tolerating him and his scab-
rous revolution because they had no option but to do so told
me it showed that he always took the greatest possible care
to avoid danger when a fight was on, or, as some put it much
more bluntly, that it showed he was a coward.

Although the episode at Moncada was futile and costly in
human life, it gave Fidel Castro a crop of martyrs and a
glamorous propaganda basis on which to build an organization
for the mounting of the revolution on which his heart was set.
The 26th of July Movement—a noncommunist affair, be it
noted, and even a nonpolitical one in the sense that it was
affiliated with no party at all—became the emblem of his revolution. And even though it was quickly submerged in the
hectic maneuverings and juggling that followed the capture
of Havana in January, 1959, it served with increasing importance year after year as an original symbol to be honored
and as an excuse for a national holiday.

The site of the formal celebration of the anniversary was
moved from one city to another each year, to bring all sections
of the country eventually within its scope, and each July 26
Fidel Castro journeyed to the chosen city to make an impassioned oration in memory of the martyrs and to exhort the
whole population via radio and television to make still further
efforts, still more sacrifices, for the revolution. This year the
site was Santa Clara, in the province of Las Villas, which had
a proud claim of its own to recognition as a revolutionary
landmark, for it was here that in the last week of 1958 two
columns of rebels led by Camilo Cienfuegos and Ernesto Guevara routed the last remnants of Batista's fighting force and
opened a way for a drive upon Havana.

Thousand upon thousand of Cubans were taken to Santa
Clara from all over the island to enjoy the celebration and to
see and hear the Maximum Leader. Many of them traveled

hundreds of miles in considerable discomfort, sitting on chairs or just boxes in Czech-made utility trucks while others relaxed in the comparative luxury of a Leyland bus. The official estimate of the crowd of visitors that overwhelmed Santa Clara for two days was half a million, and the journalists, diplomats, and others who also went there agreed that there was the usual uncertainty about the proportion that went there spontaneously in revolutionary fervor and that which went because there was no option but to obey the orders of local functionaries such as factory stewards and officials of the hundreds of branches of the Committee for the Defense of the Revolution that flourished everywhere.

Castro made two of his marathon speeches to the multitude. The first, lasting about two hours, came when he presented awards to several hundred workers who had distinguished themselves in the fields during the gathering of the sugar harvest. The only notable fact about this occasion was the preference shown by the winners for the kind of prize they wanted. There were two alternatives. They could have either a free trip to one of the communist countries allied with Cuba or they could have more material prizes such as refrigerators, television sets, or other consumer goods. Not surprisingly, 420 out of the 500 prizewinners chose the material awards and Fidel Castro, although clearly disappointed that so few wanted to see the wonders of the communistic world outside Cuba, quickly suppressed his feelings and with a show of jocularity went along, once again, with his people. "All right," he said, with an expansive wave of the arms, "next year we'll have more refrigerators and fewer trips." There were two points worth noting here. One was that Fidel Castro had been correct in sensing during the past few months that Cubans really did need incentives to keep them in line. The other was his quick sense of the appropriate in protecting and preserving his image as the understanding and beneficent father of his country.

The second speech was one of exactly three hours, made as a climax to the celebrations in the early evening, when the blistering summer sun was at last waning. It was relayed all over Cuba by television, and I was able to watch and listen to the performance at ease in a cool room in Havana. The cameras were trained relentlessly upon Fidel Castro with only a few brief respites for the whole of the three hours, and I had an excellent chance to observe and assess this remarkable man as he now was, until his droning voice so dulled my senses that I could absorb no more and was left wondering how those half-million people standing like a restless army in front of him could possibly withstand such punishment. I do have to confess, though, that the interjections and the applause were just as keen toward the end of the speech as they had been at the start.

But Fidel Castro that day was not the impassioned and inspired leader of yesteryear. For one thing, he looked much older than when I had last seen him just a year earlier. There was a look of middle age about him—he was now thirty-nine—and I thought as I watched him that physically he belonged to that common Latin type that blooms early and ages early. His delivery was also by no means as sharp and attractive as it had been, and the content of the speech was fuzzy and often tedious. There was none of the old defiance and taunting of the Yankee imperialists—not a single joke in the whole of the three hours—and even when he made such exclamations as, "All the divisions which the United States may send anywhere will not stop the world revolution" and "Revolution in Latin America is inevitable, with or without Cuba," one felt that he was saying these things not from a fiery conviction but because they were expected of him. My impression of him as he rambled on and finished his oration exactly on the dot of a duration of three hours was that here was a Fidel Castro who, deep within himself, was now worried and unsure. Was it the utter loneliness, brought home by the loss of Che Guevara, that was unnerving him? Was it the dismaying pressure of mounting financial and economic troubles? Was it an eleventh-hour realization that he could not hope, after all, to survive the relentless hostility of the United States, and that if a new challenge came soon he could not rely on rescue from the distant east? Or was it some secret knowledge, maybe only even a suspicion, that time was running out for him within Cuba itself? That the latent hostile forces which he had never been able to eradicate were growing and preparing to move against him at last? I pondered these questions as I watched him droning on, the words not cascading from him in a torrent as of old but seeming almost to be dragging themselves from him. I could not divine the answer, of course. But I was as certain as I could be that here was a troubled man on the defensive. And I had never before had this impression of Fidel Castro since I had first set eyes upon him in 1959. I had seen him petulant and off form, yes, but never so somber and preoccupied as this. Would that old resilience reappear and lift him from this obvious depression? Or was I seeing, at last, the first signs of a permanent decay?

Certainly, there was muttering in plenty in Havana, but it was not political in the sense that it sprang directly from anti-Castroism or anticommunism. It was a complaint against non-fulfillment, and only in that sense was it inferentially anti-revolutionary. People were just getting tired of privation and denial of the good things of life. The concessions by the regime in making available a slightly more varied diet and a few more things for the home and the adornment of the body had had the effect of whetting the appetite for more and, accordingly, a possibly dangerous spiral had been started. This was in essence what the reported argument between Fidel Castro and Che Guevara had been about.

But the propaganda apparatus of the revolution was far better organized to interest and influence the people than I had ever known it. The anniversary of the 26th of July Movement was used most adroitly. A series of shows and exhibitions— circuses, in some respects—were put on in the capital to be- guile the population and at the same time convey to them an impression of the marvelous feats of the revolution in broaden- ing and expanding the economy of the country. I could scarcely credit the accuracy of my ears when early on my first morning in my bedroom on the twenty-first floor of the one-time Hilton Hotel I was awakened by the lowing of cattle.

I have heard some strange noises and seen some extraordi- nary sights in Havana, but this was something I had never ex- pected. There were indeed cows quartered in stalls put up on a clearing off Twenty-third Street, three hundred yards from the hotel—about a dozen of them, labeled "half-Holstein." They had been brought into the capital as an attraction in an ex- hibition designed to demonstrate what the revolution had done, and was still doing, for the Cuban dairy industry. This was a very good exhibition indeed, even though some of the posters on the walls managed to include in the story they told of the history of the dairy industry some fairly irrelevant shafts at Spanish cruelty and Yankee greed, and for three days long queues of Cubans formed around it and people waited patiently for hours to get in and shuffle through it.

One day I joined them. I paid my few cents to enter and dutifully read the posters, looked at the ancient milk carts, butter churns, and milking stools that offset the grand new milking machines and laboratory exhibits on view, admired the half-Holsteins (splendidly manicured), and wound up the ex- perience by paying sixty cents for a container of yogurt and some delicious ice cream and cake. I ate this in the open air from a chest-high circular wooden pedestal, and as I dined with enjoyment I was able to take a leisurely close look at the Cu- bans around me.

Without doubt they were, as a whole, better dressed and hygienically smarter—better laundered, shall I say—than a year before and earlier than that. But there were one or two

anachronisms to set against the fresh print dresses, the lip-
stick, and the nylon stockings of the young women. There was,
for instance, the young chap whom I saw wearing a pair of
soccer football boots with the studs taken out. They were a
quiet crowd, for Cubans, and here I had no evidence of open
or covert grumbling, probably because of the soothing effect
of that excellent yogurt and ice cream, and perhaps also because the exhibition *did* seem to show that in this Year of
Agriculture the regime was building up the dairy industry.
But one feat it had not yet achieved was an off-the-ration
supply of milk; only rarely could the waiters in the coffee
shop of the Havana Libre Hotel produce milk to go with the
tea or coffee. There seemed to be a long way to go before the
target of a production of thirty million bottles of milk a day
would be reached.

Another exhibition on Twenty-third Street was a far less
attractive affair, but it drew just as big and possibly greater
crowds. It was a display of photographs and such relics as
bloodstained tunics said to have been salvaged from the slaugh-
ter of the assault on the barracks at Moncada. Some of the
photographs were grisly, as usual for Cuba, but others were
historically interesting, such as extracts from the log of the
yacht *Granma* and roughly penciled orders of the day issued
in the Sierra Maestra by Fidel Castro. It was while I was
touring this exhibition that I realized that the Cuban revolution now has just as authentic veterans as the campaigns of
the First and Second World Wars. I was attracted to a small
group of Cubans listening to a comparatively old and untidy
man with a stubbly beard who was telling them old soldier's
tales. He told them how, as a rebel in Che Guevara's outfit, he
had chased the terrified Batistianos from one street to another
in the Battle of Santa Clara and had then ridden in triumph
along the dusty roads to Havana. When he had finished his tale
the admiring youngsters patted him on the back and went on to
look at the next batch of photographs on the wall.

One had to probe a little below the surface of life to avoid being misled by a superficial impression that an improvement in conditions here and there meant that the revolution was prospering. One needed the evidence of friends and acquaintances whom one had known since 1959 to hear the truth. It was given to me by one particularly fearless young man who did not mind speaking out to a foreigner. "They've got a tougher stranglehold on us than ever, but they need it because they simply are not delivering the goods," he said. "Here we are seven years after liberation and we are still grubbing for enough to eat and for even the basic elements of a life worth living. I don't know how much longer he expects us to wait. . . ."

This young man had had his troubles with the regime. Some months earlier he had been so outspoken in his criticisms that his fellow workers had denounced him and accused him of trafficking in the black market. The G2 inquisitors had tried hard to fasten black marketing offenses upon him but had failed. Then, finding that he spoke several languages and knew a lot of people in Havana and a lot about life in the city, they had tempted him with an offer to enroll him in their service at a good salary. "What! Me wear that militia monkey suit?" he had told them, indignantly. Perhaps because they were bowled over by his audacity, they had let him go. Months later he was still free.

Cubans are forever surprising one with their effervescence and their lightninglike changes of mood, and this is probably the reason why it is often so difficult to predict what they will do next and how they will react to shifting circumstances. This thought came to mind one afternoon when I dropped in casually upon one of the numberless political seminars being held in the city during the celebrations. A young woman who had come to Cuba from one of the other Latin American countries as a guest of the revolutionary regime was fulminating emotionally against the deeds of the Yankees in Vietnam. She ended al-

most sobbing as she described how they had been dropping bombs
on women and children. "Yes, tiny children," she cried, wring-
ing her hands as she held them aloft. The audience was composed mostly of young men who had been given time off from
their jobs to attend the afternoon session. They rose impul-
sively to their feet and almost drowned her closing words with
their handclapping and their cries of sympathetic anger. It
was a demonstrative Latin American moment. But, to my astonishment, only one minute later these same young men were
swaying with laughter as they cracked none too delicate jokes
about the size, shape, and awkwardness of women volunteers
filmed as they helped to gather the harvest in the blazing hot
sugar fields. The bombs on the children were all forgotten now,
it seemed.

From the seminar I strolled round to a modest restaurant
on one of the arcades flanking Parque Central for an early
supper. This evening it was bean soup, a plain piece of liver,
one spotty potato, and a small fruit tart for $3.50, with an
extra sixty cents for the beer that washed it down. This price
was comparatively reasonable in the ruling conditions. One day
I was entertained to lunch by an official of the government
at La Torre, a restaurant reserved exclusively for diplomats
and official personages. We did not stint ourselves—I for one
was quite willing to use this unique chance to compensate myself for the drab nourishment I had been enduring for some
days!—but even so the bill of $22.00 was high enough. Yet
despite the high prices I noticed again, as I had done so a
year earlier, that there were plenty of Cubans paying them.
It was even more surprising that they should do so now, for
there had been a rise of at least 25 percent in restaurant
charges in the interval.

Cubans told me that a black market of all-embracing scope
was making it possible for anybody dabbling in the traffic in
smuggled spare parts and commodities of all kinds to treat a
peso as if it were a mere twenty cents instead of a dollar in

equivalent value. No wonder I found myself being importuned on all sides for American cigarettes; they were worth $4.00 a packet on the black market. A bottle of good Scotch whisky was a prize indeed, worth $40.00 and $50.00 to anybody with a bottle to sell. Even a banana fetched twenty cents when sold off the ration. And the authorities did not seem to be waging any kind of serious war against either the black market or the inflation. I was told, in fact, that rising prices in the restaurants, the bars, and the few places of amusement still open were being deliberately encouraged. A spokesman for the Ministry of Foreign Relations told me they were being used as an instrument to hasten the process of drawing back into government possession the loose money that was still in circulation. The man said that once it was seen that money was becoming tight again and that people were no longer able to spend so lavishly in the bars and restaurants the prices would be reduced. It would be good propaganda to be able to order an all-round reduction, he said, for Cubans would regard it as a sign of improving economic well-being. . . .

So the time came for me once again to leave this fantastic never-never land just ninety miles south of Miami. As dawn was breaking on the ocher city, I packed my bag and tried to marshal my impressions and make my guesses. There had been plenty to observe and estimate on the surface—but there was so much more that was hidden from the visitor. There were two thousand Russians, including quite a number of fully trained soldiers, in Cuba—but I had seen only one here and there, an inoffensive-looking civilian carrying a slender attaché case. Fidel Castro had an army of about two hundred thousand at his command, with about a hundred thousand in reserve—far and away the most powerful in the Caribbean. All I had seen of it had been a few soldiers lounging about off duty, and those bored-looking militiawomen still stationed at strategic corners, but sitting down at ease now on comfortable chairs with their rifles across their knees, waiting for the Marines.

The revolution seemed to be robbing Cuban womanhood of the fey attractiveness it had once had. I recalled with momentary depression that not once this time had I heard anywhere the uninhibited shriek or even the rippling soprano laughter of an amused woman. I recalled also the gaping empty windows of the dress shops in the midtown streets—and I recalled the grotesque sight I had noted in the window of one once-elegant establishment in Calle Neptuno. One of those wax models of the female form divine had been adorned with the black beret, olive-green tunic and trousers, the cheap black boots, and the black and red armband of the 26th of July Movement. The legend on the armband ran, *"Acción Femenina: Prov. Habana"* (Women's Division: Province of Havana). Beyond this monstrous travesty of a fashion show lay the red flag of the Soviet Union, draped on a pedestal to serve as a blending background. Was *this* what communism would do to women? Was this then the ultimate in revolutionary chic?

There was the rationing, too. Here in Cuba, after almost seven years of operation on an island so fertile that almost anything would sprout, the revolution could still only provide people with twelve ounces of meat each a week, one quart of milk per day for five persons, and three ounces of coffee for each person per week. I had understood the drabness and the shortages two or three years earlier when the eager revolutionaries had dismantled one kind of economic system and had not yet been able to replace it with another, but it was now beginning to look as if they never would do that. Perhaps the spectacular experiment in Cuba was at last betraying the inherent incapacity of communism, totalitarianism, dictatorship, socialism—call it what you will—to turn theory into practice.

Half a million Cubans could still be taken to Santa Clara to shout their huzzas and to cheer and applaud Fidel Castro, but they might not go on doing so for much longer. Castro himself was aging, like his revolution. He looked harassed, as if possessed by some secret anxiety, or was becoming worn down at last by his self-imposed burden. It had all seemed so different only a year earlier. Now, for the first time in almost seven years, I was leaving Havana feeling that he might have passed his zenith and that he no longer represented a permanence. A long line of dictators have risen and fallen in my own lifetime, and most of them have gone suddenly and violently when the game has been up—Mussolini, Hitler, Trujillo and, most recently of all, Fidel Castro's own friend Ben Bella. I could no longer convince myself that Fidel Castro might be an exception.

13 • *Narrow Options*

MY TALE is told. It has taken us a very long way since that unforgettable New Year's Day of 1959 when sudden victory turned the revolution from a hazy shadow on the Cuban horizon into a stormy reality of which the whole world had to take account. I have described the early surging years, when Fidel Castro, burning to liberate his people from the bonds of domestic and foreign servitude but (as I saw him) a bungling amateur withal, was there for the taking. I have closed the narrative with him and his revolution at a point of new danger—at a moment when it seemed at last as if inevitable wear and tear, relentless pressure and hostility from the one power capable of destroying both the man and his machine, and some inherent flaw in communistic performance, might be overwhelming him at last.

All that remains now is to take a second, reflective look at what happened in seven crowded and mostly confusing years and then to turn to the much more hazardous task of guessing at the future. As far as the first proposition is concerned, one dominating puzzle faces the inquirer: How can it possibly have happened that in 1966 the United States was still being plagued by an irrational and rather comical-looking Cuban who in 1959 was regarded by almost everybody as just another temporary tinpot figurehead in the unstable world of Latin America? In facing this question, as in making a dabble into the future, I shall be mostly expressing opinion as opposed to relating fact, and the reader will be entitled to agree or disagree as he chooses.

There is, of course, one facile way of explaining away Fidel Castro's unexpectedly lengthy survival. It is to say that the shameful failure of the Bay of Pigs invasion guaranteed his survival for years to come after 1961. Certainly that American catastrophe was about the luckiest thing that ever happened during the outstandingly charmed life of Fidel Castro, but it by no means supplies a full answer. One might just as well argue that the failure of the British and French to stop Hitler's advance into the Rhineland in 1936 made the Second World War inevitable, or that Hitler's later defeat in Russia *guaranteed* that Germany would lose that war. In the case of Fidel Castro, there were many factors operating in the development of his fortunes before and after the bungled invasion. Each played its part to greater or lesser degree. To me, two of these factors were of permanent importance and would probably have made Castro's survival certain even if the Bay of Pigs episode had never happened. They were:

1. The message that Fidel Castro brought into Havana at the beginning of 1959—one of promise for independence, emancipation, and prosperity—could not but appeal to the Cuban masses, even

though it tolled a bell for the minority, and as long as there was even
the slightest chance of its fulfillment nobody who either willingly or
unwillingly stayed in the island would do anything decisive to stop
him. After all, as I have mentioned earlier, no Cuban even felt sufficiently impassioned against him to try to assassinate him. To kill
him was, surely, the one certain way of ending his revolution—for
there was never anybody on the scene after the death of Camilo
Cienfuegos who looked likely to be able to succeed him—but he was
never even molested by a fellow Cuban for over seven years.

2. American policy toward Fidel Castro was never ruthless
enough, or even sufficiently definite and determined, to knock him
off his throne. It was indeed this lack of resolution that preserved
him at the time of the invasion. If President Kennedy and his advisers had really possessed the will to destroy the Castro revolution
and let the consequences go hang they could have done so easily and
without much further bloodshed. And, of course, they should have
done so on logical grounds, for there was no sense whatever in promoting such a venture, even by indirect and covert means, if they did
not really intend to thrust it through to its successful end.

It seems to me that one of the reasons why the United States
fared so dismally and for so long in its effort to topple Fidel
Castro was that it was simply not psychologically or politically prepared for his triumph in 1959 and never became so
for almost six years. I think I can place the moment when it
became apparent that at last the United States had done so.
This was in the spring of 1965, when the Marines were sent
into Santo Domingo. Even then, America seemed still to be
afflicted with lingering symptoms of cool feet—I won't go so
far as to call them cold feet—for it shilly-shallied and even
prevaricated about why it was doing what it did, and by most
accounts was none too skillful in the postoperative, restorative
maneuverings there. But at least President Johnson did indicate
that the United States was not going to stand any more nonsense and defiance or treachery in Latin America, and I have
no doubt that this newfound resolution was one of the reasons
why I found such a noticeable depression in the Castro camp

when I went to Havana in the summer of 1965. There were other contributing reasons, of course, but I do think that evidence of increasing American toughness was as strong as any of them.

When Fidel Castro and his *barbudos* (bearded ones) overthrew Batista and his men, they took almost everybody by surprise. Few had believed that this would ever happen. I recall that there had even been much doubt only a little while beforehand about whether Castro was still alive. It became instantly clear that neither the State Department nor America's friends and allies had any plans to deal with the crisis that the rebel victory had created. Why, the British government had only just completed a deal whereby the tottering Batista received tanks and planes with which to beat off the chronic nuisance afflicting him; and there was a mighty hullabaloo about that in the House of Commons after Fidel Castro had paraded some of the tanks that had fallen so conveniently into his hands.

Nobody knew for certain whether Fidel Castro was or was not a communist, although a lot of people claimed they knew. Most observers could be neatly arranged into two opposing lines. The argument about what he was politically when he captured Havana is still going on years afterward. One should not wonder that in all the early confusion, ignorance, and makeshift catching-up the Eisenhower administration should have been bewildered. But there does not seem to be any reason or excuse why, after a few weeks or even a few months, it should not have squared up to him and his anti-Americanism. Chance after chance was missed of either treating with him skillfully—such as by receiving him decorously and probing his mind when he visited the United States in 1959—or of warning him that he would be invaded and destroyed if he did not behave in accordance with international law and usage— such as when he seized one American-owned property after another without even giving a receipt.

The communists who, in my submission, began taking over
the revolution very soon after they saw that there was an excellent chance that they could succeed without much risk,
would have been stopped in their tracks by an early warning
that the United States did not intend to tolerate any kind of
communist establishment in the hemisphere. Time would have
been gained, at the very least, and even if all alternatives
failed and the United States had had to use force, the Cuban
people would have been spared years of trial and hardship.
Communists in Latin America would have been given a check
from which they would not readily recover, and the United
States would have achieved quickly an objective that, it seems
as I write, it intends to gain ultimately by one means or
another.

The opportunities were all allowed to slip by, partly because
of American perplexity at the unique problem presented by the
Cuban revolution, and partly because of American sensitivity
(exaggerated and unnecessary sensitivity to my mind) about
the effect on her "image" in Latin America and elsewhere if she used even a moderately big stick, or even just a
schoolmaster's cane. Hindsight confirms that as late as during
the missile crisis in October, 1962, the Cuban regime could have
been undermined, perhaps permanently, in the bargain by which
President Kennedy secured the removal of the Russian missiles.

It is now apparent that Fidel Castro and Nikita Khrushchev could have been advised coldly that unless the missiles
were removed and the sites dismantled by a certain date, Cuba
would be invaded and the job done for them by American forces.
The missiles would have been removed and there would have
been no world war. I have read that only a minority of one
among President Kennedy's advisers recommended this course.
It is a pity that the majority did not feel similarly, for it
seems to me that Fidel Castro might not have survived such
an ultimatum. He and the communists in Cuba would certainly
not have found it so easy as they did to negotiate international

trade and otherwise expand the base of the revolution between 1962 and 1964 if the rest of the world had had such conclusive evidence of American determination. A prudent man would think hard before consorting with a Fidel Castro who at last had been transformed from a valid revolutionary leader into a puppet who in future would have to take heed not only of what his Russian patrons permitted but would also be subject to invasion and overthrow if he did not toe a line drawn by Washington. In other words, American authority would have been restored.

In making this purely personal assessment of events since 1959, I do not wish it to be inferred that I am recommending any particular course or policy to be followed by the United States. I would not presume to do that. Nor do I want anybody—including Fidel Castro!—to assume that I am agitating for his downfall and the overthrow of his revolution. My thesis is simply that I believe that if the United States really does feel that Fidel Castro represents an intolerable threat to its political and military security within the hemisphere that it dominates, whether the United States likes it or even admits it, it should not shilly-shally in dealing with him as it did between 1959 and 1965. It is just as much an inexorable rule of diplomacy and politics as it is of warfare that if you set out to gain a victory over an adversary you do not hesitate or draw back from delivering the winning thrust. I happen to think, as I believe the reader will have deduced, that the revolution of Fidel Castro was entirely justified in its origins and was to be welcomed and encouraged in the early days of its triumph. I regret intensely that because of the political and administrative inexperience of Fidel Castro, plus his ignorance of economics and the lack of American vision and firmness in dealing with him, the revolution was allowed to get out of hand and then fall under communist control. Even so it achieved something of worth to Cuba, but it could have achieved so much more. . . .

Finally, we turn to the future. Is it possible or safe to make any forecasts at all? Probably not, the more so because of the notable perversity of the Cubans in bringing speculation to naught as frequently by mismanagement as by intent. But one may make some observations pointing to a few likely alternatives. First, I ask it to be taken for granted that Fidel Castro cannot hope to preserve his revolution for communism in view of the way events were shaping up in 1965, although it might take years for the process of attrition to have its climactic effect if it is left to work alone at its own slow and stealthy pace. I could not see in the summer of 1965 how eventual disintegration could be avoided, for the reasons advanced earlier in this chapter, based on what I saw and heard during my last visit to Havana.

Castro can still hope to preserve his revolution as a liberalizing and admirable influence for Cuba and for all Latin America if he can make an arrangement with the United States. At least two main considerations will have to be met. One is that he will have to give substantial guarantees in absolute good faith to the United States. The other is that he will have to rid himself of all communistic encumbrance—and this is becoming harder and harder for him to contemplate as time passes because of his ever deepening involvement with communist and other anti-American influences inside and outside Cuba. If the overture he made in 1964 was any criterion, there seemed to be scant chance of any later concord between him and Washington —unless and until pressures upon him became so unbearable that his only hope of rescue lay in surrender.

The Soviet Union was, of course, an element in the situation of which serious account had to be taken at all times after the summer of 1959, when Russian agents in Cuba began to show their strength. Immediately after its withdrawal of missiles in the late fall of 1962, the Soviet Union was morally bound to make sure that Fidel Castro, then in very shaky economic condition indeed, did not collapse. Russia honored its commitment, at vast material cost. One estimate given to me in Havana in 1963 was that Cuba was costing Russia over $100 million a day. This appalling expense was offset only in very small degree by the sugar and other commodities that it could absorb from Cuba, but one psychological dividend the Soviet Union did receive was a remarkable upsurge in pro-Soviet sentiment among the Cubans. Hungry and deprived people could not fail to respond with gratitude to the helping hand from the east. They were in any event not allowed to forget whose hand it was, for Havana became festooned with propaganda posters emphasizing the fact that Cuba was not alone, that the Soviet army stood shoulder to shoulder with the militia, and so on.

But the Soviet Union clearly could not sustain its crippling Cuban burden indefinitely and, as we have seen, encouraged Fidel Castro in 1963-64 to expand his trade with Africa, Western Europe, and anywhere else that offered. Briefly, the maneuver was successful. Then came a disastrous fall in sugar prices and, in 1965, sobering evidence to both Cuba and the Soviet Union that the United States was at last squaring up to the challenge of communism, not only in Cuba but in Latin America as a whole. It seems to me that once the United States takes a stand, the Soviet Union cannot face up to it in this area, for America still has most of the economic, geographical, and (if needs be) the military circumstances in its favor.

Certainly in Cuba the utmost that the Soviet Union can hope to achieve is to keep Fidel Castro going for just as long as he has some of his own strength left. Once he begins to wobble seriously and once the fatal cracks begin to appear in the framework of the regime built around him, the Soviet Union cannot hope to save him. It would be operating from extreme long range, six thousand miles and more away, and it would surely find that its American adversary, a mere ninety miles away, would be exploiting any opportunities offered by a looming Cuban collapse. The only terms on which it could take up such a challenge would be to run the almost-certain risk of precipitating world war; and that, I suggest, it will never do until it feels utterly certain that it can win. Clearly, that is not yet.

What, then, are the possibilities open to the United States in its lengthening tussle with Fidel Castro and communism in Cuba? They are many. They range from practicing purely passive containment to making a full-scale invasion—an irresistible one this time. The first will satisfy only a small minority of communists and so-called liberals in the United States. I cannot imagine that the second would be openly recommended by anybody, although I must say that some Americans have told me privately that they would like to see it carried out without more ado; they have always hastily added the qualification, "Don't quote me on that."

It may well be that invasion will be the means whereby the transition from the revolutionary Cuba of the Castro era to something new and, one fervently hopes, more enlightened, will be made. I do not mean a calculated brutal aggression planned and carried out solely to crush Fidel Castro and his regime because of political intolerance and blind frustration. Such an act of savagery by the United States, or anybody else, is unthinkable. I mean an invasion more in the sense of a surgical intervention to stop civil war or anarchy that could engulf Cuba in one of those swift convulsions which have been characteristic of Latin America for so many generations. One fact I have observed during the sixteen years I have been in contact with this area is that political or administrative change there is rarely achieved without a primitive commotion and usually some bloodshed, and I cannot convince myself that any future change in Cuba will provide an exception.

The Castro revolution was born in a ghastly bloodbath on July 26, 1953, with a mad and futile attack planned by Fidel Castro on a barracks at Moncada, in Oriente Province. Some sixty young Cubans were slaughtered or were afterwards tortured to death by the agents of Fulgencio Batista. The revolution was prosecuted in two years of kill-and-run warfare in the Sierra Maestra. It was inaugurated as a triumph in 1959 in even more revolting bloodletting in which hundreds of men (nobody knows the exact number) were put against walls and shot down after mockeries of adjudication. The executions went on for several years, and their toll was augmented in 1961 by bloodshed in the field while an invasion was being fended off. One can never be certain, but it seems likely to me that this deplorable sequence will be maintained to the end.

One alternative to an overnight eruption could be a repetition of the process of military attrition whereby Fidel Castro himself gained power. A force of counterrevolutionaries—not Cuban alone but including fighters from other countries in Latin America stimulated at last to resist extremist communism encroaching upon their lives—might establish itself within Cuba and erode a weakening revolution. Such an operation would not, I think, take anything like as long as did Fidel Castro's to achieve its purpose, for it would presumably be infinitely stronger than his—it would surely need to be—and there would be a reasonable chance that the Cuban population and perhaps even parts of the army and militia would support it. There was not even a glimmer of a chance of such support for the invasion of 1961, for Fidel Castro was still a savior within his country and his revolution still promised a high degree of fulfillment; but even five years later he was becoming a blemished image and his revolution had still not delivered anything like a satisfying proportion of the glorious pledges he had made for it. The gap here seemed to be widening day after day.

If a counterrevolution did prosper, I do not believe that it would be able to grasp power with such unchallenged finality as did Fidel Castro's in 1959. For one thing, the Castro revolution is a very different organism from the Batista dictatorship.

It was for a long time an inspiration to Cubans, and there would be many fanatics who would go on fighting for it after it was doomed, even though just as many might desert and join its assailants. For another thing, the United States probably would not simply look on this time and let events take their course in Havana. No, I believe the lesson of 1959 has been well learned, and the United States would make sure without delay and by whatever action seemed appropriate that a post-Castroite Cuba did not stay outside its political and economic control.

Many people, enlightened and idealistic Americans prominent among them, may claim that the time has come when countries like Cuba ought to be allowed to go their own ways, but the harsh facts gainsay them. In its unique position as the prime—and perhaps the only fully committed—resistant to communism, the United States simply cannot afford yet to let go of Latin America; and the countries of Latin America are not yet mature enough to be allowed to go. The day is obviously drawing nearer when this will be both desirable and possible, for most of them have made notable political strides in the last two decades of this century. What is to be hoped for and expected if, as I suspect, the United States finds that her self-interest demands that it intervene again in the affairs and destiny of Cuba is that it will not make the fatal mistake of going all the way back and trying to make Cuba once again its handmaiden. I very much doubt whether it would find this even remotely possible, for whatever else Fidel Castro has done or not done he has most assuredly given Cubans an unforgettable glimpse of a freer and fuller life that they might enjoy.

And even if the United States did manage for a while to reimpose a partly colonial yoke around the neck of Cuba, it would come to rue it. The United States would be like somebody trying to close a door against a gale; the moment its pressure relaxed the door would fly open, with violent and probably

painful consequences. I feel sure that the Cuban people will
never again submit for very long to the subordinate role in
economics, politics and even in social affairs that they had to
play for the first half of this century, and any attempt to
force them to do so will probably mean the emergence of an
even more determined and dangerous leader than Fidel Castro.
Although Castro forced some bitter medicine down their
throats, he did give them—as I now feel impelled to re-empha-
size—a draught of the nectar of independence.

The United States will be acting with great wisdom if it
takes account of this truth while biding its time until the
moment comes for a decisive reckoning with the Castro revolution, no matter what form this reckoning assumes. The interim
can be used to press forward quickly and sincerely with the
policy that first took elemental shape in the latter days of the
Kennedy administration: adjusting the relationship with Latin
America by recognizing that the area is ripe for self-develop-
ment and encouraging the process, not by continuing the old,
basically self-serving, programs of loans, investment of American capital, partnership with local oligarchies, and such like,
but by generous and sacrificial gestures such as the establishment of domestically owned industries, even though these would
deprive her of profitable market. Anything that will prove to
Latin America—and to errant Cuba—that at real cost to
itself the United States intends to open a new era in the hemisphere should be done. Thus will it be cutting away some of
the ground upon which Castroism and communism stand, and
it might well be hastening the day when Cuba will wish to return to the fold. In the bargain the United States will be taking out insurance against the creation of replicas of Castro's
communistic Cuba elsewhere in Latin America.

One final possibility remains. It is that Fidel Castro, defying the odds and surviving all that the United States and his
other adversaries may do to frustrate and overpower him, will
achieve the miracle of establishing a soviet satellite state per-

manently just across the Florida Strait. I do not believe he can do this. But, if he does, he will be the father of more such satellites. That is a certainty that the United States will have to face, however unpalatable it might be and however unwillingly Americans look upon it.

Index

Currency, 123–24, 147
Czechoslovakia, 97, 101, 115, 130

Daniel, Jean, 199, 200, 201
Davis, Brian ("ffolkes"), 89, 90
Diaz Balart, Mirta (Mrs. Fidel Castro), 111
Diaz Lanz, Major Pedro, 74, 78
Directorio Revolucionario, 51
Dominican Republic, 8
Donovan, James, 180
Dorticos, Dr. Osvaldo, 57, 74, 78, 94, 260
Draper, Theodore, 27, 112
Drug shortage, 181–82

Economist, 169
Eder, Richard, 245
Eisenhower, Dwight D., 85, 86, 88, (*quoted*) 89, 93, 94
El Cano, 143, 144
El Mundo, 44
Escalante, Anibal, 129
Exiles, 97, 99, 103
Expropriated refineries, 94, 237

Federation of the Students of Chile, 86
"Fifth Sugar Harvest of the People," 247–48
Food rationing, 146–47, 188, 271
Fordham, A. S., 22, 23
Foreign trade, 72–74, 95, 114–15, 235
Foreign Relations, Ministry of, 132, 140, 153, 179
Fugitives, 194

Gambling, 53–55, 91
Gitmo Gazette, 216
Granma, 261, 267
Greece, 146
G2 surveillance, 153–67 *passim*

Guantanamo, 105, 208–27 *passim*
Guatemala, 112
Guevara, Ernesto ("Che"), 27, 28, 34, 100, 104–05, 108–09, 110, 111–12, 113, 114, 115, 120, 126–27, 129, 151–53, 174, 249, 250–59 *passim*, 262

Hagerty, James, 88
Halcrow, Sir William, 236
Hart, Dr. Armando, 57, 149
Havana Hilton Hotel, 16, 22, 29, 48, 55, 91
Havana Libre Hotel, *see* Havana Hilton Hotel
Havana Riviera Hotel, 48
Havana trials, 35–42
Hemingway, Ernest, 93
H.M.S. *Victory*, 214
Honeymoons, government sponsored, 189
Hotel Nacional, 7, 48
"Humanism," 28

Immigration, Cuban Department of, 58, 59, 153
In Defense of National Sovereignty, 78, (*quoted*) 79–82
Inflation, 241, 269–70
Information, availability of, 100–01
International Telephone and Telegraph Company, 67
Invasion fever, 117–19
Italy, 146

Juvenile Rebel Movement, 131

Khrushchev, Nikita, 94, 95, 111, 140, 206
Kennedy, John F., 106, 121, 169–70, 181, 199–200, 205–06

6/13/66

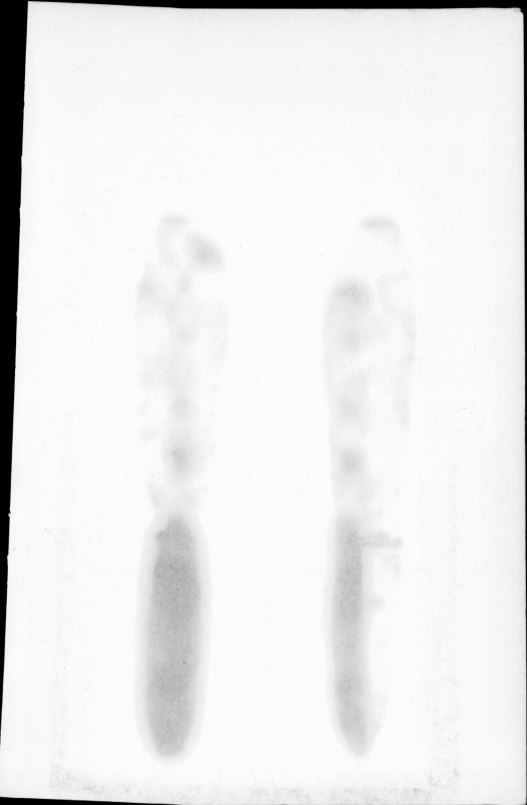

DATE DUE

Pocket inside

Gulf of

Mexico

FLORIDA

Miami • Miami
Beach

DRY TORTUGAS

Key Largo

Key West

FLORIDA KEYS

90 Miles

Straits of Florida

GULF STREAM

CAY SAL
BANK

ARCH. DE SABANA

Havana

Matanzas

Guanajay • HAVANA
Güines Camarioca • Cárdenas

PINAR DEL RÍO • Candelaria MATANZAS
C
Colón
• Pinar
del Río Santa Clara U
Sagua
la Grande

ARCH. DE LOS CANARREOS LAS VILLAS
• Cienfuegos

ISLE OF PINES Bay of Pigs Trinidad •

YUCATAN CHANNEL

N

W *E*

CAYMAN
BRAC

LITTLE CAYMAN

GRAND CAYMAN

S

C a r i b b e a n

0 *Scale of Miles* 200